"No one can speak to the intersection of social activism and the formal world of politics better than Libby Davies. Having cut her teeth on the hard streets of Eastside Vancouver, she never lost her passion for justice or her fight for the most marginalized, even when she rose to the halls of power in Ottawa. Libby tells us that one choice is not better than the other. The issue is how those who advocate for change at the grassroots level and those who seek political office work together toward common goals."

—Maude Barlow, writer, activist

"This book reminds us of Libby Davies' courageous and compassionate leadership in giving voice to the voiceless and hope and empowerment to the poor and the powerless in Vancouver and nationally. But this book also reminds us of Libby's international leadership on Palestine, and on global health issues with the IPU and The Global Fund to Fight AIDS, Tuberculosis and Malaria. Read this book, an inspiring and moving reminder that one dedicated woman can indeed change our world."

—Svend Robinson, NDP MP 1979–2004, NDP federal candidate 2019

"I've always known Libby Davies to be a principled and dedicated activist, but didn't realize she had such an interesting story to tell. From her early rough-and-tumble years in Vancouver's gritty east side to her later battles on Parliament Hill, her tale is both engaging and inspiring."

—Linda McQuaig, journalist and co-author of
Billionaires' Ball: Gluttony and Hubris in an Age of Epic Inequality

"For 18 years I was proud to call Libby Davies my MP. And her fabulous book reminds me why. Libby has always been a true champion of the communities she represented—particularly the most marginalized people of the Downtown Eastside—while walking the halls of political power at both city hall and later as MP for Vancouver East. In her utterly captivating memoir, Libby offers deep insights into how to bridge the divide between electoral politics and social movements, and issues a compelling call for a bolder NDP."

—Seth Klein, former British Columbia Director,
Canadian Centre for Policy Alternatives

"What a beautiful, page-turning memoir by an activist politician! Libby Davies advocated fearlessly, boldly, and prophetically, from the first day she set foot in Parliament, for drug policies grounded in science, health, compassion, and human rights. This book is honest, reflective, and revelatory—a true profile in courage."

—Ethan Nadelmann, founder and former executive
director (2000–2017) of the Drug Policy Alliance

"Passionate, unyielding, and strong, Libby shows how it is possible to hold on to core beliefs and effect transformative change for social justice both in the community and the political world."

—Olivia Chow, former NDP MP and author of *My Journey*

"Libby Davies has always been a beacon of light in electoral politics. Coming from anti-poverty activism in Vancouver's Skid Road, Libby brought the interests of the most marginalized people into the halls of Parliament. Now she has generously opened her life to us in an honest political memoir that provides an inside view of the most important political battles of our lifetime. *Outside In* is a fascinating read for anyone interested in how social change can happen in the halls of power."

—Judy Rebick, author of *Heroes in My Head*

"*Outside In* is essential reading for anyone wanting to make a better world and wondering what it takes to make it possible. Always from the perspective of a tireless organizer, Davies sees politics as a dynamic process of power in constant flux where progressive change is always possible if you build a united community willing to fight for it. Community activist, parliamentarian, and fearless catalyst for change, Libby Davies melds the personal and the political, the outside agitator and inside legislator."

—Elaine Bernard, Labor and Worklife Program and Harvard Trade Union Program, Harvard Law School

"*Outside In* is supposed to be the story of Libby Davies' life, but really it's a handbook on organizing. Reading about her wins and losses, her work both outside and inside of electoral politics, and her ability to swallow her fear and work for a more just community and country is not only inspiring, but a call for us all to join in that work and a blueprint for how."

—Megan Leslie, former MP for Halifax and Deputy Leader of Canada's NDP, President & CEO of WWF-Canada

"*Outside In* tells the incredible story of how Libby Davies burst into the halls of power and held the doors open for others. Along the way she introduces all the people she credits with making her journey possible. It is a generous, hopeful, and deeply personal book—I couldn't put it down."

—Kennedy Stewart, Mayor, City of Vancouver

"In these pages Libby Davies documents her life in the Downtown Eastside from its earliest days: working largely as a volunteer, fighting for the downtrodden, the disenfranchised, the poor, the forgotten, and the discarded souls she always recognized and respected as neighbours and comrades. Davies writes as a true storyteller about her time in the trenches of the political left. I wish I could vote for Libby to be our next Prime Minister, but I can't, so I will just encourage anyone who cares about our democratic system, or about changing the world from the outside in, to please read this book."

—Ivan Coyote, writer, storyteller,
and author of *Tomboy Survival Guide*

"Despite all obstacles, Libby Davies has been dedicated to confronting the most severe urban situation in modern Canadian history, the sorrows of which she bore with equal parts outrage and compassion."

—Matthew Good, musician, writer

Outside In

Outside

In

A Political Memoir

LIBBY DAVIES

BETWEEN THE LINES
TORONTO

Outside In

© 2019 Libby Davies

First published in 2019 by
Between the Lines
401 Richmond Street West
Studio 281
Toronto, Ontario M5V 3A8
Canada
1-800-718-7201
www.btlbooks.com

Every reasonable effort has been made to identify copyright holders. Between the Lines
would be pleased to have any errors or omissions brought to its attention.

Library and Archives Canada Cataloguing in Publication

Davies, Libby, author
        Outside in : a political memoir / Libby Davies.

Includes index.
Issued in print and electronic formats.
ISBN 978-1-77113-445-3 (softcover).–ISBN 978-1-77113-446-0 (EPUB).–ISBN 978-1-77113-447-7 (PDF)

        1. Davies, Libby. 2. Politicians–Canada–Biography. 3. Canada–Politics and govern-
ment–1993-2006. 4. Canada–Politics and government–2006-2015. 5. City council members–
British Columbia–Vancouver–Biography. 6. Autobiographies. I. Title.

FC636.D39A3 2019   971.064'8092   C2018-906062-X
                                            C2018-906063-8

Design by Ingrid Paulson
Printed in Canada

We acknowledge for their financial support of our publishing activities: the Government
of Canada; the Canada Council for the Arts, which last year invested $153 million to bring
the arts to Canadians throughout the country; and the Government of Ontario through the
Ontario Arts Council, the Ontario Book Publishers Tax Credit program, and Ontario Creates.

In memory of Bruce Eriksen

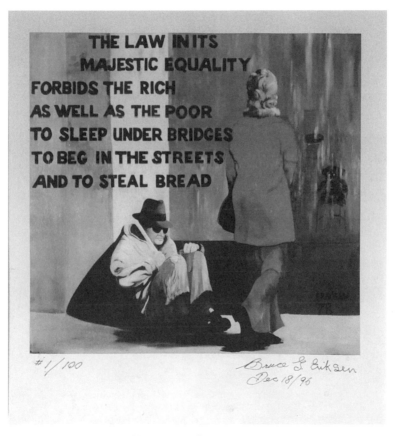

Downtown Eastside mural by Bruce Eriksen

Contents

Prologue

My first official day on Parliament Hill in Ottawa, as the newly elected member of Parliament (MP) for Vancouver East, was on September 22, 1997. Green grass stretched out in front of the castle-like buildings and the Peace Tower with its Big Ben look-alike clock. It was a beautiful, sunny day, but even so the heavy humidity was so unlike the fresh coastal breezes I was used to. Julius Fisher from BC's *working TV* followed me onto the Hill to record my first moments. An anti-choice rally on abortion was taking place, and I felt angry about it. Why did they of all people have to be here, I thought. The clock chimed eleven and it dawned on me that I was late. As I picked up my pace, Julius stopped me and said, "Libby, wait—how do you feel about being here on this first day? What would Bruce think about you being here?"

What would Bruce think? Immediately tears came. I wanted to turn and run back to my son, Lief, and the life I had known, even with the staggering absence of my long-time partner Bruce Eriksen, who had died just two months earlier. I got a flash of our lives together, as activists, as community organizers, as city councillors, as co-conspirators, as parents. A sweet team of two that was no more. And now I was far from home and far from the activist life I knew. What the hell was I doing here?

I have no idea what I said to Julius and his camera. I could only focus on cutting through the anti-choice rally—the shortest route—to make it into the House of Commons in time for the election of the Speaker, the first task of any new Parliament after an election. I dreaded meeting the New Democratic Party (NDP) caucus, most of whom were strangers to me. I felt lost and not up to the job ahead of me. It was a familiar feeling: one of being thrust into something that I felt unprepared and unqualified for. Yet I knew that people were counting on me to do important things in Ottawa.

My biggest challenge, since my earliest experiences of running for public office, had always been overcoming my own sense of inadequacy. It was almost as though I'd gotten where I was not by choice but by accident. But there was another part of me too, the fearless part that was able to push past the uncertainty, driven by a mission, by everything I believed in about making a better society for people. That day on Parliament Hill, my passion for social justice prevailed again. I forced back the tears and strode forward.

Organize, Organize, Organize

In the 1970s Vancouver's Skid Road was a no man's land. Overshadowed by the downtown Central Business District, it didn't appear on civic planning maps. No one at city hall cared about the area. Its seven thousand plus residents were left to the mercy of numerous churches, charities, and missions as they administered to the poor. To an outsider it seemed a bleak and unforgiving place, derelict in both its physical and human form. The blocks of battered, broken-down brick and wood hotels and rooming houses, built mostly at the turn of the century, with decades of soot and grime on dirty grey windows, overlooked heavy traffic arterials leading into the downtown core. It was an area of forgotten old men who were seen as down-and-outs that the city would rather ignore.

Just a block away lay Gastown, the historical centre of the modern-day city. It, too, was part of Skid Road, with heaving brick streets, old rooming houses and hotels with beer parlours containing single-room occupancies (SROs), and the Gassy Jack statue standing guard. But by the 1970s it had mostly been bought up by developers with dreams of cruise ships and happy tourist spaces. It was an uneasy co-existence for the remaining low-income residents, feeling unwelcome in their own community, next to wary tourists looking for a good souvenir.

Today, some fifty years later, although some of those rooming houses still exist and people still call them home, thousands of rooms have been lost to gentrification and thousands of people have been dispersed like parcels to lost addresses. The need for permanent social housing is as urgent now as it was in the 1970s. It seems unbelievable, but those critical housing issues persist due to decades of chronic austerity programs and unrelenting income inequality in Canada. Still somehow the neighbourhood—for it is a neighbourhood in every sense—and its community of survivors and brave souls continue to survive in a city of glass towers and flowing wealth that takes care only of itself and no one else.

My introduction to Skid Road came through a federal Opportunities for Youth summer student employment program. I applied to help establish a low-cost food store in the recently established community health clinic. I was a student at the time, and that summer of 1972 was a life-changing experience that immersed me in what was to become the community of the Downtown Eastside and a lifetime of work.

The idea of setting up a low-cost food store in Vancouver's inner city was a simple one: buy food in cheaper large quantities from local wholesalers, and resell at cost in small units so that residents of the community had better purchasing power for their below-the-poverty-line incomes. You want only six tea bags? We could do it. One cup of soup mix, or one can of sardines, one tomato—it was there. The food store was just a makeshift counter upstairs in the health clinic, with some roughly fashioned shelves displaying the basic food wares for sale. Thus began my work at age nineteen, as a community organizer in what was still called Skid Road.

Business was brisk at the food store, and many residents would pop in when attending the clinic to purchase a small can of beans, a cup of rice, or noodles. The staff were all students, Calvin, Debbie, Charlotte,

Linda, among others. We were always looking for new sources for whole-sale purchase. We'd load up someone's car with our precious goods and return to begin the repackaging and selling process.

Twice a week or so we hauled enormous plastic buckets of leftover soup from the Woodward's department store basement coffee shop about five blocks away. Woodward's was famous for its clam chowder, and it felt like we were hauling gold on the rickety trolley that held the pails of soup, trying not to slop any of it on the uneven sidewalks. Back at the community health centre, it would be served still warm. I'm sure no public health official would allow it now—and maybe not then—but we did it anyway.

Later in the summer we did a survey of Safeway supermarket stores in the city, comparing prices of the small Safeway store at East Hastings and Gore to those at Safeways in affluent neighbourhoods. Not to our surprise, the local Safeway was the most expensive—and we had evidence of how poor people got ripped off because they weren't mobile to shop around. It made us more determined to make the food store as accessible as possible, with as much food choice as we could muster. The small store operated successfully for many years after the initial group of students left.

The summer of 1972 was also the lead-up to a provincial election, and change was in the air. Old W.A.C. "Wacky" Bennett, British Columbia's longest-serving premier, had dominated provincial politics for twenty years with his populist Social Credit Party. But the BC New Democratic Party was gaining strength and hoped to form government. My father encouraged me to get involved in the campaign to defeat the Socreds. I don't remember how I met Emery Barnes—all six foot six of him—a former BC Lions football player turned social worker, turned NDP candidate in the constituency of Vancouver–Burrard, which included Skid Road. But I canvassed like crazy for him, because he was the real deal.

He would come to the food store and treat people with dignity and respect and a huge smile and bear hug. I'm sure the party considered it a lost cause to canvass in Skid Road, but Emery believed it was important and he believed in us to do it.

That campaign was my first introduction to the NDP. I had no inkling of my future relationship to the party. What drew me was the desire to see Emery elected, more than a desire overall to support the NDP. I think this is often the case, especially for young people engaging in the political process for the first time—they are drawn to a figure they know and believe in. It was my belief in Emery's commitment to fight for our community that made the difference. I never felt like a party insider then, and I still don't to this day. My politics grew like a wild tree from the community experience of organizing, not from the party.

Knocking on doors with my canvassing mate, Gary Holman (who many years later became an NDP member of the BC Legislative Assembly), I got to know every rooming house and old hotel in the neighbourhood. It was shocking to see the conditions people lived in. I got to know many folks, many of them older, forcibly retired resource workers injured on the job with nowhere else to go but Skid Road. I gained huge respect for the people I met. They were class conscious and eager for change, and they grinned from ear to ear when they opened the door and saw a young woman with a British accent earnestly asking them to support Emery and the NDP in the upcoming election. Never before had they seen someone canvass door to door in the neighbourhood. Many a time we were asked in to have a drink of the cheapest red wine, or join a happy drinking party, and but I always declined with a smile.

There were no cell phones then, no social media, no tweeting, not even personal computers. It was just slogging door to door, conversation by conversation to solicit political support. I saw every filthy rooming house and hotel, and experienced first-hand the indignities people had to put up with. We trudged up the seven or eight floors and down narrow dimly lit hallways, with decades of rot, smoke, bugs, and dirt at every step. How could anyone not be moved by the injustice of what people endured? These were people who had worked hard and had literally broken their backs building BC as loggers, fishermen, and miners. But emotion isn't worth a scrap if it isn't followed by an understanding of what you might be able to do. For me it was a burning desire to bring about change and to work for social justice. Perhaps a naive one. But that desire for transformative change has stayed with me my whole life.

Emery was elected on August 30, 1972, and became part of a new BC NDP government under the leadership of Dave Barrett. That victory was a positive experience of engaging with electoral politics. I felt very buoyed by knowing that we had helped bring our candidate into office.

The following summer, a second project—also under the sponsorship of Opportunities for Youth and with some of the same people—produced the publication the *Downtown East*. This was a biweekly community paper that we distributed for free, door to door, in the hotels and rooming houses. It was a darn good paper, and it would eventually become a powerful tool for a massive organizing effort that was emerging, as the people of Skid Road began asserting their rights and their voice by forming the Downtown Eastside Residents Association (DERA).

Those of us who worked on the paper wrote furiously about life in Skid Road: its people, their struggles, and their need for recognition. We were fervent in our zeal to produce a paper that local residents would want to pick up and read when it arrived at their room. We often interviewed interesting characters in the neighbourhood and shared their stories of dealing with abusive, uncaring landlords and working in dangerous resource industries where debilitating injuries were common. We didn't always get it right. On one occasion we heard that Buck, a colourful local guy, had died and we wrote a glorious front-page obituary about him and his hard life. It was a great piece. Only, when we ran into him the next week, he grinned cheekily and said, "I ain't dead, but thanks."

DERA held regular membership meetings every couple of weeks. Local residents came out eager to sign up for action to effect change in the community. These extraordinary meetings blew the lid off years of silence and invisibility in the community. People jumped to the mic, eager to share their experiences, their stories, and the grievances they had against cruel landlords and disgusting living conditions. The meetings were chaotic and charged, with voices echoing off the First United Church gym walls as the chair called for "Order!" I would scribble as fast as I could to write down what people were saying.

Residents wanted better housing, better run beer parlours that weren't havens for violence and for overserving by management, and improved street lighting and a ban on knives to improve community safety. The biggest threat was fires in the old hotels and rooming houses. At many a meeting there was intense discussion about the rooming houses and the fear of another fire. Whatever the issue was, DERA took it on. We demanded enforcement of the city's fire bylaws that required sprinkler systems on every floor and room. The landlords wanted no such thing; they cried poverty and threatened to close down their rooms and evict long-term residents rather than upgrade to meet the law. This is where the brilliance and strength of Bruce Eriksen, an unemployed ironworker and lead organizer at DERA, emerged. Bruce figured out that the numerous beer parlours were required by law to keep their residential rooms if they wanted to retain profitable liquor licences. He called their bluff. He fought city hall and organized rallies and demonstrations demanding enforcement of civic bylaws. So the sprinklers went in, and as a result no one died in fires any longer in what had been death traps.

In those early days of community organizing at DERA, we were driven by the imperatives of life and death. People dying in rooming-house fires. Murders in beer parlours. Back then we were driven to make change any way we could, no matter whom we pissed off and no matter what the risk. We just did it. Like there was no tomorrow, like we were wild. I had no fear. No one taught us and we learned from

Marcy Toms, Libby Davies, Vancouver Centre MLA Emery Barnes, and Bruce Eriksen tour Skid Road pubs on Hastings Street (Ovaltine Café in the background)

experience and mistakes, success and failure. I loved that period of my life—it was earth shattering and vivid like a multi-coloured dream that flew by in minutes. And it was the towering force of Bruce Eriksen that drew me to it all.

The day I met him, in the summer of 1973, I had been dispatched by my co-workers to cajole him into doing some cartoons for our little paper. We'd heard about the fiery figure who was organizing and becoming visible in the media as he bulldozed his way through barriers and the ancient stereotypes about Skid Road. We'd heard he was a self-described artist too. "You go and see him, Libby," my co-workers said. "You're so nice he won't say no to you." So off I went to First United Church at East Hastings and Gore, where DERA's first office was located, to make my pitch. We sized each other up. I was twenty and he was forty-five. I was polite and he was gruff. I smiled and he didn't. But I could see his interest and a bit of a grin as he realized that doing a few cartoons for our paper would give him a useful organizing tool, especially if he could get us to cover the issues he was working on. And of course, we delivered the paper door to door—five thousand copies each issue.

I was very struck by Bruce. Something told me that behind the tough exterior was a unique individual of enormous strength and creativity. Intense blue eyes, a small goatee, slim and wry and impeccably dressed—white shirt, dress pants, and polished shoes—and slender, artistic hands, this is what I saw. He wasn't a man of many words but he had an aura of passion and drive that was charged with energy. I don't know what he saw in me, and in fact, he discouraged my interest at first, saying he was too old. It didn't matter to me. I loved him the first day I met him.

My mother was horrified. She flipped out when she learned I was living with a man twenty-five years older than me, in a rundown old house on East Cordova Street that we shared with cockroaches and people who came and left. She could see no future for me living in such a debilitated neighbourhood and working, mostly unpaid, for what was at best a marginal group. For a while it was difficult to visit her at home; I felt like I'd betrayed her hopes for me to become a social worker or teacher. I resisted her questions and concerns whenever she raised them, refusing to understand why she was upset.

In many ways, as Bruce drew me into a world of fighting for people's rights, we had a tumultuous relationship. He was a natural organizer and leader who was proud of his grade three education. He was a self-taught man who liked to read a dictionary at night. He had been an ironworker, miner, logger, and, as he used to laugh, a grave-digger too. We'd had totally different life experiences. He liked country music and I didn't. He'd had a very rough life and I hadn't. He liked to drink in beer parlours (I didn't) and monitor what was going on; his "inspections" became legendary and the beer parlour owners hated him and the exposure of how they broke the law and created misery for people. He got stats from the police department showing that the murders, knifings, and violence in the beer parlours and out on the street were perpetrated mostly by people from outside the community. He exposed how the deliberate overserving of alcohol created vulnerable low-income residents as victims—overserving by beer parlours made people intoxicated and thus more susceptible to crime. He broke every stereotype about Skid Road and bugged the hell out of every reporter at the cop shop until they covered the issues he was raising.

He attended coroner's hearings on fire deaths and had an uncanny instinct on how to use the law itself to attain social justice. He would study little-known civic bylaws on public health, fire, maintenance standards for rooming houses, and safety, and use them as a weapon to expose the indignities that people suffered and demand enforcement of the law.

Skid Road was a non-entity—without any political voice or clout—until Bruce emerged like a megaphone that would not be silenced. City hall was politically dominated at the time by The Electors Action Movement (TEAM), made up of mostly middle-class liberals and some New Democrats who sought to bring more liberal policies to city hall after decades of power by the Non-Partisan Association (NPA), a pro-business and pro-developer group. By the time DERA became a powerful community and political force, only two NPA city councillors remained on council, alongside legendary left-wing lawyer and city councillor Harry Rankin of the Committee of Progressive Electors (COPE).

Ironically, DERA fought harder with TEAM than with the NPA. Mayor Art Phillips and his TEAM councillors saw DERA as a militant, unruly protest group that never learned to get along with anyone. Time and time again we would charge up to city hall demanding bylaw enforcement and better housing. And time and time again we would be met with hostility and brick walls. We hurled ourselves at those walls until the bricks crumbled. We had screaming matches, we tore city hall up and down, we raised hell like there was no tomorrow. And we made change in ways that still matter.

For the next decade the transformation occurred of what had been ignored as "transient" Skid Road into the community of the Downtown Eastside. It had always been there, of course, but it was invisible as an established community of long-term residents. Bruce's drive and sheer force of will made for many enemies and detractors. The beer parlour owners, landlords, cops, and city politicians, and the myriad of social service providers, churches, and missions in the community all had their reasons to dislike the guy. (Though a chief of police told me decades later that as a young beat cop in the Downtown Eastside, he had admired and respected Bruce's guts.) Bruce was a threat to the established order of things as he gained strength and stature, and DERA became like a union; militant and raw with an attentive and active membership. He became president of the organization, which at this point was 3,500 strong. I remember Bruce saying, "They want you to get up out of the gutter, but only as far as your knees." Harry Rankin described Bruce as a "diamond in the rough."

We were an unlikely crew, three of us in particular: Bruce, Jean Swanson, and I. Jean was a beer slinger in the Patricia Hotel on East Hastings Street, and a single parent of two young kids. She'd heard about Bruce Eriksen and was warned by her boss to not overserve him, as he was always on the lookout for violations. I was with him the day Jean was sent to his table to ask for my ID—in the hope that her boss could catch him drinking with a minor. She came over with her tray laden with beers, tall and striking with beautiful hair, and in a slightly embarrassed way asked for my ID. I looked very young, but I was not a minor. Later she had conversations with Bruce and was interested in the organizing work he was doing in the neighbourhood. She told him she wanted to do more than serve beer and boldly asked for a job at DERA. He promptly hired her when she said she had some high school newspaper experience. The *Downtown East* paper was still operating and had been taken over by DERA. Jean wrote incredible stories—researching who owned the slum hotels and how the Salvation Army operated. She interviewed people in food lineups at missions "singing and praying for their supper," and she helped write briefs to city hall about enforcing the Standards of Maintenance Bylaw.

At times Jean and I had a stormy work relationship with Bruce. He was volatile. He would come up with crazy ideas and charge at city hall. We took on the role of good cop to his bad cop. He'd stir everyone up and get social workers and others furious at him and DERA, and then Jean and I would try to calm things down and explain why we were going after particular people and issues. It made sense to us that we would fight the landlord of the East Hotel at Gore and Pender, who was trying to evict elderly Chinese residents. It made sense to fight city hall to save the old Carnegie Library at Main and Hastings, which was threatened with demolition, and turn it into a community centre. And it made sense to us to fight for federal funds to clean up the neighbourhood's only park—the historic Oppenheimer Park, formerly the Powell Street Grounds, where many a labour rally had been held during the Depression of the 1930s and the famous On to Ottawa Trek of unemployed workers began.

Slum landlords were a favourite and obvious target of ours in DERA's early days. Many were absentee landlords. It took Jean hours of research to figure out who owned and was making exorbitant profits off the cockroach- and flea-infested hotels and rooming houses, some with huge beer parlours—where the big money was—in tow.

We held annual Crummy Cockroach Haven contests and awarded slum landlords their prize of a beat-up garbage can lid. We went door to door in the old hotels and rooming houses, following up on complaints and meeting with residents to find out what was going on. We fought tooth and nail to make sure Vancouver's Standards of Maintenance Bylaw was enforced, demanding that inspectors do their job and that City Council have the backbone to do its job of upholding the law to ensure livable conditions. We often attended Vancouver City Council meetings after we had demanded "show cause hearings," where the onus was on a city business licence holder to show why their licence shouldn't be revoked due to flagrant and ongoing bylaw violations. We saw slum housing at its worst—hot plates hooked into the single lightbulb fixture, twenty people to a filthy single bathroom, no hot water, peeling paint, and impossibly small rooms.

DERA was controversial in those formative days. The problem wasn't us—though our enemies tried valiantly to make it so. The problem was the class issues we raised that the middle-class city councillors refused to deal with. We found more support from the old-time NPA city councillors than the liberal TEAM members. Harry Rankin, the lone city councillor from COPE, was already a staunch ally.

"The law in its majestic equality forbids the rich as well as the poor, to sleep under bridges, to beg in the streets, and to steal bread." Thus said Anatole France, writer and social critic, in 1894, and DERA took up the law in its majestic equality and challenged every prejudice of poverty, injustice, and discrimination. We did it blatantly and without apology. It was our lack of apology that got so many so angry at what we were doing. We refuted the notion of charity as an option. We railed against food lineups, even against the highly respected Franciscan Sisters of the Atonement and their sandwich line that had existed for fifty years. The relationships we had with social service agencies were at best fragile, and most organizations and churches in the community viewed DERA with suspicion or even dread. We didn't play their game and we were pretty self-righteous about what we were doing.

Even worse, we were "political"—way too political for their liking. That was a threat. We detested the social service agencies, which we saw as counter-progressive. The agencies, we believed, were responsible in part for maintaining the status quo of inequality and the notion that people in the Downtown Eastside were "clients," not citizens. We couldn't tolerate that. Residents were citizens first and they had rights. Maybe we could have done more to reach out to the social service providers and make them allies on some issues, like better housing. But we were impatient and intolerant. If they didn't agree with DERA and its tactics that was their problem.

Bruce's loathing of the well-intentioned social service providers came in part from his own history of running away from the Knowles School for Boys as an orphan in Winnipeg. His father, Oscar Eriksen, a railroad worker, had been unable to raise five very young children after his wife's early death. It's very likely DERA would not have become such a catalyst for transformative change had it not been for Bruce's supreme impatience with the status quo and his guts to forge ahead.

Bruce was an impetuous man, but also a disciplined one. He got up every morning before six and, with a Sportsman unfiltered cigarette in hand, he would walk to the coffee shop across from the cop shop and meet Harry Rankin. Harry ate porridge and Bruce always had eggs and bacon and too much coffee. Often Jack Webster—an old Scottish hound who barked out his radio talk show on CJOR every morning and later on BCTV—would join them. What three unique characters they were; it was like a reality TV show way before its time. I would sometimes force myself to get up and trudge along and listen to these guys, as they cut the crap out of everyone, dissected politics, and judged everyone and everything they came across. Harry would launch into court cases he was working on, and then use the foulest language to describe his fellow city councillors. Webster would laugh his socks off and, in his deep voice and burly Scottish accent, share the latest cop shop talk among reporters. Bruce was a bit of a sideline to these two professional gossips, but he would test out his latest ideas for fighting city hall and whatever grunge he had dug up in the beer parlours. After about forty-five minutes it was done and they parted ways. Some days, a few young politicos would show up too: Mike Chrunik, Dave Stone, Rosemary Rankin, and Fred Lowther. They were my age and we'd all listen in as the three stars mouthed off. It was a great way to start the day and we learned a lot.

Life with Bruce was unusual to say the least. By 1975, the DERA office was only a block away from our rundown old rental house on East Cordova Street (the second location of many moves for DERA over the years), and my life revolved around organizing, advocacy, and writing for the *Downtown East*. There was no training; the learning came from doing and figuring out what worked. We followed up rental grievances and helped people take landlords to court, and we began to advocate for the three levels of government to commit to the development of affordable non-profit housing—social housing—to replace the ancient, filthy rooming houses and hotel rooms. There was no personal social life to speak of, and I've often joked that my young adult life was devoid of the usual parties and drinking. I never even thought about that social part of life that most young adults revel in. I went once to a Ravi Shankar concert, but that was about it. But I never felt bored or distracted, because organizing and political activism were already defining my life. We would often attend meetings at night, working for the establishment of a ward system for Vancouver, or organizing for better neighbourhood planning and better housing. I shopped sporadically at local stores: the Pacific Bakery on Powell Street, Sunrise Market on Powell and Gore, where you could pick over the cheap and abundant vegetables, and the local meat store across from Oppenheimer Park.

Vancouver was full of emerging activism in the 1970s. Groups like the Vancouver Status of Women—which included Rosemary Brown, who became a well-known political figure—were powerful voices for women's liberation. But we had little to do with these other forces for change. There was a disconnect between the women's movement and the anti-poverty movement; we saw other organizations as too middle class and there seemed to be no natural affinity to work together. We had a closer connection with a few neighbourhood groups, in Hastings Sunrise, for example, as they too were organizing around neighbourhood issues.

Despite our fractious relationship with the local social service agencies and missions and with city hall, DERA had important allies. Harry Rankin, who had his law office at Main and Alexander Street in the Downtown Eastside, understood what DERA was about. He understood the class struggle, and he willingly assisted us in our mission to take on every power that be—whether it was city hall, the provincial government, the federal government, or slum landlords and others who were ripping people off. It was with Harry that we learned a basic political lesson: Don't shy away from the institutions of power even if they oppress you; rather, learn how to use them for what you need to do.

Many a time we would meet Harry at his law office, the brick walls displaying an impressive collection of West Coast Indigenous art given to him by his Indigenous clients. We would talk about issues and motions that we wanted to be moved at City Council meetings. Sometimes Harry scoffed at whatever crazy antic we were up to at DERA, but he knew that DERA was having a transformative political impact in the city. Sometimes we would run into Ben Swankey, Harry's wise political confidant, who ghost-wrote weekly columns that we also published in the *Downtown East* under the heading Rankin's Law.

Harry was our inside guy, along with city councillor Darlene Marzari (later a provincial cabinet minister in Mike Harcourt's NDP government). Originally a member of TEAM, she quit the organization over a contentious rezoning in the Downtown Eastside and showed her strong support for DERA. Darlene was the first progressive woman I met in elected office. I thought she was pretty cool and admired her greatly. She was young, energetic, and welcoming, and I enjoyed interviewing her for the *Downtown East*. Getting to know Darlene at city hall was the first glimpse I had that women could be successful in politics, though at the time I never thought it was something I might do. Harry, on the other hand, intimidated me until I got to know him better. You had to say what you wanted fast and not waste any time with frivolous talk. But he was always there for us. Once, as deputy mayor, he ordered the city to turn the heat back on in the East Hotel when the landlord deliberately shut down the furnace to try and force elderly residents out.

When we had the epic battle to save the old Carnegie Library building, built in 1903, Rankin agreed to our suggestion to chair what turned out to be the pivotal City Council committee meeting inside the musty, long derelict building. Civic workers had to clean off years of dust and cobwebs and hastily set up a committee table and chairs for the meeting to be held. It was a brilliant but simple tactic to have the committee meet inside, as it brought attention to the pressing need to retain the building for local community use. Being there made it real. That meeting resulted in a positive vote by the committee—moved by Darlene—to earmark capital funds for a full renovation program to restore the building for a community centre for local residents.

Earlier we had secured a visit with businessman and mayoralty candidate Fred Wyder, who had put in a bid to the city to demolish the Carnegie Library building to make room for a restaurant. We wanted to stop that and see if instead he would donate money to help renovate the grand old building. It was a far-fetched idea, but typical of DERA's creativity—and good for media. The meeting took place in his corporate office in the Bentall Centre, in the heart of the downtown business district, only a few blocks from the Downtown Eastside. Bruce, Jean, and I made our pitch that he could gain huge political support by helping renovate the beleaguered building for people who needed it. He listened politely in his beautifully furnished office, and then said, "You wouldn't want me to rob her of her future, would you?" We looked with interest to where he pointed, and gazed upon the portrait of a young girl (presumably his daughter), whose future was apparently in peril.

Jean is still closely connected with the now flourishing Carnegie Centre, and when I recently asked her what she remembered about that meeting with Wyder, she recalled the funniest part that I had forgotten. After the meeting, Wyder volunteered to drive us back to Main and Hastings and we thought, why the heck not, it would save us bus fares, and so we accompanied him to the underground Bentall Centre parking lot, full of luxury cars. It was the first and last time we were driven to the neighbourhood in a Jaguar. People gaped in disbelief as, embarrassed, we got out of the car and said goodbye to Mr. Wyder.

The campaign to save the Carnegie building took about six years. It taught us a lot about how city hall worked and what we needed to do to secure an ongoing commitment from the city. Even when the city agreed to an initial contribution, we fought unsuccessfully for

Bruce Eriksen begins painting his mural "The Law in Its Majestic Equality" on the hoarding of the to-be-renovated Carnegie Centre at Main and Hastings, June 11, 1978

federal funds. The civic works department put up a hoarding around the renovation construction site and Bruce, upon learning that local MP Ron Basford, a powerful Liberal cabinet minister in Ottawa, had secured federal funds to repurpose industrial Granville Island to a public market, seized the opportunity to paint the Carnegie hoarding at night. In garish lime and white paint, he painted for all to see: "$6 million for Granville Island—$0 for Carnegie." The city, unimpressed, quickly hired a co-ordinator to "help" the community develop murals for the hoarding. Even that became a political statement: Bruce painted his mural "The Law in Its Majestic Equality" and David Lane, a young organizer at DERA, created a mural on the need to raise welfare rates.

Emery Barnes, our provincial representative in Victoria, and the guy I had campaigned for in 1972, became another ally. We maintained a close association with Emery, and he stood by us even when the NDP government that he was part of, under Premier Barrett, changed the law eliminating long-term hotel and rooming-house residents from tenancy protection. He spoke out in solidarity when we took our protest to Victoria, demanding that long-term residents of single-room occupancies have the same rights as all tenants. I am sure he paid a price for his unflinching support of DERA, especially when others in the NDP government admonished us for "shitting in our own nest." It wasn't easy to take on an NDP government that we supported in many respects, and that did many excellent things, such as establishing the Agricultural Land Reserve in 1973 to preserve valuable farmland from suburban development. We made our causes for social justice very public, as well as our criticism of any wrongdoing or lack of action, no matter who was in power, and that made for an uneasy relationship with the NDP. The trust we had with Emery was essential to our survival, and his understanding of the political structure in the BC legislature helped us understand how to navigate a sometimes complex political world.

᳘

Community organizing is an ill-defined job—it can mean pretty well anything. But creativity is at its core. No one taught us how to do community organizing for change. We taught ourselves. And the more creative we were and the more we employed the media on our side, the more we got done.

In 1976 Oppenheimer Lodge—the first social housing in the Downtown Eastside—was due to finally open. The opening was delayed because of a labour dispute with unionized electricians. We were desperate to get people who had waited so long moved in. Bruce's creative brain went to work. He found out that Mayor Art Phillips—not a fan of DERA's, to say the least—had cut a deal to have work finished on his favourite civic project, the construction of the Granville Mall. So Bruce approached the union and struck a better deal. If we put up a picket line on the mall, would they honour it, because a work stoppage there would pressure the mayor to get work finished on Oppenheimer Lodge? Yup. They were up for it. They much preferred the idea of helping low-income folks, most of whom were former union members who had been injured on the job, to helping the mayor with his fancy mall.

So we hurriedly made our picket signs to announce what we were doing and got up early every day to be on the mall before 6:30 a.m., when the workers arrived, to set up our picket line, which they then refused to cross. It wasn't far from the Downtown Eastside to the Granville Mall construction site, and it seemed an adventure to walk uptown so early in the morning, the rush-hour traffic not yet at full steam, hearing the birds sing as we cut through the cenotaph and up the hill. Despite being almost mowed down by a furious contractor in his pickup truck, our action was a success with good media coverage. Bruce grinned from ear to ear as the mayor was forced to get Oppenheimer Lodge open on schedule. This was community organizing!

In another instance, Bruce had been forcibly thrown out of beer parlours as an "undesirable" under the *Innkeepers Act*. To draw attention to the absurdity of this, and the fact that beer parlour owners were really trying to prevent his exposure of their flagrant violations, he got Rankin (a non-drinker) and Barnes to accompany him on a beer parlour tour up and down East Hastings Street—so they too would be thrown out as undesirables. They were indeed duly thrown out, as reported to full effect by the media. Ingenious community organizing to draw attention to, in this case, the misuse of the law. Bruce became such a threat to the liquor-licensed establishment that the police showed up one day and said an informant had given information that there was a contract out on his life. He noted a similar incident in his diary, which my son Lief found recently:

> **8am** While having coffee at the Ovaltine Cafe I was approached by Peter Pezel who stated to me "It is now just a matter of where and when. You are costing me money." This is the second time he has made veiled threats. The first time I reported to Inspector Fish who made a note of it.

The police told Bruce to leave town, and he did for about two days, staying with his brother in Victoria. But he promptly returned and declared the best policy for his safety was to announce publicly that his life had been threatened. The announcement garnered front-page news, and then work continued as usual.

One day, as Bruce and I walked down the back alley by the Empress Hotel, a big black car came speeding at us. If we hadn't smartly jumped aside, it would have been a hit and run for sure. Community organizing wasn't without its dangers. Many a time I would wait up very late, in the minute apartment on East Hastings Street next to the First United Church that we had moved to in about 1976, waiting for Bruce to come home after his beer parlour rounds. He came home one night particularly late, gasping in pain—his ribs cracked from a run-in with a bouncer who had been ordered to evict him from the premises. The beer parlour owners hated Bruce.

Bruce had a nose for a good story and how to get the media on board. He'd hang out at the cop shop where the reporters were waiting for police updates and feed them great lines and stories. They were game. Bruce was good drama and any story about booze, dying in fires, crime, and the like, was good for business. I listened many times to Bruce phoning the news stations at night, saying, "I got something for you." He knew that if he got it on CKNW news radio first, other outlets would pick it up too. Funny thing is, he never said who he was; they just knew his voice. Often they'd tell him to get lost, but he was never deterred. He had a breathtaking drive to get the story out. Later, after Bruce died, reporters told me that he nearly drove them mad, but they, and he, knew a good story when they saw one.

In 1976, provincial welfare minister Bill Vander Zalm, in the Social Credit government of Bill Bennett (W.A.C. Bennett's son), made an infamous comment about people on welfare: "Pick up a shovel and work." We kicked into gear. Vander Zalm owned a chain of garden stores, so we headed out, unemployed people from the Downtown Eastside, shovels in hand, to demand work at his store. Of course they weren't hiring, and the minister looked a bit sheepish as he had to admit that work was hard to come by. The media covered it in full, as Vander Zalm was a colourful figure who we knew would attract attention. The action exposed the rhetoric of poor-bashing by a powerful minister in the Social Credit government—a line of rhetoric we hear even today. And it exposed that unemployment levels were high and people actually did want jobs, not welfare. We had many run-ins with Vander Zalm and delighted when in 1978, the *Victoria Daily Times* published a political cartoon by Bob Bierman that portrayed the minister picking the wings off helpless flies.

When "taxbuyer" businesses popped up and starting ripping people off for their meagre tax refunds, we were furious to learn there was no law against it. It was another example of lack of protection and discrimination against poor people. Most people of average income were satisfied to file their income tax return and wait for any refund due. But if you lived far below the poverty line and were desperate for cash today, then unscrupulous businesses were ready to take advantage and "buy" your refund in advance, keeping most of what was due to you. So another high-profile public campaign began to change federal laws that eventually led to changes that forced taxbuyers to refund 85 percent of any refund.

DERA attended the Berger Commission hearings on the Mackenzie Valley Pipeline in May 1976. Bruce gave powerful testimony prepared with support from DERA researcher Lawrence Bantleman, showing the linkage for Indigenous people between loss of land, rights, and culture in the North and in the Downtown Eastside. It's astonishing to reread the brief today—more than forty years later—to see how visionary and prescient DERA's statements were:

> Right now we are sitting in a hall that symbolizes the extravagant sophistication of our western civilization. The Hyatt Regency Hotel is a lavish example of our architectural aptitudes. It is one result of our progress and development. Another result is less than a mile from here in an area of Vancouver that I and 7,000 other people call home. It's the Downtown Eastside known otherwise as Skid Road.
>
> You may wonder what DERA and Skid Road has to do with the Mackenzie Valley Pipeline. Well, I'm here to tell you because I believe they are directly related.
>
> Skid Roads as they exist in all cities across Canada, are the devastating side effects of progress and economic development. Of the 7,000 residents of the Downtown Eastside, I believe there are close to 50% native Indians.
>
> They once enjoyed the benefits of living in their own communities and settlements in the interior of BC. But with the slow and persistent needs of the white settlers who came to

BC, the native Indians were divorced from their homeland, stripped of their traditions, culture and rights, and forced into the white man's society. As past governments and private industries expanded and developed the interior for logging, mining, and agriculture, the native Indians were pushed aside and left to struggle alone.

Stripped of their resources and land, many coastal Indians came and still come to the cities in the south in the hopes of finding work and a new life. What they find and now have to live with is Skid Road.

Faced with substandard housing, unemployment, and disorientation in the city, many native Indians end up in jail, in the drunk tank, and on welfare....

It is not from freedom of choice that native people end up on Skid Road or in jail. It is the result of loss of dignity, self-determination, and economic independence.

We will be aiding that process further if we allow the oil companies to interfere, tamper and exploit the northern lands....

Because we are involved in our own struggle for survival, we express our solidarity with the native people of the north. We demand that our government recognize the right to self-determination and political security for the Dene nation, the Inuit, and all the natives of the north.

Their culture, heritage, economic independence and survival as a nation are dependent upon a fair and just land settlement. Because of that we say "No" to the Mackenzie Valley Pipeline.

We weren't lawyers, professionals, or experts. We were ordinary people deeply committed to defending people's rights and dignity.

Formative Years

I've been asked many times: How did you become so fierce about what you do? Personally, I suffered no trauma or hardship that forged my character. On the contrary, I was brought up with my two sisters in a relatively secure and stable middle-class environment. But looking back I can see that both my parents were strong willed, independent, and very unconventional.

My father, Peter Davies, ran away from an unhappy home environment when he was fourteen and became a soldier in the British army. He was a firebrand socialist, whose fellow soldiers called him "Red." He remained a soldier until we emigrated to Canada in 1968. (Until I was fifteen we lived mostly outside the UK, in Cyprus, Germany, and Malaysia until finally Canada became home.)

My mother, Margaret Davies, has wonderful stories of how she became liberated from her small-minded conservative working-class father, when she joined the army as a young woman in the Second World War. There's a beautiful photograph of her in uniform in London, where she worked underground in the War Office in Whitehall as a Morse code operator taking messages from the front. When we were growing up, she loved telling me and my sisters stories of how, even during the horrors of wartime bombing in London, there was excitement too, attending dances and social gatherings for the young women in the Women's Army Corps. Ironically the war freed her from the gendered constraints in her family. It was also where she met my father, who was in the Royal Signals.

Two characteristics of my parents stand out: a sense of compassion and care for people, and a fierce independence and desire for change. These qualities were formative for me. Life in the British army was very conformist, but my parents were never satisfied with that. Wherever we lived the family immersed in local culture and even politics. The first friends that I can remember at three or fours years old were Loolya and Denya, Greek Cypriot kids who lived next door. We played in the schoolyard close by and watched Charlie Chaplin movies at their house. My mother says I would come home at night talking about "Chubbly Chubbly" until she figured out who it was. There was a civil war going on in Cyprus and my father slept with his army pistol under his pillow. Every night we heard gunfire, and often I would lie in bed listening to the sound of bullets as I slowly fell asleep, with not a care in the world. One night we were awakened by a blazing fire in the civic works yard across the street. The night watchman was tied up and in danger of burning to death. My father fearlessly leapt the high wire fence to rescue the terrified man. I stood at the front door in my nightdress, watching wide-eyed as fire trucks and police rolled up. When my father came home, I asked about what had happened but he just told me to go to bed.

In our small Hillman Minx car, we would take day trips outside Nicosia and come back after curfew. My father had a knack for running out of petrol as we explored new places, and I developed a lifelong habit of always watching the petrol gauge in the car and looking out for petrol stations to fill up. He would coast down hills in neutral gear to save petrol. On one such outing, we finally came to a halt. The tank

Libby hangs out with her father, Peter Davies, as he fixes the car, Cyprus, circa 1958

was empty. My father got my mother to knock on someone's door to see if they would give us a little petrol to get us home; not exactly the safest thing to do in the middle of an emergency.

My father took me in an army jeep up Mount Troodos, where a few days earlier a British soldier had been shot. And my mother was perfectly okay to go into the city centre with me in tow during curfew hours to buy a heavy Murano glass paperweight she wanted, with a fish in it. She said later it was good as a defensive weapon if need be. Every time I visit my mother's house, I see the fish paperweight, sparkling blue and iridescent, vigilant on the coffee table.

Many decades later, in 1987, I returned to Cyprus with my son and my older sister and her daughter to visit our father, who was working for the Middle East Council of Churches in Limassol. We visited many of the old places we had grown up in; the city of Nicosia was now divided and patrolled by UN peacekeeping forces, including Canadians. It was extraordinary to visit our old white, flat-roofed house and say hello to our former neighbour, who still lived next door. She remembered us well and said she used to babysit us. I looked at the high white wall around her house in disbelief—it looked ordinary now, about six feet high. What happened to the massive wall I had jumped from at five years old because the boy next door dared me to? I can remember running in to my mother, my eyes streaming, and she thought I was hurt. "I'm not crying," I exploded—it was limestone dust that had produced an outpouring. I was only mad at the kid because he wouldn't jump too.

Later in Germany, we lived in a big square army quarters house on a civilian street. My favourite pastimes were riding a pony called Honey and biking up and down steep hills in the local woods nearby. One day the military police came by and searched our gardens, and others, looking for a knife that had been used as a murder weapon on a body found in those woods. I was fascinated and desperately hoped it might be found in our garden. But they searched on. My parents strictly forbade me to go back to the woods on my bike. But I ignored them and, as I was flying up and down the steep hills, my heart would beat faster as I looked into the misty shadows between the trees, wondering who or what lurked there.

From Germany we took a family camping holiday at Lake Garda in northern Italy. We drove through Austria and, leaving Innsbruck, began to climb the mountainous roadways. As he used to do in Cyprus, my father coasted down in neutral to save petrol and then, as he switched gears to go up the steep inclines, we screamed in horror and delight convinced that, as the car lurched backward, we would fall off the mountain. We continued this way onto the Brenner Pass and into Italy, arriving at our destination at sundown. Everyone at the campsite looked nicely settled in, but for us it was time to set up shop. A disaster in the making.

Since we had no camping equipment of our own, our father had borrowed a crushingly heavy green khaki army tent that we struggled to put up. As my older sister and I tried to hang on to the heavy metal poles, my poor mother tried to follow military-like orders from her husband. Time and again the tent collapsed. It got darker and darker, and our tiredness and desperation got to a breaking point, which the local Italians thought was very funny. Finally the tent was up, secured by its main centre pole, though looking rather precarious. We fell into scratchy and smelly army sleeping bags. Things got a little better with day trips to Verona, where my sister cried her eyes out listening to the story of Romeo and Juliet. Later in Venice we ate wonderful ice cream and took a ride in a gondola under the Bridge of Sighs, imagining what it must have felt like for the convicts who were dragged over the bridge hundreds of years before.

Later, when the family moved to Malaysia, I would sometimes go out with my father into the jungle as the Gurkha soldiers under his command did their military exercises. It was likely against the rules to have a ten-year-old child with you, but it didn't stop my father. I rode on low boats up rivers, tramped through the jungle, found snakes, listened to the monkeys howling in the trees, and took ghastly tasting antimalaria pills every day.

Despite their army life and social connections, my parents always voted Labour, while most other military parents were staunch conservatives. Even knowing this fact at an early age is an indication of the importance of politics in our household. Dinner at eight was first eaten in silence to listen to the BBC World News on the radio. And then discussion would follow, with us kids listening to our parents as they sorted through the day's current affairs.

Sometimes I would accompany my father to local night markets, where we would sit on small stools in the street, rangy dogs prowling around, and eat from bowls of steaming noodles. He met mostly with ethnic Chinese Malay political activists, and I would listen to their charged and lively political conversation about the massive changes taking place in the country, as Merdeka—Malay independence from the British Empire—was underway. I have no recollection of the specific conversations, just that they mattered and that political change was exciting and even dangerous. Somewhere and somehow, the politicized environments we lived in, and that my parents cared about, whether in Cyprus, Malaysia, or Germany, seeped into me. And from my earliest memories, the state of global affairs and politics and the need for change were part of my life.

I attended the local British army school in Malaysia and was mostly bored out of my mind. Each day I longed for classes to end at 1 p.m. so I could go "swimming like a fish," as my mother said. That's where I felt most free and alive. My blond hair became sticky and took on a greenish colour from the chlorine, and my eyes were always red from swimming underwater—there was no such thing then as swimming goggles. Sometimes on weekends my father would take us to Port Dickson to swim in the sea, and I'd sail with him in a small boat. On one such occasion, the rudder broke, and we drifted for what seemed like hours in the blazing sun as the shore receded in the distance. Overall these were glorious days: the endless heat of the sun, the waves rolling over us, and later eating my mother's delicious cold cheese and onion pie. Here too in Seremban, where we lived, I had local friends and I couldn't understand why other army kids didn't. It seemed natural to me to have these friendships, but I also felt the looks from other British kids who frowned upon them.

At age eleven, my parents sent me from Malaysia to join my older sister in boarding school back in the UK. True to form, my parents rejected the norm of sending us to public school (as private school was known in class-conscious Britain); instead, we were packed off to one of two state-run boarding schools, and the only one that was co-ed. My first night there, when most of the kids were homesick, I started a pillow fight. I ended up in detention walking around the quadrangle, where the dormitories were, in my slippers and dressing gown. Many more detentions followed for breaking the rules.

While my sister Jane and I were at school in the UK, our family experienced unexpected events in Malaysia. My father suffered a serious accident in a military jeep on a twisty mountain pass and broke his neck, ending up in traction in the military hospital in Kuala Lumpur for many weeks. He was lucky to survive. A few weeks later, my mother suffered a brutal, near-fatal attack in our home by three men with knives. Incredibly she fought the attackers off and survived the long ride to the military hospital. Once stabilized, she was wheeled in to see her husband in an adjoining ward. She was also lucky to survive. Neither parent made a big deal of these events. My older sister was flown home from our boarding school outside London, to help both parents and my younger sister, Helen. I was left at school, utterly fuming that I'd been left behind.

I was an average student, who only excelled when I liked the teacher or the teacher liked me. From a French teacher who would ridicule students and bully us, I developed a lifelong aversion to learning languages. It made retention of new foreign words seem impossible. Even decades later as an adult in Ottawa, attempting to learn French, I failed miserably, time and time again. I couldn't get Mr. Wolfe (yes, that was indeed his name) out of my head.

But I was an avid reader. By age thirteen I had read *War and Peace* and *Anna Karenina*—still my favourite novel—and many other Russian novels by Gogol, Turgenev, and Dostoyevsky. I was enthralled by the tragedy, romanticism, and sweeping drama in these books. My father introduced me to George Orwell at an early age, and still today I find Orwell's spare writing revealing and memorable.

As a young adult, I was captivated by books by Jean-Paul Sartre and Simone de Beauvoir, Albert Camus, and Franz Kafka. These authors shaped my thoughts about life and the choices we are responsible for. If books are a mirror of who you are, then I was to be the fierce idealist who believes in the power of each of us to do things that mean something. I loved scouring the bookshelves in the living room, reading everything I could—including novels about India and the Far East, like John Masters's *Bhowani Junction*, where my ten-year-old eyes goggled at the graphic sex scenes, and *The Malayan Trilogy* by Anthony Burgess, describing the crushing weight of British colonialism. I was also fascinated by astronomy and delighted when my father bought me a book by Patrick Moore that unfolded the stars above. I decided to make my own telescope, and messed around with lenses and cardboard and glue until it fell apart. I also had a subscription to *Look and Learn*, a children's magazine of knowledge and science; I carefully built up the volumes in red boxes that I still have today.

I spent my childhood days as a wild spirit, out on my bike, exploring a deserted, mysterious old house with ancient photos strewn on the floor, or playing with friends in the rubber plantation, with the heavy smell of white latex dripping into small cups attached to the trees. I realize now that I was given great freedom of movement and was mostly left to do what I wanted—unless my mother caught me out.

I had very different relationships with my parents. I greatly admired and loved my father. He let me do whatever I wanted, and I loved the adventures and activities we undertook together. It seemed like we were always getting into trouble. In Germany we lost the car keys while riding horses in the dense forest a couple of hours from home; I have no recollection how we got back, but we did. Later in Malaysia, while visiting the Cameron Highlands to cool off from the stifling summer heat, my father and I walked through the vast tropical forest, the sun rays barely reaching us, surrounded by massive vines, beautiful flowers, and sounds of the jungle everywhere. All was serene until he suddenly yelled, "Run, Libby, run!" I had no idea why, but we took off at breathtaking speed, careening down the steep path. Then out of the corner of my eye, I saw the cloud of hornets chasing us, and I could hear them buzzing furiously. My father had apparently stepped on the nest. He suffered thirty-two nasty stings that swelled up and had to be treated at the local clinic. I was lucky and received only three. But the adventure stayed in my mind long after the stings were gone.

Peter Davies was a charismatic and powerful personality, which made him popular and interesting to be with, but we knew he had a dark side too. He would erupt into disturbing tempers and then slide into deep remorse and retreat from those around him. But he always cared for us, and he taught me important things about injustice and the impact of colonialism. It almost broke my heart when, many years later, sick with Parkinson's disease, two years before his death, he told my older sister and me that he deeply regretted that he had been a terrible father. I cried in protest and told him it wasn't true, that he had been a source of wonder and extraordinary love. He didn't believe me. I reminded him how he had taken me to visit the Cheshire Homes, near Colchester, England, when I was about seven years old, where he volunteered to help soldiers who had been wounded and disabled by war. He would talk with the soldiers and help fix things around the home, while I helped weave baskets. I tried to tell him how much I'd valued this and the many shared experiences we had. How many fathers would bring home a live tortoise from Libya, tucked safely in the suitcase, and small curled-up pointed-toe leather slippers in white and pale blue with gold etchings? He looked at me sadly. It was the last serious conversation we had before the disease took over his body and mind.

My mother, on the other hand, I saw mostly as the person holding me back. I was always in trouble, and she was the one left to dish out the punishment. When I sprayed a garden hose through the house window in Malaysia—apparently on purpose—and ruined the week's clean laundry, she grounded me for a week. She let me out a day early to go with the family to the officers' mess for the weekly lunch, where I promptly got locked in the toilet and couldn't get out. After much banging and yelling, the formal luncheon was disrupted as various people tried to unjam the door. She looked at me and rolled her eyes.

Libby and Margaret Davies at May Day rally, 2001

"How could you," she said, looking embarrassed at the fuss. She freaked out when I brought home a long snake on a stick (alive and wriggling) to show her, and she refused to come out of the bedroom until my father came home. She tells me that when I left for boarding school I never looked back to wave goodbye, and that I shrugged off her entreaties to be polite at all times. I spoke my mind to the point of rudeness and made it very clear when I didn't want to do something. Though she always defended me when relatives clucked their tongues and raised their eyebrows at my unorthodox behaviour.

Even in her advanced years, my mother always dressed beautifully. I recall when she attended parents' day at our boarding school in the UK, dressed to the nines. I watched in wonder as she walked carefully across the grass field toward me, making sure her blue high heels didn't sink into the grass. Her Thai silk day coat in royal blue had deep slits up the sides, and her bright fuchsia hat with small silk flowers was fitted perfectly. The other parents looked drab and boring next to her.

Not embarrassed in the least—as teenagers often are about their parents—I marvelled at her elegance and style.

I think now that I am more like my mother than my father. She too was rebellious and independent as a child, and as a young adult threw over her narrow working-class environment, escaping, like many young women of her generation, to a new life in the army. But in my childhood and even into young adulthood, I could only see her as someone who held me back. It has taken me years to fully comprehend that she was always looking out for me, only fearing that my unorthodox decisions would get me in trouble, as they often did. She became a rebel in her own way, and in her eighties talked up a storm about the gigs she did with the Raging Grannies in Vancouver, protesting against war and injustice.

We came to Canada almost by accident. My mother told us they had applied to be interviewed in London at Canada House and Australia House, either country being a possible place to live. My parents didn't seem very enamoured with Britain, and it appeared we were destined to follow the great migrations of emigrants. Canada House came up first and became our destination by default. My father secured a job in northern Alberta through an old army friend, and in October 1968, after landing in Montreal, we travelled across the country by train to Edmonton. On our first morning in Montreal, already cool and frosty, our father marched us at a brisk military pace up Mount Royal, where I promptly threw up at the summit. We were later treated to the new experience of Canadian pancakes with maple syrup, which seemed a very odd thing to us girls to eat for breakfast.

At the Queen Elizabeth train station waiting to board our trans-Canada train, the three sisters squeezed in a photo booth; there we were, eighteen, fifteen, and six years old, ready for another adventure. We were worldly wise, having lived in many cultures and environments, but nothing prepared us for the vastness of northern forests, lakes, prairies, and wetlands that moved silently by. Each night on the train, we were tucked into our neatly made bunk beds and the curtains were drawn. My older sister looked in horror when she ate a turkey sandwich smothered in pale gravy. At brief station stops, we looked in amazement at the rough-and-tumble men on the platform in their red checkered padded shirts and enormous boots. It was a long way from London, from where we had come.

The three sisters—Jane, Libby, and Helen—at the Queen Elizabeth train station photo booth, Montreal, before boarding the trans-Canada train to Edmonton, October 1968

The first evening in Edmonton, my parents left us in a motel as they went out to explore the city and I watched my first movie in Canada—*The Birds* by Alfred Hitchcock. We were terrified and for the first time thought, what if our parents didn't return? Here we were in a city and country we knew nothing about, and the looming enormity of our situation closed in. We huddled on the bed and tried to shield our youngest sister from the scariest parts of the movie. Of course our parents returned, having sized up Edmonton, and we felt safe again.

My father bought a huge American car, a Plymouth Fury, in a solid beige that melted into the grey skies as winter approached. We piled in and began our journey to a place called Lac La Biche, hours north. Eventually the paved road gave way to gravel, and I remember looking out the car window thinking, how can there possibly be anything at the end of this road? The muskeg stretched as far as the eye could see. I have this picture in my head of the Davies family arriving: a small motel room, suitcases in hand, the air colder than anything we'd ever felt before, and our feet freezing. My older sister and I were proudly wearing our tall black leather boots from London boutiques. They looked distinctly out of place compared to the fur-lined winter mukluks people wore in the very small town. But nevertheless we set off up the street to Tomboys, the only grocery store, with our shopping baskets in hand. The grocery clerk looked curiously at us, with our fine British accents, and an old man peered into our baskets and said, "What you got in there, babies?" My mother politely advised him they were for our shopping, of course.

Life in Lac La Biche was a marvel and a strange dream. The lake was frozen, and we watched in astonishment as people with nothing better to do on a Sunday afternoon drove in wide circles around and around the lake. My younger sister remembers us taking her to skate on the lake in her new second-hand skates that were duller than a bread knife. Unbelievably we sat in the car as she plowed through the snow on her own. I can't imagine why we didn't help her. And no one had said you needed to clear the snow first to get to the ice. It was a year of the deep-winter freeze, and even locals complained bitterly about the minus-forty temperatures. My father commanded me to walk to the local convenience store that was open on a Sunday morning, "only a few minutes away, Libby," to pick up his *Edmonton Journal* newspaper, which was apparently essential. I sniffed at the frigid air, was hit by the swirling gusts of wind and snow, and barely made it back with the damn paper clutched under my arm. "Thank you, Libby," he said with a smile, as my mother tried to warm up my frozen toes and hands. "She nearly got frostbite," my mother threw at my father. He seemed unconcerned.

We adjusted to our new place. My older sister got a job as a clerk in the local hospital, which seemed a far cry from the drama school she had left in London. On weekends she and friends would drive to Edmonton for coffee. The great distances didn't seem so great after all. Jane and I took Helen door to door along the motel rooms for our first "trick or treat" Halloween experience. As it turned out, it was mostly construction workers who stayed in the motel and, my older sister remembers, they had no sweets so they gave us dollar bills instead.

I ventured into new territory at the local high school—bumped up one and even two grades in different subjects, for some strange reason no one would explain. I didn't fare well. I always knew I was different—but here I was downright odd. They thought I spoke in a very funny way, and I couldn't understand very well what people were saying in their rush of jumbled words. Just what was a "restroom," and why was hockey played with skates on ice and not on a field? It helped me appreciate the hardships of settlement for new immigrants—our family was lucky to at least share a common language and familiar culture with Canada. Still, the transition to a remote northern community was not without its bumps.

My father had a job at Alberta New Start, a government-funded initiative to teach Métis people the niceties of modern life. It was an ill-conceived and disastrous model for engaging Indigenous people, and when we heard later, having moved to Vancouver, that there had been protests and a sit-in to take over the facility, we all cheered. My father later worked in Fort McMurray as a college administrator, and the rest of us bore the winter in an ATCO mobile home still in Lac La Biche, wishing for warm weather.

We arrived in Vancouver on Dominion Day—July 1, 1969—and my father, never content to just arrive, announced we would go immediately to the famous Stanley Park to experience the true Vancouver. Of course, as every Vancouverite knows, Canada Day (as it's now called) in Stanley Park is bumper to bumper, and so we crawled along admiring the sea in the monstrous Plymouth Fury, hot and sweaty from our long journey. Then it was takeout Chinese food on Denman Street and finally, as darkness fell, arrival at our rental home at Dunbar and West 49th.

The recent history of Canada is the story of immigrants and their settlement, and our story was a familiar one—adjustment, lack of work, and ups and downs. My father had a hard time finding employment in Vancouver, and it was my mother who held us together after she was hired as a clerk in the welfare office run by the City of Vancouver. She worked her way up to the position of social worker, and became a powerful force helping single men on welfare. She would try to bend the rigid rules as much as she could to get people more money. She later ran the emergency bed bank single-handedly and helped many people in the inner city (still known as Skid Road). My father, on the other hand, joined a radical group of unemployed people—the Unemployed Citizens Welfare Improvement Council (UCWIC) and, as they campaigned for better social assistance for single people, ended up in protests outside the same welfare office where my mother worked on West 8th Avenue. This didn't seem odd to us—my mother working valiantly on the inside and my father protesting on the outside. Maybe I am the product of a perfect blend of my parents, working inside the system and protesting outside too.

It was during this time that my father met a fiery Hungarian refugee, Alex, who was the organizer of UCWIC. Although Alex loathed the welfare office and what it stood for, he had a close affinity to my mother and maintains a friendship with her today. Alex, it turned out, was in some trouble with the police and had to go into hiding for a while. Never one to shirk from responsibility fraught with risk, my father brought Alex home and he was adopted into our household on West 49th. We were told in clear terms not to speak of his presence to anyone. I don't remember feeling the situation was out of the ordinary at all, and the unusual patterns of life in our family continued. Alex had a great influence on me—I was now seventeen and he helped me write a paper on Marxist theory in my first year at the University of British Columbia (UBC). A fervent and passionate leftist, he was like a big brother who had the patience to explain what was going on in the world.

My school life has always been up and down and dimly experienced, possibly because I went to so many different schools and was never grounded long enough to fit in. It was no different in Vancouver. I attended only one year of high school—grade twelve—and immediately decided I didn't like it. Yet again I felt that I didn't fit in—but I was content to be a loner who was into my own thing. I boycotted the graduation and refused to have my photo taken, admiring the blank hole with Elizabeth Davies written underneath. Only a handful of students knew me, and barely at that. Even then, politics was in my blood; I remember writing a high school law class paper on Vancouver's Rental Grievance Board, the rights of tenants, and the need for rent control. My father took me to city hall, where the Rental Grievance Office was located, and I nosed around and picked up what information I could to write my paper. We also visited the third floor, where the mayor's office is located. I had no inkling that one day I would become a city councillor and even run for mayor.

I was the first person in my family to attend post-secondary education—but finishing a university degree was not in the cards. In later years we would all cheer when my younger sister, Helen, received her PhD from the University of Manitoba in 1999. But in 1970, I was intent on learning philosophy and political theory and I enrolled in Arts 1, a multidisciplinary liberal arts program at UBC. I loved hearing the lectures and attending the small-group sessions, and I remember listening to a young David Suzuki from the zoology department. I soaked it all in, but the second year was a disaster, with large lecture halls and what I felt was dull course work with little interaction. Skipping classes didn't seem such a big deal. As in my primary school years, I became bored and unsettled.

One night in 1971, I went home to a news story about underground US nuclear testing in Amchitka, part of a remote string of islands off Alaska. My attention was immediately seized when the news story said Greenpeace was looking for volunteers to go on the high seas to protest the testing. I phoned the number that was listed right away and said I knew how to sail. After a few brief questions—when it became clear my experience was in a tiny sail boat as a kid, and that I was eighteen—the Greenpeace volunteer co-ordinator politely dissuaded me. I wasn't what they were looking for. Even my father agreed it was a stretch and I didn't have the experience needed for such a mission. Disappointed I trudged back to UBC, and the lifeless lectures went on. But I knew I wasn't cut out for academia and I felt ready to leave.

By about 1970 or maybe a little later, my father had found part-time and then full-time work at First United Church in the heart of Skid Road. It was his initiative that started the community health clinic, the first of its kind in Vancouver, and my subsequent connection to applying for the summer student youth program of setting up the low-cost food store. He later became a social planner at city hall and helped with the formation of DERA and its precursor, the People's Aid Project, where Bruce was first hired. Peter played a role in DERA's early struggles to define itself, helping to write the association's objectives to "expose the injustice of the law...and uphold the rights and dignity of residents." My father likely hoped I would return to UBC—though he never said so explicitly. Maybe he already knew that my future lay in organizing and political change.

The Good Fight
at City Hall

With our extensive work in community organizing and fighting city hall, it was probably inevitable that Bruce, Jean, and I would get involved more formally in civic politics. It certainly wasn't planned that way; it was a natural evolution of our work in the Downtown Eastside.

Bruce made his first run for civic politics in 1974, running for alderman. Jean and I followed two years later, in 1976, both running for City Council too. We joined the Committee of Progressive Electors, of which Harry Rankin was still the lone elected representative on council. COPE, formed in 1968 by the Vancouver and District Labour Council, was the left alternative to the liberal TEAM organization. When we ran, Art Phillips was the mayor of the TEAM majority on City Council—and we ran because we were pissed off. After many battles with TEAM and their lack of response to critical issues in the Downtown Eastside, we figured we could do as good a job as any of them to make sure the needs of our community were being met at city hall. The only major city in Canada without a ward system of electing representatives, we had to run "at large" for one of the ten City Council spots available. This was a daunting challenge, not only in terms of the money needed to run a successful campaign across the city, but also because there weren't enough votes to get elected in the Downtown Eastside, which had the lowest voter turnout in the city.

The tipping point for my decision was an "order" from Harry Rankin. A group of us were sitting on his living room floor discussing the COPE slate for the upcoming 1976 civic election, and he pointed a finger at me and said, almost accusingly, "She should run." I turned around thinking he must mean someone behind me. But no, it was me. I was unsure that I had the experience and confidence to be a candidate, even though, like Bruce and Jean, I was pissed off at the way the community we worked in was so often ignored by city hall. Maybe it was my naïveté that pushed me on. Or maybe I was just taking direction from people like Harry, who knew better.

I don't think we even expected to win. We just wanted to make a difference and put our community on the political map. Bruce was elected in 1980 on his fourth try, as a city councillor. I was elected as a parks commissioner to the Vancouver Parks Board in the same civic election and then in 1982, at age twenty-nine, as a city councillor.

For that electoral success, we needed support in almost every neighbourhood. We were well known in the Downtown Eastside, but it took several elections to broaden our appeal to other communities across the city. Many of the issues we worked on went beyond the Downtown Eastside, especially the desire to support local community planning and stop the demolition of affordable housing. These issues were being grappled with in many neighbourhoods and they gave us a connection to neighbourhood activists in different parts of the city. We had also been very involved in city-wide campaigns to implement a ward system for electing civic representatives (something that still eludes Vancouver today).

Libby, Lief, and Bruce, circa 1980

We raised a few dollars here and there, hand-delivered flyers, and had yellow and black matchbooks made that urged people to vote for us. In these days before social media, matchbooks and bumper stickers for cars were popular promotions. We managed to book a few radio ads, but our work was mostly what we had always done—person by person, organizing, speaking out, connecting, and soliciting support for the issues we championed. There's no question, too, that the organizing work in the Downtown Eastside was gaining city-wide attention. More and more voters questioned why such a poor neighbourhood was being written off by the powers that be.

For several years the battle for what became known as the DERA grant took on mammoth proportions. DERA had a small amount of civic funding to pay for its community organizers—positions that Bruce, Jean, and I shared at various times. A grant from city hall required a two-thirds vote of council—thus eight votes were needed to approve a grant. Each year, as we became more aggressive in our community organizing, it became harder to secure the modest financial support we relied on from the city. The annual grant appeals became legendary, as the TEAM council endured listening to hundreds of delegations late into the night who supported DERA's work. The anti-DERA councillors squirmed in discomfort at the political theatrics underway in the council chamber. The most famous of these was in about 1980, when in taking the vote it was clear that seven councillors were finally on board to support DERA funding. The mayor, now Jack Volrich, was the last to vote. There was a deadly hush in the chamber as the seconds ticked by and the mayor pondered whether he would be the eighth vote to approve the grant or the fourth vote to defeat it. He took stock of the public galleries filled to overflowing with DERA supporters, and he made a pragmatic decision to be the approving vote. Cheers broke out, but he didn't look happy about it.

To this day I marvel that people from such diverse communities in Vancouver gave us their confidence. It was a manifestation of the understanding of DERA's work and people's desire to see social and economic conditions improve in the Downtown Eastside, whether they lived there or not. It was incredible to know that the work we undertook had value for the broader community. It was an affirmation of democracy that the hard work for social justice can be shared and supported in a popular way by many different people.

So what does a new and inexperienced city councillor do? For Bruce it meant grasping the new rules in play and learning to apply them from the inside. We had always been on the outside, and here we were, voting members of Vancouver City Council with an opportunity to directly influence the political agenda, for the benefit of not only the Downtown Eastside but also the city as a whole. Bruce became a champion for bylaw enforcement that improved people's quality of life. He became a strong defender of civic services, especially the fire department, and fought tooth and nail to save Vancouver's old fireboat—which would eventually be sold to San Francisco in 1987. He also defended people's rights and fought to remedy historical injustices.

For me it meant widening my horizons and seeking new allies and partners in other neighbourhoods, and I became particularly interested in community planning and housing. We became champions for meaningful citizen participation and tougher rules for developers, and strong advocates for city-supported social housing. My two years as an elected parks commissioner prior to being elected to City Council had helped me understand how the city worked and gave me valuable insight into moving motions, seeking support in the community, and arguing my case. Patricia Wilson was the second COPE parks commissioner. Together we took on the old boys at the Parks Board every Monday night—the two of us against the five NPA commissioners who mistakenly thought we were inconsequential. That is, until we started winning battles to keep recreation fees reasonable, and challenged the copious public dollars going into privately run facilities such as VanDusen Botanical Garden and the Vancouver Aquarium, where we took on campaigns to oppose the captivity of whales.

Bruce and I had a steep learning curve, with only our gut instincts to guide us. We picked up what we could from Harry Rankin, who had years of experience both as an accomplished lawyer and as a city councillor. But ultimately, it was sink or swim on your own. I learned to wade through reams of City Council reports that showed up every Friday night, to be debated on the next Tuesday. I learned to understand how city budgets worked, and the complexities of zoning changes and land use development.

At times it was daunting to understand all the facets of civic government. But I learned quickly, and eventually it became easier and more familiar to debate issues in council meetings and committees. But there was always an awareness that we were "outsiders," and a part of my brain questioned what right we had to be there. Elected office in those days was a seriously male domain, and my political mentors were men, particularly Bruce, Harry Rankin, and Bruce Yorke, also a COPE city councillor. There were few progressive female role models that I related to in my early political life: Darlene Marzari at city hall before I was elected, and later, Margaret Mitchell, a strong feminist and NDP member of Parliament for Vancouver East. Margaret had been a social worker and showed much compassion for the people she represented. I don't recall facing sexism in the political world I was in, but I am sure it was there—I just didn't recognize it as such. It was only years later in Parliament that the pervasiveness of sexism and its damaging impact became clear to me.

In the 1980s massive changes were underway in the city. Vancouver was getting ready to host the world Expo '86 on the north shore of False Creek, and the city's hundredth birthday. Development pressures were unrelenting, as local neighbourhoods fought the demolition of affordable housing and many communities wanted to bring in community planning and controls on developers (sound familiar?). The newly elected progressive majority on City Council in 1982, which I was part of, was led by Mayor Mike Harcourt. We rejected austerity programs from the Social Credit provincial government, and, at our first meeting in December 1982, the six progressives on City Council voted to maintain jobs and public services at the city level.

I remember that first council meeting very well. Feeling nervous and excited, sitting in the red swivel chair looking at the richly panelled wood interior of the council chamber, ready and eager to cast my vote against cutting civic services. I looked at Bruce and marvelled that we were both there together, having run so many times against all the odds. Lief, our son, not quite four years old, was close by, as was my mother, keeping a close eye on him. Lief was to attend many meetings after that, poking around our offices and keeping himself busy with the "meeting bag" that Jean Swanson made. He would be carried along at numerous rallies and

Bruce and Lief at the annual Walk for Peace, 1982

marches for peace and justice, with his small sign made by our friend Judith Gould that said, "Let me grow up, not blow up!"

At night Bruce would tuck him into bed and sing a lullaby and tell him he should sleep now to grow up big and strong. "I don't want to grow up," said Lief one night, in a small voice. "Why not?" asked his dad in surprise. "I don't want to blow up," replied Lief immediately, eyes filling with tears. Bruce and I looked at each other in dismay as it came home to us just how real and scary it was for a little boy experiencing the fears of the world. The world was gripped in the height of the Cold War and a frightening nuclear arms race. It was in the civic arena that cities for peace reached out to one another and Vancouver led the way.

In April 1983, Vancouver declared itself a Nuclear-Weapon-Free Zone (NWFZ)—the first city in Canada to do so. COPE had the political will and four votes to make it happen with Mayor Harcourt and councillor Bill Yee. It took just six votes out of eleven. But it was the powerful coalition of End the Arms Race (EAR) that made it possible. A massive movement representing tens of thousands of citizens from faith groups, unions, peace organizations, and more, EAR, led by Carmela Allevato and Frank Kennedy, gave people hope that a world free of nuclear fear was possible. Each year in April, tens of thousands of people came together to walk for peace, beginning at the south end of the Burrard Street Bridge and winding through downtown streets to Sunset Beach for speeches and music. When I spoke at one of the mass gatherings, I experienced my first bout of severe stage fright.

From behind the stage, clutching my meagre notes on a crumpled piece of paper, I could hear the crowd roaring its collective voice. Feeling sick to my stomach, I wondered if I had the might to get up there and speak out to so many. On this and many other occasions I experienced the stress of speaking to large gatherings, but somehow, amazingly, once up there, the passion of the moment would propel me to find my voice.

These rallies for peace were extraordinary examples of grassroots mobilization, coupled with civic action that gave meaning to the slogan "Think globally, act locally." Where else did a city council direct its medical health officer to write a pamphlet outlining the dangers of nuclear war and distribute it to every household? It was a bold and necessary move. It was a pioneering example of civic government taking on a global issue because it affected the lives of people in the city, notwithstanding federal jurisdiction. In the new millennium, it's quite expected for municipalities to be involved in issues of a global proportion, particularly climate

City councillors Libby Davies, Bruce Yorke, Harry Rankin, and Bruce Eriksen celebrate Nuclear-Weapon-Free Zone posting, Vancouver, December 1983 change, because the massive implications are obvious at the local level where people live. But back in the 1980s, city councils were expected to confine themselves to potholes and dog shit (to cop a phrase from Harry Rankin). Not so with the COPE city councillors, Bruce Eriksen, Bruce Yorke, Harry, me, and later Patricia Wilson. We considered it our civic duty to connect the local and the global, despite right-wingers on council who considered these issues quite beyond the realm of civic responsibilities.

I was fortunate to chair a Special Council Committee on Peace that brought together activists from the peace and justice movements. I later met Jack Layton, a Toronto city councillor, at the Federation of Canadian Municipalities (FCM) conferences, and we naturally gravitated to each other. We were working on common issues to do with peace and disarmament, housing, socially responsible development, HIV/AIDS, and community health. In 1989 we were both involved in initiating a project to develop a Nuclear-Weapon-Free Zone network in Canada. Jack was fast moving, fast talking, and filled with passion for change. Along with me and councillor Michael Fainstat from Montreal, we worked on getting other municipalities on board as Nuclear-Weapon-Free Zones. We called for ethical purchasing policies to ensure that municipalities were not buying goods and services from the military industrial complex.

The NWFZ wasn't just a symbolic declaration—we did everything we could give the declaration meaning. Vancouver was a favourite port of call for US warships to give navy personnel rest and relaxation. The city demanded to know if these ships carried nuclear weapons, but the policy of "neither confirm nor deny" was the standard response.

In August 1989, training for an upcoming swimming event in English Bay, my swim coach, Lesley Beatson, and I were at Spanish Banks so I could get used to swimming longer distances in the ocean. In the early morning sunlight against the grey-blue North Shore mountains, we could see the massive warship and aircraft carrier USS *Independence* anchored in Burrard Inlet. I mentioned to Lesley that the city was opposed to the hundred or so nuclear weapons on board. "We have to do something," she said and proposed a swimathon around the ship to protest its nuclear weapons. She assured me that she could gather up other swimmers—and she did. I contacted Janos Mate at Greenpeace, who thought it was great idea.

The famous Greenpeace zodiacs ferried out about twenty swimmers to the middle of Burrard Inlet, and we jumped into the very cold water and began our swim. Most of the swimmers were experienced triathletes and great swimmers; I lagged behind, but I was in! I had also roped in a swimming buddy from my local community pool, Barry Morris, a minister at First United Church who optimistically joined the action. We swam and swam, and realized just how bloody enormous this warship was. The uppermost deck, an overhang where aircraft could land, was a giant shadow that blocked the sky. Every time I lifted my head for a breath I could hear the insults the sailors hurled at us from above. They were clearly neither enthused nor impressed with our swimming skills—but we continued anyway. We came to shore pretty damn cold but pumped that we had swum the entire circumference of the vessel. I don't think I will ever do it again, but it was good to experience tiny human arms and legs moving like crazy against a monstrous symbol of the military industrial complex.

Other life-and-death issues in the city were close to home. The issue of street prostitution, as it was referred to at the time, had plagued Vancouver for years. A national campaign led by big-city mayors across Canada took hold, seeking new federal laws to ban street soliciting for the purposes of prostitution. The mayors and many city councils in Canada's major cities were under intense pressure to stop street prostitution and its impact on local neighbourhoods. Angry, locally organized citizen groups sprung up, some of whom displayed nasty public shaming tactics. These were vicious campaigns that, despite their claims to the contrary, targeted sex workers.

It was a time of heated emotional debate, and much of it took place at City Council meetings in Vancouver. Citizen groups demanded action and protection from street prostitution, believing the only answer was more cops on the streets and tougher laws. The so-called nuisance impacts of street prostitution garnered much media attention and increasing action by citizens who were determined to rid their neighbourhoods of sex workers and their customers. On one occasion in 1984, late into the night, with many irate citizen delegations speaking, there was intense debate on a motion supported by Mayor Mike Harcourt. Mayor Harcourt was a leading advocate calling for new federal laws to be passed to control street prostitution. The four COPE councillors, Harry Rankin, Bruce Eriksen, Bruce Yorke, and I, refused to vote for the motion. We were screamed at by angry residents, who said that we had betrayed them. But we refused to be part of the mass hysteria and reasoned that the proposed new laws would be unworkable and dangerous.

The new federal "communicating law" that resulted in 1985 contributed to the dangers that sex workers faced. Under this law it was illegal to communicate in a public place, including a car, for the purpose of prostitution. Although prostitution itself was not and never had been illegal, activities such as living off the avails and keeping a common bawdy house were.

It was after that, when the new communicating law was enacted, that stories of missing women began to circulate in the Downtown Eastside. And although missing-persons complaints were made to the Vancouver Police Department, the community felt strongly that the complaints were not treated seriously because many of the missing women were sex workers. The position the four COPE councillors took on defending sex-worker rights, refusing to jump on the simplistic and misguided law-and-order bandwagon, was a significant experience for me as an elected representative. I was learning to withstand vitriolic public opinion that too often led to draconian measures—something I would see again in Ottawa as a member of Parliament.

It would have been easy to just go along with it all, to appease people's fears and frustration, and say yes, more cops and tougher laws are the answer. But we knew it was the wrong approach. It was these days and issues that taught me about leadership and principle. I was thankful to be part of a small civic caucus that knew what we had to do and had the gumption to carry it through. We had to push back against the hyperbole and angry rhetoric and maintain a firm and reasoned position that was based on evidence—and not on undermining the rights of the sex workers, who were being scapegoated in this debate.

The situation became horrifying when the body parts of a sex worker were found in a dumpster at Powell and Salsbury in east Vancouver. I remember vividly that first community march in 1992 from the dumpster to the Carnegie Centre, about a kilometre away. On a cold February day we walked along the streets, many of us holding hands, as we grappled with the issue of missing and murdered women, most of whom were sex workers and many Indigenous women. A smudge ceremony was held at the Carnegie Centre, and I wept as we saw the family members who had come into town to pay their respects. With the smell of sweetgrass and sage drifting through, the theatre of the Carnegie Centre was so full you could hardly move. The emotion in the room was palpable. The murder of Cheryl Ann Joe and the community march that day to the Carnegie Centre brought home the enormity of the disappearance of so many women. This gathering for Cheryl Ann Joe began the annual Valentine's Day Women's Memorial March that continues today.

It was soon after this event that community members, including me, became convinced there was a serial killer at large, and we called for a special police task force to investigate the disappearances. We were told repeatedly not to worry and that investigations were in progress. The ongoing tragedy of missing and murdered women and the risks faced by sex workers had a profound impact on me. I grappled with how to respond to the issue amid the divisive public and political discourse, and to come to terms with a society where some people—because of their

Speaking at the Missing Women Commission of Inquiry (Oppal Commission),
January 19, 2011

trade, gender, ethnicity, health, or economic circumstances—are considered human garbage to be disposed of and forgotten.

Over the years I have tried to be aware of the spiritual aspect of life, but it's been a tenuous thing. I can get close to it by being in a beautiful west coast forest with tall trees that reach for the sky, weathered but unbroken. The branches stretching out with drops of rain, sunlight dappled and luminescent green. Alongside the massive trees, graveyards of stumps so enormous it would take six people to reach around. The stumps are alive, even though the trunks have been cut down and sold for profit long ago. By nature's force they regenerate and harbour new growth, and they might have a spirit within them. The forest floor is covered with thick ferns that ebb and flow with the seasons, and the softness of the ground is layered deep with generations of change and transformation. A silence as disturbing as it is comforting. I am a small speck within nature that, despite human degradation, continues to exist. But it's up to me to go outside of the forest to make a difference in my community and world. I can't do it alone. Belief in a better world is what motivates me.

Thinking of that forest helped me get things in perspective when working on sex-worker rights. In those early days of growing public consciousness about missing and murdered women, there was a strong acknowledgement that most of the missing were sex workers, and most Indigenous, and that the laws pertaining to prostitution were harmful and horrific. Twenty-five years later, as the National Inquiry on Missing and Murdered Indigenous Women struggles to ground itself with the community, much of the discourse on sex workers has been quietly dropped. It is accepted now, finally, to speak about Indigenous women and girls and the systemic racism and inequality they face—but it's still unacceptable to name the sex workers as sex workers. The language is sanitized. I often wonder if this is because of society's moral judgment and the stigma of being a sex worker.

The 1980s, when I was first elected to City Council, was also a time of massive development in Vancouver. COPE became the watchdog of the impact of Expo '86 on the city. There were human tragedies, as local hotels cashed in by catering to visitors and tourists attending the Expo fair, evicting long-term residents from their homes. In the 1986 election, Harry Rankin made an unsuccessful bid to be mayor, leaving Bruce and me as the only left-wing survivors. A pro-developer City Council led by newly elected mayor Gordon Campbell paved the way for the development of the Expo lands on the north shore of False Creek and the old Marathon lands in Coal Harbour. We endured many a late-night public hearing where citizens argued for lower-density developments with a higher mix of affordable and social housing, similar to the successful development of the south shore of False Creek a decade earlier. This was something that Harry had campaigned on arduously in 1986. But after the election, it was usually nine votes for the developers and two votes against.

Campbell's style of leadership at city hall focused more power in the mayor's office in a more cabinet style of government. The rules for citizen delegations to appear before council became strict, and he ruthlessly forced through cuts to civic services, including the fire department and libraries. The biggest change at city hall was his love of zoning changes that conferred massive densities in massive developments that benefited the development industry with millions of dollars in profits. I had learned earlier from Harry Rankin that the most powerful tool a municipal council had was the power to create enormous wealth through rezoning, whether or not it was in the public interest. Most often it was a battle between private development interests and community or public interests. Bruce and I had a firm view of what represented the public interest, and although we did vote for some rezoning, if there was a conflict between community and neighbourhood interests versus developer interests, we always knew which side we were on.

Nevertheless the early COPE years on City Council, 1982 to 1986, where we were part of a progressive majority, saw significant gains for community planning, good housing, fair wages, and preservation of public services. During the massive construction of the world Expo site, prior to its opening in 1986, non-union contractors consistently underbid unionized contractors and wages fell dramatically as more and more of the Expo building sites went non-union. We worked hand in hand with the building trade unions and, in a move led by councillor Bruce Yorke, Vancouver City Council adopted a fair wage bylaw (based on an old federal statute) to level the playing field. It generated enormous opposition from the non-union part of the construction industry and from conservative politicians who accused us of meddling in the free market. But it was an excellent example of a successful collaboration between progressive forces—elected and non-elected—to achieve a community benefit and value. Today the campaign for a living wage, which has led to living-wage policies being adopted by municipalities including the City of Vancouver, is further evidence of the positive role municipalities can play in working with the community to close the income gap.

Those years in municipal politics taught me a lot. They matured me politically and deepened my conviction for social justice and human rights. So many times we'd take the plunge and speak out, whether against nonsensical anti-soliciting laws on prostitution, racism, mega-developments being rammed through, or illegal suites that tore neighbourhoods apart, as Campbell and his crew made it virtually impossible to keep secondary suites in homes. Civic duties are a twenty-four-hour-a-day job and often our home phone would ring off the hook (in those days before voicemail) as we answered noise bylaw complaints or people just wanting help.

Beyond the day-to-day work at city hall, I also got involved in broader issues for social justice, including ensuring reasonable access was allowed to abortion clinics in Vancouver. In 1988, the Supreme Court of Canada struck down Canada's abortion law as unconstitutional. The law was found to violate section 7 of the Charter of Rights and Freedoms, ruling that it "infringed upon a woman's right to life, liberty, and security of the person." Dr. Henry Morgentaler came to speak in Vancouver at John Oliver high school not long after the decision. Tensions were still high in the city. I introduced Morgentaler at the pro-choice rally—it came after an injunction had ensured that anti-choice protesters could not block access to women attending the Vancouver abortion clinic. This injunction preceded what would later be known as bubble-zone legislation. There were hundreds of supporters at the rally, but also many anti-choice protesters outside.

My horizons also expanded internationally. In 1978, before my successful run for City Council, I attended the world youth festival in Havana, Cuba. There I experienced the thrill and vigour of a massive political gathering that included delegates from socialist countries. The excitement of hearing Fidel Castro speak in Revolution Square, with a million participants attending, was an awakening to a larger world of politics and change. Cuba was the first socialist country I had visited, and Castro, its charismatic, controversial leader, had stood up to the US for decades already by this time. I can easily remember the heat and the spicy scent of cigar smoke that seemed to permeate every corner of Havana. Castro spoke of justice, economic self-sufficiency, and the power of the human spirit. While an imperfect political system—there is no excuse for the treatment of gays and lesbians or Castro's political opponents, for example—Cuba nevertheless showed that there were alternatives to capitalist economics. I met extraordinary women who participated or had leadership roles in the Cuban revolution, and they reinforced for me that change could happen in powerful ways, beginning at a grassroots level.

Later I attended the 1985 UN Decade for Women conference in Nairobi as part of a global delegation organized by the Women's International Democratic Federation—including the African National Congress (ANC) and the Palestine Liberation Organization (PLO). I was thrilled to meet Angela Davis, the passionate African American political activist and academic, who was staying in the same compound as our small delegation from Canada. She was fiery and confident, and I recall listening to her in awe as she gave a press conference outlining the issues facing women in our struggle for equality. The media in attendance tried to rattle her with their questions, but she was undeterred and unwavering. Later that day in the shower facilities, I ran into her and was able to briefly mumble my admiration for her leadership and courage. She smiled back at me and said, "Never give up." At both international gatherings I soaked up the politics, heated discussions, and passion for groundbreaking change. I came home with a greater motivation to work for equality and social justice.

I had also learned much from Bruce—not only about organizing in the Downtown Eastside, but also later at city hall. My admiration for what he was able to accomplish is limitless. By any mainstream standard he was uneducated and not trained in any way to play a leading role in the life of Vancouver. Yet his strength of conviction, even when he was wrong on something, moved him ever forward, usually by instinct. He took on so many issues as a city councillor, even the archaic title of "alderman." We were both elected as aldermen, and for years he campaigned to change the name to city councillor. He researched the history of the name (rooted in an old British practice of the Alder—an elder in a local parish). Because he was a man, he was made fun of for wanting to change the name, even in media cartoons. It upset tradition and people didn't like it. But he said the term was sexist and outdated, and submitted resolutions to the Union of BC Municipalities conventions until eventually there were enough votes for a name change.

Later on, as a city representative on the Pacific National Exhibition (PNE) board, he fought tirelessly for historical recognition of the unjust internment of Japanese Canadians at the PNE during the war. At the time, most of the directors just wanted to forget this shameful past. But Bruce was relentless and would not take no for an answer. I learned to rely on my gut instincts of what was right or wrong, and from Bruce I learned to never shy from the truth or take bribes, or love power for the sake of power. He was guided by the straightforward imperatives of honesty and principle, and he showed me and many others that you could engage in the political world and not be corrupt.

In Bruce's six terms on City Council and my five, we were a pretty good team. We lived and breathed politics. In the beginning when we ran for civic office, it was a novelty to the media. By some it was seen as wholly inappropriate to have both of us running for civic office. Worse, we weren't married. Still worse, he was older than me—and then I got pregnant too. It wasn't planned. I just about died of embarrassment when Bruce wrote a letter to the editor of the Vancouver *Courier* weekly newspaper during the 1978 civic election when I was pregnant with Lief. He was responding to a columnist in a local paper who decried the fact that we were "living together" and how scandalous that he was trying to get me elected. (I presume the columnist thought I couldn't get elected by myself and that the voters couldn't make up their own mind.) The reply was pure Bruce Eriksen—no holds barred and straight up,

My private life
by Bruce Eriksen

page 2

Mr. Editor, Sir!

Upwardly mobile

The best-kept secret of the recent civic election was that two aldermanic candidates filed sworn nomination papers listing the same address of residence.

This was a "first" of its kind to my knowledge. By most standards of reporting of a public event by a free press, it would have been thought that some notice would have been taken of the coincidence. None was. This says something about the public's "right to know" and about voluntary censorship.

Neither of these two candidates was elected, although both came well within the upper range of the also-rans. Both are prominent by their own names. Had both been elected, their aldermanic indemnity cheques combined would have placed their joint address well into the more-than-comfortable bracket of Canadian incomes.

Aldermen are paid $9,702 a year plus $4,851 in non-taxable expenses, plus $607 extra for the one month they may expect to serve as deputy mayor. This means that two aldermen would get a total of $30,320 of which $9,702 would be tax free.

The two candidates with the same address were Bruce Eriksen and Libby Davies of COPE.

This is my life
by Bruce Eriksen

BRUCE ERIKSEN   LIBBY DAVIES

Mr. MacKay, Re: Mr. MacKay's Nov. 30 article in The Courier, "Upwardly mobile".

You (Mr. MacKay) say "the best kept secret of the recent civic election was that two aldermanic candidates filed sworn nomination papers listing the same address of residence . . . By most standards of reporting of a public event by a free press, it would have been thought that some notice would have been taken of this coincidence. None was. This says something about the public's "right to know" and about voluntary censorship".

Libby Davies and I ran in the 1976 and 1978 elections as COPE candidates. In both years we filed nomination papers listing the same address of residence. I don't know how you missed it.

I didn't realize that you were interested in gossip and serilities as well as biased ultra right wing political reporting. However, since you obviously do have a penchant for scabrous yellow journalism, I suggest you go whole hog and do a first class job. Don't let me be a spoil sport; after all the next election is only two years away.

Your commentary pertaining to myself and Libby Davies could have been much more exciting and titilating if you had done your research properly and included the following juicy tidbits:

I am 50 years old. Libby Davies is 25 years of age. Libby and I have been living at the same address since 1973.

Libby is pregnant and the baby will arrive in Feburary 1979. I am the father. We are not married. I was unemployed seven months last year.

I am a former alcoholic. I consort with conservatives, liberals, socreds, communists, socialists, journalists, publishers, reporters, bankers, rich people, poor people and immigrants. Sometimes I am known to use naughty language. I have had hemmorrhoids, measles, mumps and scarlet fever. My father is a Danish immigrant.

There are all kinds of other personal juicy little tidbits I could include. While I agree that the public has the "right to know" I believe that as a hard working conscientious journalist you should uncover them yourself.

Three cheers for good journalism.

Bruce G. Eriksen

P.S. You could point out to the public that I only attended three years of elementary school. That should get them.

Bruce's letter to the editor responding to "City Council candidates living together," Vancouver *Courier*, November 30, 1978

announcing that he was the proud father of the baby yet to be born.

Most everything we did became public—sometimes by Bruce's own doing. In February 1979 he proudly announced to the media that his son, in keeping with his Danish heritage, would be named Lief Eriksen. The only problem was he didn't tell me first. I was mad at Bruce for making the decision, but then embraced it as a wonderful name. As I read the news of his announcement, he lined up a photographer for a shot that was later printed in the paper of newborn baby Lief in his Vander Zalm diapers, made by David Lane as a baby shower present. Yes, even our diapers were political. These special diapers had a dartboard printed on them with Bill Vander Zalm's face and famous flashy smile, centred at just the right place to receive baby poop.

Lief was born in the Salvation Army Grace Hospital maternity home. My stay there was eye-opening. I left furious. As I arrived with Jean Swanson in her car, to check in at the admissions desk, the clerk asked me if I was keeping the baby, no doubt having seen on some form that I wasn't married. It was astonishing to be asked such a personal question—water broken, already in labour—and breathlessly I said, of course I was keeping the baby. The day after Lief was born, a social worker stopped by my bed to probe if I wanted to give up the baby and to ask who the father was. I told her to fuck off. I was twenty-six years old and it served to remind me of the vulnerability of single mothers, maybe facing postpartum depression, who were pressured by religious people with an agenda.

The only thing that made my short stay in the maternity hospital palatable was the daily entrance of Bruce the new dad. Ignoring strict visiting hours, he would march in, in his raincoat, briefcase in hand, with an air of such confidence that the nurses at the ward desk thought he was one of the doctors visiting his patients and didn't question him. Another slice of sexism, but at least this one worked in my favour. It maddened me that in a ward full of mothers, from multi-faith backgrounds, we each got a written message on our breakfast tray saying our baby was a gift from God. I knew it was from sex. Thus began my life as a mother.

Our life on East Hastings Street after Lief was born brought routine to our little world. I immediately returned to work at DERA and would walk around the Downtown Eastside past all the beer parlours, with baby Lief in an old-fashioned blue pram with four white wheels that Jonnie Rankin, Harry's wife, had given me. It must have looked pretty funny, and often the old guys would grin at me and stop to look at Lief sleeping peacefully. It was a treat to walk the few blocks to the Woodward's store at East Hastings and Abbott, and stop in the spacious lounge and mother's room to feed Lief. We rarely took time off. In all the time I knew and lived with Bruce, we seldom left town; once to Disneyland for three days and another time, an overnight visit to Nanaimo.

Bruce was a doting and loving parent. There was a joke in our family that Lief's feet never touched the ground until he was three years old because he was proudly carried everywhere by his dad. Bruce became a familiar sight, catching the bus every day at Pender and Main, briefcase in one hand, his son in the other arm, headed for city hall at 12th and Cambie. The first stop was the City Hall Day Care, across the street from city hall, where Bruce would reluctantly leave Lief before he crossed the street for his third-floor office. The City Hall Day Care, housed in a small portable building, was, like all licensed not-for-profit child care centres, staffed by excellent trained staff and filled to capacity with long waiting lists. (Unfortunately still a reality today, after decades of promises for a national childcare program.)

In those early years, I would leave the DERA office at Main and Hastings, pick Lief up, and pop across the road to the council chamber, where Bruce might be in mid-afternoon tea break from a City Council meeting. He would stuff his pockets full of cookies for Lief, who eagerly scooped them up. We had no car, no savings, no property, and few material possessions, and it was rare that we went out even to a movie. But we had a richness of love for each other and our work; life was good, and breathtakingly busy. We had no ambitions other than to serve the city and fight the good fight.

Vancouver has never elected a woman mayor, though many qualified women have put themselves forward. Jean Swanson ran for mayor in 1988 and I ran in 1993. Jean ran on the COPE ticket against incumbent Gordon Campbell and did what needed to be done—oppose his developer agenda. The city was in the grip of a housing crisis, with a near-zero rental vacancy rate, and ongoing demolition of old apartment buildings amid massive redevelopment. Bruce and I were running for re-election in 1988, part of the COPE slate with Jean. It is usually politically necessary to run a progressive mayoralty candidate in civic elections to promote a strong platform and garner attention from the electorate and the media. Often the odds of winning, especially against a powerful incumbent, are slim, but nevertheless it is an important action to present a credible alternative. Jean's campaign was valuable for all of these reasons, and she became a champion for a fairer and more inclusive city, where renters and low-income people had a right to live. We didn't imagine then that some thirty years later she would run again and, in 2018, be elected to Vancouver City Council.

In the 1990 civic election, I received more votes than the mayor (Gordon Campbell), and there seemed to be an expectation that with Campbell not running again, having exited for provincial politics, we had a rare opportunity in 1993 to gain a clear majority on City Council, including the mayor's seat. COPE had regained strength on council with the election of Patricia Wilson, an experienced and capable representative. So now there were five of us, with Harry Rankin and Bruce Yorke back after earlier defeats in the face of Gordon Campbell's 1986 win. But as the 1993 election drew closer, Patricia, Harry, and Bruce Yorke didn't run, and Bruce Eriksen too decided it was time to leave civic politics. That left me as the only left-wing incumbent seeking re-election, but this time for the office of mayor.

The decision to run for mayor wasn't easy. My old fears and doubts about whether I was up to the job came to the surface. But, propelled by circumstances, I was thrust into a role I didn't know if I was ready for. We had no money in the bank to speak of, and with a federal election also underway, the campaign team was thin too. I was very used to running in a civic election, having run eight times before. But I had never experienced the additional responsibilities involved in running for mayor. Mayoral debates, media interviews, policy releases, campaigning, door knocking, and fundraising—I did it by the seat of my pants. There was little by way of briefing notes, message boxes, or communications support. It would be unheard of to operate this way today. Yet, having lived and breathed civic life as a councillor for eleven years, I knew the issues deeply and instinctively.

I was well known and respected across the city and had a strong sense of what we were fighting for—affordable housing, democratic governance, excellent community planning, and strong rules for development and developers to protect the public interest. Facing the *Vancouver Sun* editorial board was not your everyday media interview, and I remember being grilled on finances and the city budget, and future development in Vancouver, in particular. I know they wanted to

trip me up and show me as inexperienced and too left wing. But I think I held my own even if I wasn't the well-heeled, well-financed, mainstream mayoral candidate.

Nevertheless our campaign was a disaster, both the campaign itself and the consequences for COPE. Campaign donations trickled in and the campaign team was short on resources. Desperate for cash, we approached a number of people to see if they would be willing to use their house to back up a campaign loan. The only bright light was Joy MacPhail, a vibrant and well-known provincial representative from east Vancouver who, without hesitation, said yes to putting her house up for the bank. That was one moment when I thanked my lucky stars for wonderful friends.

I had a popular grassroots following across the city, and some media predicted I

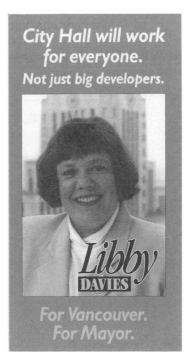

City Hall will work for everyone.
Not just big developers.

Libby DAVIES

For Vancouver.
For Mayor.

Running for mayor of Vancouver, 1993

would win as mayor but face a hostile council. Neither happened. Vancouverites elected Philip Owen from the NPA as mayor. That year, 1993, was also coincidentally one of fractious national debates on constitutional changes following the collapse of the Charlottetown accord, and a federal election that took place only a few weeks before the civic election. Our local mayoral campaign deflated as volunteers pitched in for the federal NDP campaign. It was deeply in trouble with the rise of the Reform Party, which successfully exploited voter suspicions that the established parties, including the NDP, had lined up in tandem on unpopular constitutional changes. Much of the traditional NDP vote in BC swung to Reform, and Margaret Mitchell was defeated in Vancouver East, along with many other NDP members of Parliament across the country. We were stunned by her defeat, only to be hit by another loss at the civic level, which left only one COPE candidate, young Jenny Kwan, who made it onto City Council.

Timing is always a factor in the success of political aspirations, and certainly the timing of that 1993 election, both locally and federally, had a disastrous impact for the NDP nationally and for COPE locally. Sometimes these issues are beyond our control. But still, had we been more experienced and sophisticated in our approach, we might have developed strategies for the federal and local election that were mutually advantageous. For example, we could have encouraged progressive organizations to get more involved in both campaigns by linking national and local issues.

Although I was disappointed by the election outcome, and the lowest recent voter turnout in Vancouver, I didn't feel personally devastated. I had given it my all and done my best. I felt saddened that I had been the only incumbent running for COPE. Most of all I felt relieved that I'd held my head high despite a struggling campaign team and inadequate campaign resources. Like many women in the political arena who experience defeat, I picked up fast and moved on. I only mention this because I've seen many men defeated over the years, who are utterly crushed as a result—nursing bruised egos and hurt from failed attempts to get elected. Women are typically more pragmatic about our victories and losses; we are able to see ourselves in the broader political context and maintain a more grounded perspective. Even so, men are much better at promoting themselves into their next venture—unabashedly asking for money, work, and contacts.

I was ready to move on but didn't have a clue how to do it. It felt awkward and embarrassing to ask people for employment help, and I did a rather pathetic job of shopping myself around. It was a difficult time financially, when the small stipend of a city councillor ended abruptly a few weeks after the election. Neither Bruce nor I had a civic pension, and our meagre savings paid the basics for a month or so. It was the aid of amazing friends—Ruth Herman and David Chudnovsky, Mike Chrunik and Sue Lockhart, and many others—who took up a collection to help us get through the next few months. Bruce was now officially retired and eventually I secured some short term work, returning to Main and Hastings and the Downtown Eastside to oversee the development of a community health plan under the auspices of the newly appointed Vancouver Health Authority. And later, Joy MacPhail helped me yet again by securing a short contract with BC Transit to do a safety audit of SkyTrain stations. I had previously been a city representative on the BC Transit Board and, as an avid user of public transit, I was familiar with the issues.

After the 1993 civic election, the left was in disarray. Federally the NDP lost its party status in Ottawa, sinking from forty-three seats to nine, below the twelve seats required for full party status. With a demoralized left, hard lessons about the challenges of unity and co-operation on the progressive side of politics came to the surface in Vancouver. We had had success as grassroots activists turned politicians, but on the other hand, we were inexperienced and even naive in our understanding of attaining and maintaining power.

COPE fell into fractious infighting, with people blaming each other for what seemed like forever. Ruth Herman and I became co-chairs of COPE and struggled to hold the organization together. For the first time I experienced the downward drag of internal politics. How do you describe the swamp of mudslinging, where people lose sight of who the real political opposition is and indulge themselves in emotional—even hysterical—name-calling, paying no attention to the need for resolution and recovery? I am always so surprised when someone's personal grudges or self-important analysis overtakes the need to move forward together in a collaborative and respectful way. I'm afraid the left suffers terribly from a self-righteous judgment imposed on each other that displays a debilitating and unforgiving harshness. It was always this kind of politics, the instant denunciations and moralistic judgment, that got me down the most. It still is today.

Concerning 1993, only later did I fully comprehend how immature and downright silly the infighting was. It was a waste of precious time and energy as one person, or faction, sought to destroy the other. It came home to me more recently, when I attended a book launch for Cynthia Flood, and listened to her illuminating discussion about her book *What Can You Do*. She deftly captured the "dysfunction of the left" as she described politics in the 1970s, and the lack of emotional intelligence that left people unable to work through conflict. I was intrigued by her phrase to be "calm and resist" that spoke to the need for radicalism with composure—a great feminist analysis. What a sensible idea and so much more mature an approach. What if on the left we focused on supporting each other and seeking ways to lift each other up?

For COPE there was a brief recovery a few years later, when Larry Campbell was elected mayor in 2002 with a COPE majority on City Council. The left felt energized and strong, before it busted apart again in an even worse way. A harder-line faction within COPE had serious differences with Campbell, and the organization eventually split, creating Vision Vancouver in 2005, which began what was seen by many as a successful move to the more politically palatable centre ground. Vision Vancouver dominated the civic field for a decade or more. But the history continued to play itself out with a further split in COPE as another breakaway group left, unable to contend with the organization's increasingly hard line, to form OneCity in 2014.

My run for the mayor's job in 1993, despite its challenges, was important to my political development. We always think of what we learn when we win, but we also learn when we lose. I learned to be better prepared, and to make sure to have the key elements of a team in place who are ready to go into action. I remembered a conversation that I'd had a few years before with Jack Layton, still a city councillor in Toronto, and Brian Mason, a progressive city councillor in Edmonton (and later leader of the Alberta NDP). We mused that one day we'd all run for mayor. It didn't turn out so well for Jack, either; he lost his mayoral bid in Toronto in 1991. The next time we saw Brian, we let him know that maybe it wasn't such a good shot for him to try.

Endings, Beginnings

Leaving civic politics at age forty left me unclear about where to go and what to do. After working on the community health plan for the Downtown Eastside and later with the Hospital Employees Union (HEU), I had no long-term plans. My association with the HEU had begun years earlier as a part-time human rights investigator, and I was proud to work as the union's co-ordinator of human resources in 1995. It wasn't until there was talk in 1996 of a federal election on its way that I was encouraged by friends to think about running to be the member of Parliament for Vancouver East, our home community. The seat had been won by a Liberal, Anna Terrana, in 1993; she defeated New Democrat Margaret Mitchell, who had held the seat for fourteen years. Once again, political circumstance drew me along a path that I had not even contemplated. But things were very different this time.

Bruce fell ill from cancer in January 1996 and was given only a few months to live. He valiantly kept going for close to fourteen months. During that time I got to know him more deeply than ever and marvelled at his resilience and good nature. He never complained and was incredibly grateful for every comfort and assistance family and friends gave him. Lief and Bruce and I did so much together, and small things like driving in the car or going to Lee Valley hardware, where he was a staunch and loyal customer, became very special. Each day and moment became precious. Dear friends helped as I continued to work part-time at HEU, and Margaret Mitchell helped us secure a spot in the Adanac Housing Co-op near the Burnaby Hospital, where Bruce's doctor was located.

The night he became seriously ill, I was at a provincial NDP convention in downtown Vancouver. Lief had come home from school to find his dad on the bed in terrible pain. For Bruce to complain about anything meant it was serious. My brother-in-law came to the convention, and Shane Simpson, our local provincial representative, came over to see me at the constituency table. I knew something was wrong as soon as I saw the look on Shane's face, and the feeling of dread only increased when he said my brother-in-law needed to see me urgently at the door. We rushed to the emergency room in Burnaby Hospital and waited late into the night as tests were done.

Nothing prepares you for such news. Lief and I went home late that night feeling lost and hopeless. It seemed unimaginable that Bruce had terminal cancer. When I woke up in the morning, the world was a different place. Suddenly my priorities had changed, and I couldn't even think where to begin. My brain was churning with one burning question: How long had Bruce been sick and why didn't we know sooner how sick he was? I kept thinking back to how he had been the previous year. He'd been tired—but he worked so hard it didn't seem surprising. Then I remembered he often came in the house with his hand on his back, saying his back was aching. And I'd say, over and over, you have to rest. But Bruce never rested; even when he retired, he stood for hours in the garage with his beloved tools and gadgets making beautiful furniture, doing it over and over until it was technically correct. No one had taught him and he struggled with the math, and we nearly went mad as he tried repeatedly to work out the proper compound angles with his mitre saw. It seemed easy to see why he was tired and aching, but I missed it totally, and he was never one to complain or see a doctor regularly. Thinking of it afterward, I tended to beat myself up. Why didn't I see? Why didn't I put the pieces together? But beating yourself up doesn't change anything, I wish it did.

For many months we continued our life in the fullest way possible. Bruce continued to travel up to Gambier Island in Howe Sound, where we were building a cabin not far from Vancouver. We had planned for it to become our principal residence, where Bruce would live while I would commute part-time to the city to work. Our next-door neighbour at Gambier, Gloria Massé, kept a close eye on Bruce, as we both knew how much he would overexert himself and not admit that he was tired and in pain. She never fussed over him, but I felt enormously relieved that she was there as the best neighbour and friend you could hope for.

During these months of illness, Bruce also embarked on another big project, redoing the mural that he had painted so many years earlier on the Carnegie Centre hoarding. "The Law in Its Majestic Equality" had been taken inside once the building had reopened as a community centre in 1978. For years it remained hidden behind a heavy curtain in the theatre, and most patrons of the building forgot it even existed. Plans for a new social housing development across the street, to be named Bruce Eriksen Place, prompted Jim Green—who had been hired by Jean Swanson and me after we left, as DERA's community organizer, and was now a community development consultant with the NDP government in Victoria—to propose that the mural be displayed permanently in the new building. The building, designed by Gregory Henriquez Architects, later won a Lieutenant-Governor's architecture award for its innovative design and the creative use of powerful words such as *vote, respect, democracy,* and *courage* on the tile work on each small balcony.

The building facade displayed a large tile mural, created by artist Blake Williams, depicting historical images from the neighbourhood as well as Bruce himself. In describing the mural, Williams said it was "to honour the work of Bruce Eriksen in the Downtown Eastside—to portray the struggle for the rights of the community—to show the defiant nature of Bruce, and in turn allow his image to act as a metaphor for all who worked with him and those who continue the fight for the residents of this neighbourhood—for this façade to act as an ongoing thorn in the side of those whose priorities negatively affect this community."

Although he never got to see the finished building before his death, Bruce worked diligently on redoing the mural that was temporarily mounted next door in the old Bank of Montreal building at Main and Hastings. For many weeks I would take Bruce to the intersection before I continued on to work, and he would painstakingly redo the brushwork and lettering that had faded and been damaged over the years. Here again, I relied on generous friends like Kathleen Boyes, who kept an eye on Bruce and made sure he ate and took small rests She told me how tired he was and also how determined to keep painting. It was his parting gift for the community that was so integral to his life and times. I remembered, too, the original zeal and determination when he first created the mural twenty years or so earlier, spending evening after evening with his bucket of paint to get it just right.

In December 1996, we met about the upcoming federal election with political ally MP Svend Robinson at a café at Main and Broadway. Over breakfast, we discussed the possibility of me running. He was supportive of the idea of me seeking the federal nomination for the NDP in Vancouver East. But I looked at Bruce and wondered how on earth that could work. We had no idea how much longer Bruce would live, never mind what it would take to work on a nomination campaign. We went home and I made up my mind that it was impossible to run—despite the support I was getting from people who thought we had a chance to win back Vancouver East for the NDP. I let the thought go, but Bruce kept coming back to the idea. And after much discussion, it was he who finally changed my mind. Bruce told me matter-of-factly that I needed to do it, not only to win the seat and fight for the things we believed in, but also because it was right for me. I always felt that he knew instinctively it was the opening of a new door for my future without him. He never said it, and I never told him I knew what he was thinking; we just focused as we always did on the here and now.

Affordable housing was still a critical issue in Vancouver, and the governing Liberals' elimination of highly successful federal programs for the development of new social housing had a devastating impact in neighbourhoods like the Downtown Eastside. For two decades the city had relied on federal funds for co-op housing, social housing, and special needs housing. Fighting for decent housing was at the core of what we believed in and worked for. At city hall we had made full use of federal dollars for social housing, both in the Downtown Eastside and elsewhere in the city. But these great programs were obliterated in 1995 by federal finance minister Paul Martin's drive for austerity. The loss of these federal programs, and the demise of the Canada Health and Social Transfer, also propelled me to run. Along with many others, I was downright mad that the feds had abandoned housing.

The Canada Mortgage and Housing Corporation (CMHC) 1993 annual report had projected 75,000 new social housing units to be constructed across Canada by 1997, but Martin's fiscal agenda killed all that. We knew first-hand how transformative good housing was in people's lives. The fact that it was seen as politically expedient to cancel opportunities for new housing made me feel that I had something very necessary to do in Ottawa. It would take decades and enormous political work inside and outside Parliament to recover from that disastrous decision to axe social housing. Many homeless people would die—and still do. And many Canadians would suffer the intolerable insecurity and anxiety of being one paycheque away from homelessness.

I was getting close to making a final decision to seek the federal nomination, but I knew I needed to phone one person first. I'd heard that Jim Green might also be interested in running for the NDP nomination for Vancouver East. The only way to find out for sure was to contact him. Jim Green was a tough character, who had many friends but also detractors in the Downtown Eastside. He had accomplished much at DERA when Bruce, Jean, and I left. He was responsible for the development of hundreds of good social housing units. I suggested we meet, but he declined. I told him I didn't think it was a good idea for us to compete against each other for the nomination and we should talk about it. He was very reluctant to say what he was thinking and clearly didn't want to talk about it. After several unsuccessful attempts to communicate, I felt I had to make a decision. So in December 1996, I announced my intention to seek the nomination. Jim was very put out, and for several years we had a strained relationship.

It was one of those difficult times—he clearly had wanted to run and felt I'd taken his opportunity. A part of me was saddened that it happened that way, but another part of me also felt, why do we as women so often feel we have to defer to men and what they want, even if they won't come out and say it? Why do we sit back and wait? Why do we ask for forgiveness because we acted? I wrestled with these emotions and knew my working relationship with Jim after that would be hard. It reinforced for me the different—often gendered—paths that could be taken in politics and how important it is to try and maintain relationships, even when things got in the way. Jim was later elected as an outstanding city councillor and played a key role in Larry Campbell's civic administration. But it took many tries and much effort to rebuild our personal ties.

It's one thing to announce that you're seeking to run as a candidate for your party—and quite another to launch into a heated nomination battle. Nominations can be testy affairs, and the more winnable the seat is seen to be, the more difficult the nomination. Such was the case for Vancouver East. Twice in recent history, the riding had been won federally by Liberals. But generally it had been considered an NDP stronghold.

People had been shocked by the loss in the 1993 federal election, and there was a determined mindset in the community to win back the riding.

Vancouver East—comprising the communities of the Downtown Eastside, adjacent Strathcona and Chinatown, Vancouver's oldest residential neighbourhoods, the sprawling working-class community of Hastings Sunrise to the east, and the old low-rise apartments of Mount Pleasant, along with Grandview Woodlands, another great historic neighbourhood—made up the northeast part of Vancouver. The riding's working-class history, strong and vibrant immigrant settlement, and rock-solid community activism made it a very special place. The northern boundary of the Port of Vancouver and Burrard Inlet gave East Van much of its labour history, in maritime trades, and many historic labour battles had originated in its communities. East Vancouver was also home to many waves of working-class immigrants from Europe and Asia. The riding was diverse, socially active, and the heart of many social movements. It also included Vancouver's lowest-income inner-city neighbourhoods and schools.

Three other candidates, all from the Italian community, declared their intention to seek the nomination. They weren't well known, but they had a belief that someone from the Italian community had the best chance to defeat incumbent MP Anna Terrana, who was well respected in the Italian community. I forged ahead anyway, hoping my years of community activism and time at city hall would garner support. Over that Christmas, as Bruce became more ill, I would spend evenings at home phoning the existing NDP membership and signing up new members. As we moved into January and February 1997, we had a hospital bed in the living room, and Bruce would watch me on the phone every night and make jokes about our "campaign" office. I honestly couldn't have done it without him and his steadfast belief in me. Many a time I sure didn't feel up to it. Many nights I would cry by myself and wonder what on earth I was doing. But we kept going—fortified by that stubbornness I knew so well in Bruce.

A great team worked their butts off on the nomination campaign, led by the legendary Glen Sanford, whose mum, Karen Sanford, had been a member in Dave Barrett's provincial government in 1972. Glen had NDP blood in his veins. He knew much more than I did about the NDP and how nomination battles were won. In fact, although I had long been an NDP member, I had never been very active inside the party—only helping at election times, beginning with Emery Barnes's campaign. Glen's insight and organizing skill were essential; I am still grateful to him and the folks who helped me. Svend Robinson, who was on the NDP's provincial executive at the time, also helped by arguing for a later nomination date in March, allowing more time to organize. This period is a blur in my mind—I was working, taking care of Bruce, and stressing about the upcoming nomination. If Bruce had second thoughts about me running he never said it; Lief, as he always had, tolerated his parents' unconventional life. He was in his last year of high school and spent much time with his dad, worrying about him as Bruce tried to convince him, not very well, that he was fine.

The nomination race became tense and tight. One candidate dropped out, claiming he had been blackmailed by another candidate. And it was clear my main opponent, Rocco Di Trolio, was signing up masses of new members, focusing on seniors in the Italian community who still lived in east Vancouver.

The night before the nomination meeting of March 13, 1997, Sharon Costello, a good friend from the BC Nurses' Union, came over to help go over my nomination speech. Fred Wilson, Patricia Wilson's husband, had looked over drafts of the speech and given me helpful feedback to improve its substance. Sharon, who had a background in communications, pushed me to practise over and over, until we were both so tired—but it had to be just right. It was tough going; my mind was on Bruce in his hospital bed downstairs, suffering uncomplainingly through pain and discomfort.

So many people planned to attend the nomination meeting that it had to be held in the Garden Auditorium at the PNE. I barely remember the night. Glen Sanford told me later that he was madly phoning our supporters as the speeches were still underway, saying, "Get your ass down here or she's going to lose." My supporters thought I was a shoo-in, but Rocco's supporters came out in big numbers. His team handed out red roses to his supporters as they entered the vast auditorium with its rises of bleachers. Looking glumly at the roses throughout the crowd, we knew he had the numbers to win. But it wasn't over yet. Practice, practice, and more practice had paid off and I gave the speech my all, distracted as I was by what was happening at home.

We went to three ballots and later learned that some of Rocco's supporters had switched their votes to support me. I won the nomination by a handful of votes. I went home late that night and told Bruce. He was in a semi-conscious state and it was unclear if he understood fully what I told him. And three days later, on March 16, he died. Lief and I reckoned at the time that he might have thought I'd won the election itself, rather than the nomination, and decided he could let go. These were the toughest three days of my life.

It is painful, but also incredibly intimate, to watch someone you love die. The closeness and depth of feeling at every moment is a rare gift. I was heartbroken that the man I loved so much had gone, and Lief and I picked up the pieces, as you are somehow programmed to do. I had also learned in that year what an incredible child we had; Lief acted with supreme maturity and care helping his dad and me get through every day. He was barely eighteen when Bruce died. Sometimes you hear that the child becomes the parent, and I felt that about Lief many times. Very often I experienced the dread that the person I most wanted to talk to about my grief was the person I was grieving. How cruel is that.

Many friends had helped us during Bruce's final weeks. We'd set up a roster of care to ensure Bruce was never alone, and so that I could keep working at least part-time. Sandy Cameron and Jean Swanson, Nathan

Edelson, Mike Chrunik and Sue Lockhart, Eileen Mosca, Jim Kinzel, and other good friends were steadfast in their care and love for Bruce. I also learned how amazing palliative care nurses are. They came to our co-op unit and made Bruce as comfortable as possible in his last days. After one of the nurses alerted me that death was close, Lief and I each spoke to Bruce and told him what he meant to us and that we wouldn't ever forget him. I remember Bruce's last breath as he drew it in, sharply, and a frown appeared on his brow. I didn't know if it was pain or his stubbornness refusing to let go. You hear about people peacefully slipping away, but I never felt that with Bruce. He was still fighting.

A week later we held a memorial and celebration at the Maritime Labour Centre, big enough to hold the six hundred plus people who came to say goodbye to a man who had given much to Vancouver. A man who was loved, feared, even hated, but always respected. He'd pissed off a lot of people in his time, but he'd changed the course of Vancouver's history in many ways for the better. Skid Road and its people would have been wiped off the map, as was the case in most North American cities, but Bruce didn't let that happen. He was determined to show the community as it really was, resilient and strong, even as the struggles continue today. He always fought for people and their rights, and he deplored injustice. Many people spoke at the memorial. Takeo Yamashiro, who had been at DERA in its early days, and later at the Tonari Gumi drop-in centre for Japanese Canadians on Powell Street, played a soulful classical Japanese lament on his wooden flute for his old comrade. Even the Salvation Army showed up and presented me with a photograph of one of Bruce's early paintings. They said Bruce had painted it—depicting Jesus on the water— while at the Harbour Light as a recovering alcoholic. Knowing how Bruce felt about religious missions and the church, I didn't know whether to laugh, cry, or yell in protest. But I quietly accepted the gift, acknowledging that Bruce had had many lives and I was only part of the later ones.

With the federal election day only two and a half months away, it became my mission to bury myself in election campaign work and not think about what we had lost. This was a mistake; it caught up with me later as I struggled to cope with ongoing grief and loss. I worried, too, that I was leaving my son to mostly fend for himself. Lief had been through many civic elections with us, but this time the absence of his father cast a sorrowful shadow. Neither of us spoke to many people, and my long-time dear friend Jean Swanson and her partner Sandy Cameron, who lived a few doors away in the co-op, kept an eye on us and checked in regularly.

It was a massive campaign effort, led by Glen Sanford. Hundreds of volunteers rallied to win back Vancouver East for the NDP. Our warehouse campaign office on East Hastings Street at Commercial, across from the Vancouver Aboriginal Friendship Centre, was buzzing with canvassers, sign makers, and phoners seven days a week, late into the night. Glen was a hard taskmaster who took nothing for granted. In the first week of the campaign, Anna Terrana's campaign manager contacted us and suggested we meet to discuss the campaign overall. We were open to it and several days later we met up at a local coffee shop on East Hastings near Nanaimo. Glen had his bike with him, and his pants and shoes were well worn and the trouser edges frayed. I saw his smartly dressed young Liberal counterpart look him up and down, and I could see the mental note he made: They don't know what they're doing. Looking at Anna, very stylishly dressed, I felt shabby in comparison, but I was also smiling inside. Glen and I might have looked like Eastside layabouts, but they had no idea what they were up against. I consider myself a ferocious campaigner. I run like my life depends on it. And Glen was no slouch for sure.

We put up a ferocious campaign. It wasn't mean, but it was hard hitting and tough. Terrana's team decided their strength was that she was the incumbent and part of the Liberal government. In their campaign material and in local debates, we heard over and over that as a government member of Parliament, only she could get things done for the community. The subtext was that if you elect an opposition member you get only that, opposition. We thought through this strategy of theirs and decided the best defence was a strong offence. What's the point of electing a silent backbencher who accomplished virtually nothing, we said. Vancouver East needed someone who would kick ass in Ottawa, be visible, and fight like hell for the riding's issues. We needed an experienced advocate who wouldn't let Ottawa get away with anything. That, naturally, was me! I knew it was true too, and so did many in the community. Being a member of the sitting government doesn't necessarily mean anything. In fact, that's an arrogant, anti-democratic argument, often used by Liberals in power, to presume that only someone in government can be effective.

By the final week or so of the campaign, a TV station did a story on the close race in Vancouver East. It showed Anna going door to door looking dejected, as several residents said they didn't know if they were voting for her again. By contrast our campaign was gaining momentum and strength, and we were cautiously optimistic. But it all came down to E-day—something the NDP excels at. Glen figures we had close to a thousand people volunteer on the campaign overall, and nearly that many on election day, pulling the vote, knocking on doors, phoning supporters, working as polling station scrutineers. It's always an exhausting day, but you know it's going to end one way or another, so you just get through it by giving it your all. We did that and then some. That election night we won by just under a two-thousand-vote margin. Good enough, for sure.

Many old friends came out to help during the campaign. And I was very happy that when I knocked on doors, people would say: I know you; you and Bruce helped me at city hall with a permit, or to stop an eviction, or to help put in a pedestrian crossing. It affirmed my deep belief that politics isn't just about big-P politics and all the insider goings-on; it is truly about helping and serving people and the community. Too many elected people get caught up in the intrigue and forget that they are there to serve, support, and help their constituents. I learned that at city hall.

I also had the good fortune to campaign with new friends—one of whom was Bud Osborn. Bud was already a legendary poet in the Downtown Eastside. I had first met him at the groundbreaking ceremony for Bruce Eriksen Place about a year earlier, probably the last public event Bruce attended. Bud was on the board at DERA. The organization had changed significantly over the years, focusing more on the management of its social housing. Gone was the small collective of organizers I had been a part of. The organization still did advocacy work, but it had taken on more of a social agency role rather than militant rabble rousers and activists. Still, DERA was a powerful force to reckon with. Bud wanted to learn about DERA's early days and what it had been like organizing and working on so many life-and-death issues. He visited us several times at Adanac Street, usually to chat with Bruce about his early work. I could see that Bud was struck by Bruce and eager to learn from him, seeing him as the fierce crusader that he was.

After Bruce died Bud came back to visit, and with the election campaign getting underway, I vaguely asked him if he'd like to help with door knocking in the Downtown Eastside. I was mightily surprised when he said yes. He'd never canvassed before, and I'd never canvassed with a poet before. Off we set, clipboard, canvass sheets, and pamphlets in hand, knocking on doors in Oppenheimer Lodge, the oldest social housing building in the Downtown Eastside, as well as at Pendera Housing, and Tellier Tower, run by DERA, the Four Sisters Co-op, and various rooming houses.

I don't think Bud knew what to expect, and he reacted strongly when people would slam their door in our faces and tell us to get lost. "How can you keep doing this when people are so angry?" he asked. I told him I knew people weren't angry at me personally, they were angry and cynical about a political system and governments that let them down time and time again. I told him, "It's not about getting people to vote, it's about getting people to know they can change things—and then voting is a natural outcome of that." He nodded and we continued down the long hallways, seeking out conversations.

Bud was a singular figure in the Downtown Eastside. He spoke at many gatherings, his resonant voice calling people to action through his poetry. He had a long, narrow face and shoulder-length hair that was unruly but somehow perfect. He smoked constantly and shared his extraordinary life experience through his writing.

When I think back on this time—the nomination battle, Bruce's death, and the election—it's with a sense of disbelief and even dismay. Did it all really happen? It seems unreal to have contemplated running for a highly competitive nomination when my partner was dying. What was I thinking? I was deeply divided—and already grieving for what I knew would be lost. It felt deeply unsettling, yet I was driven to win a nomination that felt like another struggle to take on. It was not so much regret I felt about the decision to run again for public office; it was more like: How can this possibly be? How can these things be happening at once? How do I get through it? I told people that running in that federal election saved me from the despair and pain of losing Bruce. But it didn't really save me—it only allowed me to throw myself at something that took all my attention so that I didn't have to feel what was hurting the most. No working day was too long, no task too difficult, so there was no time for personal attention. It's not a good course to follow. My emotional health was stifled, and a part of me became closed off and hard to reach. That election campaign took all of my energy like no other, and I would return home each night exhausted, still thinking about Bruce. I knew Bruce would be proud that we had won back Vancouver East.

Off to Ottawa

One summer day after the 1997 federal election, Lief and I were walking toward Main and Hastings, and we talked about Bruce and the election result. We had many conversations like this, and we'd often say, What would Bruce think? It became a way for us to stay connected to his memory and to each other. On that day, walking along that familiar street, just a block from where Lief spent his first years, with so many people milling around displaying their wares for sale, we passed the Empress Hotel. And as the heavy noise and the traffic fumes settled around us, we agreed he'd be pushing like hell, saying time to get moving. No time to waste. And that became my mantra: No time to waste.

The riding had urgent needs. Hundreds of people were dying from drug overdoses. Before I first left for Ottawa as a newly elected MP, I attended an event in Oppenheimer Park, known as the Killing Fields. One thousand wooden crosses had been erected in memory of people who had died of drug overdoses. The event had been planned by Mark Townsend and Liz Evans of the Portland Hotel Society (later renamed PHS Community Services Society) along with activists in the Political Response Group (PRG) that Bud Osborn was a part of. This powerful gathering of people who were drug users, and still alive, brought home the severity of the drug and HIV crisis in the community.

Oppenheimer Park, just one small block, is the only park in the Downtown Eastside. The gathering began at Main and Hastings, the heart of the community and also a very busy intersection. A banner was unfurled across the street, and commuter traffic and crowded city buses came to a halt. For a few minutes, it felt like the whole city stopped in its tracks and let out a deep sigh at the loss of so many lives. A slow procession began down the street toward the park two blocks away. As we approached, the thousand wooden crosses came into view lined up in tidy rows on the green grass—a graveyard for the community. It was a sad but in some peculiar way uplifting affair, as people gathered quietly in awe of the thousand crosses. The magnitude of the deaths weighed on us heavily. Bud recited his poem "A Thousand Crosses," which I later read from in my inaugural speech in Parliament on October 2, 1997. What other newly elected MP had been propelled to Ottawa by such an event?

A Thousand Crosses in Oppenheimer Park *(excerpt)*

when eagles circle oppenheimer park
who see them
feel awe
feel joy
feel hope
soar in our hearts
the eagles are symbols
for the courage in our spirits
for the fierce and piercing vision for justice in our souls
the eagles bestow a blessing in our lives

but with these thousand crosses
planted in oppenheimer park today
who really see them
feel sorrow
feel loss
feel rage
our hearts shed bitter tears
these thousand crosses are symbols
of the social apartheid in our culture
the segregation of those who deserve to live
and those who are abandoned to die

these thousand crosses silently announce
a social curse on the lives of the poorest of the poor
in the downtown eastside....

Alexa McDonough was the leader of the federal NDP, having won the 1995 leadership race. She brought the party back from oblivion with new MPs from Atlantic Canada. The NDP now had twenty-one members, a respectable number compared to the previous nine and enough to regain party status. I didn't know Alexa at all and had in fact supported Svend Robinson in the leadership race. Nevertheless, I was eager to work with her and loved the fact that the NDP had another woman leader, after Audrey McLaughlin set the bar in 1989 as the first woman leader of a national political party. But as things turned out, we got off to a bit of a rocky start.

The elected members of Parliament of a political party are collectively referred to as that party's caucus. The first order of business for the newly elected NDP MPs was the election of our caucus officers. Svend asked me if I would nominate him for the position of House leader. I didn't personally know any of the other elected members, but

I was well aware of Svend's long history and groundbreaking work in Parliament. I said sure. He seemed like a good choice to me. At the start of the meeting, the leader announced she was naming Bill Blaikie, another veteran NDP MP, as her House leader. Undeterred I jumped in and said I'd like to nominate Svend for the position. That was seconded by Pat Martin, the new MP from Winnipeg Centre, whom Svend had also talked to. There was silence, and Bill Blaikie gave me a withering look from his great height and made it clear this was not an elected position within the caucus (as is the case for the whip), but the leader's prerogative. A heated debate followed, with conflicting memories of what had happened in previous caucuses. Finally it was agreed that research would be undertaken and information reported back at a subsequent caucus meeting. Ah yes, it was the leader's decision…and I learned a lesson about doing my homework.

The caucus later had a retreat meeting in Alexa's home city of Halifax to plan for the upcoming session of Parliament. I had never visited Halifax and immediately loved the people's laid-back charm and friendliness. It had the same coastal vibe as Vancouver. I don't think I was very vocal at the caucus retreat; I felt new and somewhat vulnerable. Even so, I was dispatched by communications staff to be on a CBC panel with another new MP, Conservative Peter MacKay from Nova Scotia, to discuss our aspirations and thoughts about being new MPs in Ottawa. Caucus staff told me the CBC studio was just the other side of the Citadel park, where our hotel was—maybe a fifteen-minute walk. I should have taken a taxi. The park loomed larger and curved around and around, and the minutes ticked by. I realized I was going to be late for my first national TV interview since the election. Not the fastest walker at the best of times, I hopped along and finally found the street where the CBC was located.

I rushed in hot and sweaty, hair askew. MacKay was already in the studio looking calm and very MP-like in his suit and tie and nicely combed hair, miked up in his seat and ready to go. Breathlessly I mumbled my apologies, as the studio staff threw my microphone on as best they could. I saw MacKay look me up and down, and here again I felt the silent judgment, just as I had with Anna Terrana's people. I didn't really look like MP material—and I certainly didn't have a suit on. I saw it in his eyes: inexperienced woman poorly dressed NDPer from BC, versus pure pedigree Nova Scotia boy and son of former cabinet minister. Piece of cake and no contest.

But he didn't know I had years of scrapping with political opponents. As the interview unfolded and he eased out his smooth talk about being a glorious MP, I waited my turn. Then I launched. I had come to Ottawa to fight for people. To fight against disastrous policies that were hurting people in my community and across the country. I wasn't interested in grand aspirations—I was looking for action. MacKay made the tiniest movement of his eyebrow and looked at me down his long nose, and I could see that he wasn't impressed. But I left feeling quite okay and a tiny bit gleeful that I had held my own for the NDP, against the traditions of Conservative politics in the media.

Arriving in Ottawa that late summer of 1997, I was more concerned with learning how to be a member of Parliament than finding a place to live. But getting accommodation was on my list of things that needed doing. Catherine Prince, who had earlier worked for Margaret Mitchell and had tremendous experience on Parliament Hill, helped me look for a place. Still numb from Bruce's death, I had little enthusiasm for the task myself. Catherine said she'd contact the owner of a three-storey brick house on Flora Street in Centretown, where Saskatchewan New Democrat Len Taylor had stayed. Lief was visiting Ottawa, and we rented a car to find the place. The owner of the house, Dan Hara, and one of the tenants, Kim Elliott, a grad student in comparative literature, raised their eyebrows as they watched us arrive late, driving the wrong way up their one-way street. We had circled the surrounding streets trying to get to the right block, the right way, but every damn street was one way and not in the direction we needed. So we gave up, ignored the one-way sign, and carefully drove up and parked the car. I learned later that there was only one way (which we had clearly missed) to approach this particular block in a maze of one-way streets.

It was a hot night, and we sat on an old couch in the high-ceilinged living room, across from Dan and Kim. Kim told me much later that we'd looked like two lost souls hanging on to each other. In fact she wondered about us—arriving late, not very talkative, and stuck together. In those pre-Google days, we all knew very little about each other beforehand. I answered questions from a co-housing questionnaire Dan, an economist, had prepared. It felt more like a grilling than a friendly conversation. Did I agree with co-living arrangements? What were my views on cleaning, pot, parties, and food sharing? Though I loved the old house, I was dubious about the place—there were three Carleton University graduate students living there, including Kim, with a shared kitchen and facilities. Kim nicely described the social gatherings she had, along with her dinner parties. I couldn't see how I would fit in with the students and had visions of all-night parties and drinking. We left for Vancouver without getting back to them.

A week or so later, Kim phoned me in Vancouver asking about my interest in the room rental. Feeling guilty for not having gotten back to them, I assured her I would let her know one way or the other in a couple of days. I told Lief it wasn't the right place to live. He looked at me and said, "Mum, you have nowhere to live and Parliament starts in a couple weeks." He added, "You can always move out if you hate it." True enough, he was right. So I phoned Kim back and said yes, I'd be happy to move in. My room on the second floor came unfurnished— I had a mattress on the floor, a pair of sheets from Zellers, and no personal effects. That reflected my state of mind; I was feeling lost, with serious doubts about being in Ottawa as an MP. Plus, I'd left Lief to fend for himself. It all seemed a big mess. I was eager to get to work, but every time I was by myself there was a gaping hole and the future seemed bleak and empty.

And so began my new job. I felt lonely and sad but seized with the issue of stopping the criminalization of people who use drugs, which underlay the startling number of drug overdoses and the intolerably high rates of HIV infection. I wasn't exactly sure how to tackle these issues, nor did I know anything about how things worked in the Canadian Parliament. But I knew something had to be done to bring attention to the crisis in Vancouver's Downtown Eastside. Before arriving in Ottawa, I had already had many conversations with Bud. His deep knowledge of the issue and his own experience as a former drug user had led me to understand the gravity of the situation and the necessity to save lives and improve people's health. By 1997 the Downtown Eastside had the highest HIV infection rate among injection drug users of any place in the Western world. The loss of life was staggering, and the lack of basic rights to health care and housing and treatment destroyed the lives of thousands of people who were still alive. The stigma of illegal drug use and the impact of criminalization of people who used drugs took an enormous toll. So many things needed to happen at once and in a hurry that I didn't quite know where to begin.

As luck would have it, an opportunity arose with the opening of the new Parliament, September 22, 1997. The same day I rushed through the anti-choice rally to get to Parliament on time, as Julius Fisher filmed me. The speech from the throne is delivered in the Senate by the Governor General, and by custom MPs traipse down the marble hallway and crowd into the Senate chamber entrance to hear the speech that outlines the government's agenda and intentions. I dutifully followed along with the crowd of MPs from the House of Commons, not feeling too enamoured of the pomp and ceremony. It seemed a waste of time to me, and I felt slightly irritable and not at all in awe of the long-held tradition. Turning to look at the person next to me, I realized it was Allan Rock, the minister of health. Without thinking I introduced myself. We were walking down the stately hall squeezed closely together like a sedate mob heading toward the Senate chamber. In a breathless rush, I stammered that I represented the riding of Vancouver East and that people were dying from drug overdoses and we needed to stop that. It was a life-and-death situation, I told him, looking him straight in the eye. I asked if I could meet him to explain more. He smiled and said of course—just contact his office. I have no other memory of the speech from the throne, only jubilation that the minister of health had agreed to meet me on this critical issue.

I had just hired new staff, and we immediately followed up by sending a letter to the minister's office to request the meeting. I waited in anticipation, excited that it had been so easy to at least raise the issue. No response came. We wrote and emailed again. No response. We phoned. He was too busy.

I headed back to the riding in Vancouver and a few days later, on September 27, held a press conference in my small community office on Main Street. The storefront office was already busy with constituents coming by to ask for help, and on that day, reporters showed up as Bud and I talked urgently about the drug crisis and need for a health-based response by the federal government. The *Province* newspaper gave a lively headline: "Give junkies drugs, says MP."

"Doctors should be permitted to prescribe hard drugs—heroin and cocaine—to addicts," Libby Davies, NDP MP for Vancouver East said yesterday. "It's time for politicians to really stand up and deal with the issue fair and square and some new approaches are needed," she said.

The headline was a bit startling, but so far, so good, I thought, at least we're trying to get people's attention. A few weeks later, after an interview with *Vancouver Sun* columnist Barbara Yaffe, Yaffe wrote:

When I asked her about potential controversy surrounding the issue of safe houses and shooting galleries—a notion rejected by BC Health Minister Joy MacPhail, she replied firmly: "There's probably 1000 reasons anyone could throw at this issue and say it won't work. I'm saying, well, we have to make it work because the fact is, drug overdoses are now the leading cause of death for men and women between ages 30–44 and there's an HIV epidemic."

I didn't like disagreeing with Joy MacPhail—she was long-time friend and political ally—but I felt compelled to speak out for federal action. Back in Ottawa we had not yet had a response on my promised meeting from Rock's office. The realization sunk in that of course it wasn't so easy for a new opposition backbencher to secure a formal meeting with a government minister. So much for my naive jubilation. I stewed over it a bit and tried to think what Bruce would have done to get a meeting. Then I got it.

I walked down to the minister's office after question period and carefully opened the door. I put on my best smile and explained to his office staff that we had tried repeatedly to follow up the minister's agreement to meet me on the dire situation in the Downtown Eastside. They seemed completely unaware of this and said they would look into it and get back to me. I knew they wouldn't. I politely told them I wasn't going to leave their office until they booked a time to meet within a reasonable time period of say, a couple of weeks. There was silence. Then I added that I had media waiting outside the door. This wasn't quite true, though I had talked to Gary Engler at the *Vancouver Sun*, who was on standby to hear how things went. More silence. I stood there waiting and then sat down with a determined look on my face. It was now clear that I wasn't leaving until something happened. Within a few minutes a staffer came back and said, yes, absolutely, a meeting could happen and named the specific day and time. I said thank you and left. My hands were shaking and I felt a rush of adrenalin and relief that I hadn't been kicked out. It felt pretty good that, aided by Bruce's example, my community organizing instincts had kicked in.

I had my first meeting with the minister on November 19, 1997. I don't remember much from that meeting, only that I implored him to allow a safe-injection site to be set up and to allow doctors to legally prescribe heroin to chronic users. And that housing was a priority too.

The main thing was to stop the criminalization of drug users and convince the minister of health that a health-based approach was required. This included the need for heroin maintenance drug trials and the opening of a safe-injection site; both required federal approval. I made statements in Parliament, wrote letter after letter to Allan Rock, even after our first meeting, pleading with him to move on the necessary approvals. Later, there were more letters to Anne McLellan, who replaced Rock as the federal minister of health. In an article in the *Hill Times* in October 2002, I asked why she was "stalling and holding up critically needed health interventions like supervised injection sites and heroin maintenance trials for chronic users who are dying daily. These interventions have strong backing locally but we've not heard a peep out of the new Health Minister."

At home it was a controversial issue too, especially in the early days of the crisis. The Downtown Eastside was very divided on the issue, and there were people in neighbouring communities, too, who wanted nothing more than for the "the problem" to disappear. Every day my inbox was overflowing with irate emails from constituents who were outraged at what was going on. They wanted more police intervention and accused me of pandering to junkies who were criminals.

I did everything I could to meet with individual constituents, local groups, and business people to listen to their fears and genuine concerns about the open drug trade. The visibility of drug use on the street was freaking people out, and the automatic reaction from many was to call for tougher laws and tougher law enforcement. I felt the full brunt of this pressure, as did my staff who fielded constituents' phone calls and volumes of communication. But I just couldn't go along with the idea that more cops and rounding people up would solve anything. In fact, I was sure it would only make matters worse.

I learned fast that working to end the criminalization of people who use drugs and bring about a different approach was a controversial thing to do. Politicians were expected to quiver with rage about law and order and promise tougher laws and sentencing. That's the way it had always been. Like sex workers, people who used drugs were seen as almost subhuman and without rights.

It's painstaking work to begin a process of education, understanding, and a change of direction. But if anything was going to get better, that's what was needed, desperately, both in the political arena and in the community most affected. On the one hand elected officials were unaware of the issue and happy to ignore the growing crisis, or worse, encourage a law-and-order approach. It's the oldest political trick in the book—exploit people's fears, divide them, and call for simplistic solutions like tougher laws. On the other hand, local residents wanted a quick fix (excuse the pun), and by and large weren't interested in thinking about how to deal with serious, chronic addiction issues and the impact of criminalization on people's lives. If you'd had your car broken into too many times, or sidestepped needles on the street, you wanted action and immediate results. So many times I would endeavour to reasonably talk through what was happening and explain that the most urgent response needed was to focus on the health emergency in the Downtown Eastside.

But there were also voices of encouragement. Community agencies like the PHS that supported the work of a newly formed association of people who used drugs, led by Bud Osborn and Ann Livingston. VANDU—the Vancouver Area Network of Drug Users—brought enormous creativity, energy, and an active membership to the need for massive changes to save lives and stop the war on drugs. The passion and daring of VANDU's work reminded me so much of the early days of DERA—taking risks, speaking truth to power, and not taking no for an answer. It was easy for me to immediately understand what VANDU was about and to want to work closely with them. It was essential for VANDU, as it had been for us at DERA three decades earlier, to have allies in the political arena who would carry the message forward and not be deterred by opposition.

I spoke to the media often and held press conferences to maintain pressure and visibility. We organized public forums in the Vancouver riding and in Ottawa, to discuss the issue and call for support for safe-injection sites, health support, and housing and other measures. I spoke at conferences, even at the Fraser Institute, a right-wing think tank, because they supported drug policy reform. And I took meetings with doctors, scientists, police officers—anyone who could be influenced and be convinced, or who could help me to understand the issue better.

In our community office on Main Street near Broadway, Bud and I met with Dr. Martin Schechter, who was in the process of setting up and seeking federal approval for heroin maintenance trials for chronic drug users. His words stayed with us: the drug crisis and HIV epidemic among injection drug users in the community was akin to the tainted blood scandal, he said. Thousands of Canadians who received blood products had been needlessly infected with HIV and hepatitis C; in that tragedy the government finally acted, ordering a royal commission into the scandal.

Dr. Schechter emphasized once that the knowledge of harm was evident, the failure of any government to act was the same as knowingly leaving people to die. Eugene Oscapella, too, a lawyer and lecturer at the University of Ottawa, provided expert help in his analysis of the war on drugs and the impact of prohibition. He gave testimony on Parliament Hill before the Senate and House of Commons committees and, at my invitation, also presented a slide show to the NDP caucus showing the connection between prohibition of drugs and organized crime.

It was a joy to connect with people like Eugene, who had vast knowledge and clear arguments about the need for drug policy reform. Senator Pierre Nolin was also a great ally; his 2002 report on marijuana, as chair of the Senate Special Committee on Illegal Drugs, was a reference point for the changes that were needed. Nolin, who died in 2015, was an old-time Conservative. He and Larry Campbell, former mayor of Vancouver and now a Liberal senator, were strong advocates for drug policy reform.

The City of Vancouver, led by Mayor Philip Owen—the same guy who had defeated me in the 1993 mayoral race—called for new and bold harm reduction measures, as outlined in "A Framework for Action: A Four-Pillar Approach to Drug Problems in Vancouver," released in 2001. He was supported and briefed by Donald MacPherson, the city's first drug policy co-ordinator. Formerly the director of the Carnegie Community Centre and someone who was very familiar with the blooming drug scene at Main and Hastings, MacPherson had an amazing grasp of the crisis. He wrote groundbreaking reports to City Council outlining what needed to be done. Owen was the first mayor in Canada to call for a humane and public-health-based approach to the drug crisis, and his leadership helped change the tone of the debate in Vancouver and across the country. I would often run into him at public meetings on the drug crisis, and we always had a chuckle that here we were—former political adversaries who had run against each other— now working together on the same issue.

My biggest connection, though, was with VANDU through Bud and Ann. I attended VANDU meetings often and listened to what people had to say. They told me in excruciating detail what their lives were like on the street. No place to go, harsh daily survival for the next fix, harassed by police and often arrested, virtually no access to health care, and fear of overdoses from deadly cocktails on the street. VANDU emerged as a powerful force in the community, challenging stereotypes about people who use drugs and countering the war on drugs. It was a revolt against oppressive norms that denied people their basic human rights. Bud was a figure similar to Bruce—one a former drug user, one a former alcoholic, both determined to break a system of control and injustice. VANDU also served to remind me that the Downtown Eastside had changed since the 1970s—the old retired union guys were still around, hanging on in the rundown rooming houses and hotel rooms, but with a massive influx of illicit drugs amid growing homelessness, the street scene was very different. It had become commonplace to see people visibly destitute and homeless on the street, in distress, or lying cold on the sidewalks from an overdose.

In October 1998 I brought Bud to Ottawa to meet Allan Rock. Bud communicated to the minister like no one else could the urgency of the situation and the need for federal action. He also presented the minister with one of his books of poems, which chronicled the reality of life and death on the street.

Bud and I met almost every week, as I shuttled back and forth between Ottawa and Vancouver. I helped him navigate the politics of the regional health board that he was appointed to, and we worked on wording for an emergency resolution that the board eventually passed in response to the HIV/AIDS epidemic in the community. We found some allies in the Vancouver Police Department in Kash Heed and Gil Pudar. And we spoke out against dreadful police operations, where users and low-level dealers would be rounded up with sensational media coverage. Bud was overwhelmed with media attention—everyone wanted his take on things, and he told me he suffered from anxiety and sometimes depression as he tried to live up to people's heroic expectations.

Sometimes when I returned from Ottawa, we would drive from the Downtown Eastside to the British Properties in West Vancouver, of all places, winding up higher and higher past multi-millionaires' luxury homes, until we reached as high as we could go by road. It was always at night, often very late, and we would look down at the sparkling lights of the city spread out before us. Bud loved the Downtown Eastside. But it was also stifling, physically and emotionally. The cool air in the open space on the North Shore mountains was literally a breath of fresh air for him. And he would have a smoke, leaning against the car and listening to the trees move in the soft breeze. Sometimes we'd laugh at the irony of it all, the two worlds apart—the inner city with its twenty-four-hour cacophony and urgency as people rushed to survive, compared to the serene quietness of the British Properties, with its veil of secrecy behind all those expensive gates and walls. He would remind me, "There are drug users here too, they just don't get caught."

VANDU made me an honorary member, and I developed a clear understanding of the harsh life my constituents lived. It made me want to help in any way I could. It was an emotional time. My grief from the loss of Bruce transformed into a deeper empathy of the turmoil and hardship people were facing. My own suffering and loss became inexorably connected to that of the community. It felt like a process of witnessing death all over again—but this time there was a cure. The war on drugs could be beat. At the same time, Lief began working at the Washington Hotel and the Sunrise Hotel, run by the PHS, where many users lived. He was still very young, barely nineteen, but his connection to the community was strong and he became a valued worker at the PHS. Often on the weekend when I was back from Ottawa, I would pick him up at six in the morning, at the end of his twelve-hour graveyard shift. Exhausted, he would tell of the incredible experiences and situations he'd had to deal with.

Liz Evans and Mark Townsend of the PHS became pioneers in providing secure and caring housing and programs for people, with no judgment attached. They would eventually be responsible for running Insite, the first safe-injection site, where Lief would work too. Lief told me about the older residents he would run into on the street who would smile and say,

I remember when your dad carried you around the neighbourhood when you were little. Lief Eriksen is not a name you easily forget. I knew Bruce would be proud of his son and the work he was doing.

It was a tight-knit community, and my advocacy in Ottawa to bring about change that would help the community relied on the alliance and support from VANDU. In those early days, junkies were seen as nothing more than criminals. And the standard response was, Lock 'em up. We had many detractors, and even my own campaign manager, the same Glen Sanford who had helped me win my nomination and first election, feared I would never be re-elected because I was too focused on the issue. He might have been right; I was aware that I was walking a risky line, politically. The strong prevailing view, in Ottawa and in the community, was that tougher law enforcement and sentencing were the answer to an increasingly visible drug scene. The war on drugs was in full swing, not only in the United States but also in Canada. I was ridiculed, openly challenged, and told I was useless.

Leo Knight, a columnist in the local *North Shore News*, responded to my calls for change with outrage in October 1997:

> Libby Davies suggested it's time we provided free heroin to them. If that little nugget of brilliance wasn't enough she went on to say we should set up "safe houses" for their shelter and use. I would suggest "shooting galleries" might be more appropriate terminology. Not that I'd ever accuse Davies of being a deep thinker, but this latest gem shows just how superficial and ignorant of reality she really is.

He ended the column with "What are you smoking Libby?"

The connection with VANDU and Bud and Ann kept me confident that we were on the right path. It was the first-hand knowledge of the experience of users themselves that propelled us. I didn't see down-and-out junkies who were untouchable, I saw real people who were taking caring of each other and incredibly resourceful in the face of massive discrimination and hardship. I am convinced that if I hadn't had a background in the very same community that was now the epi-centre of the HIV/AIDS epidemic of injection drug users in the Western world, I would have wavered. I would have been pulled into the Ottawa vortex and the scepticism of my own caucus, who wondered what the heck I was up to. But my political instincts came from the street, not from inside a political party. That made me see the issue differently and act differently.

A number of critical issues, including housing, had brought me to Ottawa. When Alexa McDonough made me housing and social policy critic for the NDP, I willingly seized the challenge. In the 1970s in the Downtown Eastside, "street homelessness" had not been an issue. We'd fought to get social housing built in the community, and as bad as the single rooms in the old hotels and rooming houses were, at least they were shelter. But by the late 1990s, homelessness became a crisis across the country, and it seemed every senior level of government was obliv-ious to it.

I was still figuring out my role as an MP. Being part of a political party caucus can be both helpful and ... weird. Suddenly there were many others to consider, not the least of whom was the leader. Where did I fit in? How could I make things happen? These were some of my struggles as the new MP for Vancouver East. It seemed like you had to get someone's permission to do just about anything; the restrictive rules and procedures were very different from those a city councillor faces. I figured out that if I went *outside* Parliament and got active in the real world, I might accomplish something. Looking back I can see that it was the years of community organizing and working in alliances that drew me outside the marble halls of Parliament to do my work as a parliamentarian. I was still an organizer at heart.

Calling for a national housing program with Michael Shapcott (*left*) and Cathy Crowe (*in white jacket*), Quebec City, outside the Château Frontenac for a meeting of federal, provincial, and territorial housing ministers, 1999

Thus I embarked on a national housing tour in January 1999, as NDP housing and social policy critic, to draw attention to a national disaster that originated not from forces of nature but from terrible public policy decisions made by people in power. I was already working closely with great people like Michael Shapcott of the National Housing and Homelessness Network, and the tireless Cathy Crowe of the Toronto Disaster Relief Committee. Both Michael and Cathy are still active, and still inspiring, today.

I visited large urban centres and small northern communities and talked to and met more than a hundred housing advocates, providers, and homeless people. Looking today, twenty years later, at the recommendations in the report that I submitted to the Liberal government, "Homelessness: An Unnatural Disaster," is rather shocking. The recommendations are as urgent and relevant today as they were in 1999: "Housing is a Human Right...Develop a national housing strategy…Meet the goal of providing an additional 1% for housing… Begin at the grass roots and re-build our communities using the wealth of non-profit sector housing skill and expertise…Housing is a health issue…Establish national housing objectives and standards…"

The tour gave me a better understanding of the issue of homelessness and lack of housing affordability in Canada. The hard part, as always, was gaining political traction to influence the political agenda in Ottawa. But pressure was mounting, and the Liberals—who were loath to acknowledge until many years later that their decision to eliminate social housing had been a disaster both politically and socially—were forced to establish a minister responsible for homelessness in 1999. It frustrated me and others to no end that they wouldn't re-establish a proper housing program and would only respond to "homelessness" on a project-by-project basis. But still, progress was made.

The minister, Claudette Bradshaw from New Brunswick, was a social worker and a very decent person. But her analysis, and that of the government, was that homelessness was really a "social problem," implying it was about people who had individual problems related to addiction, mental illness, and hard times. That is true only in part. First and foremost, homelessness is a lack of affordable housing for people who need it. It is about public policy (or the failure thereof) and the priorities we assign to the funding of various initiatives and programs. The name of an Ontario group led by activist and writer Matthew Behrens said it all: Homes Not Bombs.

The social work analysis belied the fundamental structural problem that the housing marketplace is beyond the reach of many Canadian families. This was understood decades earlier. When Canada's veterans returned from war, there was an urgent need to provide affordable housing, as well as access to post-secondary education. These building years produced thousands of small but livable family homes for veterans, which you can still see in many urban centres today. But by the mid-1990s, the obsession with deregulation, privatization, and austerity stripped Canada of its honourable record. Under neoliberalism, the needs of ordinary people were subservient to trade deals and the free flow of capital.

Nevertheless, Claudette worked hard and she told me, "Libby, keep going after me in question period because it gives me the leverage I need to push at the cabinet table." So I did. As hard as I could. I fought to get questions assigned to me within the small daily NDP allotment for question period, and spoke as often as I could in Parliament about the housing tour, the need for housing and for ending homelessness, and the urgency for the government to act. These were the years of Jean Chrétien's majority Liberal government, and there was a strong expectation by housing activists that the government would uphold liberal values, do the right thing, and bring back previously successful housing programs they had axed.

It was tough going. Over time the campaign for 1% of the federal budget for housing, organized by the National Housing and Homelessness Network and the Toronto Disaster Relief Committee, was gaining strength. The campaign called for an additional 1% of federal investment in affordable housing. This was a reasonable and achievable goal, to augment the existing 1% that was assigned to ongoing mortgages and subsidies the feds had committed during the 1980s when social housing and co-ops were developed across the country. Michael Shapcott contended that a relatively small federal investment in good housing could have a big payoff in terms of jobs, economic prosperity, and most of all, good quality housing for Canadians who needed it. I raised the campaign whenever I could, promoting it in material I sent out from Ottawa to my housing lists across the country and ensuring that the New Democrats were firmly in support.

At a meeting of the NDP's federal council (the party's governing body), a number of young activists approached me and said they wanted to do a sleep out on Parliament Hill, by the Centennial Flame, to draw attention to the issue. It was a creative idea, and it wasn't too cold out yet. When they invited me to participate, I said yes; if there was any trouble, having an MP there might help. About twelve of us assembled our sleeping bags and headed off for the Hill. Sure enough the RCMP let it be known that the young activists would be arrested if such an action took place overnight. But I had a hunch that they'd want to avoid the media optics of arresting an MP for peacefully having a nap by the Centennial Flame. We stayed all night, garnered some good coverage about why we were sleeping out, and experienced stiff joints from lying on the cold, damp stones. And we heard every single quarter-hour chime of the Peace Tower clock. I can recite the Westminster clock chimes with precision to this day.

Those days on Parliament Hill were very different from what we see now. It's hard to believe now, post 9/11, but there was no security screening upon entering the precinct and its buildings. Security presence at demos and rallies was minimal.

I participated in housing rallies and demos, and I recall now, with regret, once yelling at Joe Clark, then leader of the diminished Conservative party, because he dared to show up and try and speak at a big rally on Parliament Hill to end homelessness. I was furious because he had been prime minister when the cuts to housing first began. How dare he show up, I thought, when he'd been part of the problem. I cringe now to think of it; his presence in fact demonstrated multi-party support for housing. He looked at me in bewilderment, no doubt thinking, Who the hell is this crazy woman who thinks she's an MP? Later that same day, I strode into Centre Block arm in arm with some of the organizers, and we made it to the prime minister's third-floor office to demand to see him. We didn't get to see Jean Chrétien, but at least we made it to his door.

During that first term on the Hill, only three NDP MPs were from the West Coast. My colleagues were Svend Robinson from Burnaby and

Nelson Riis from Kamloops. They both helped me understand my new role as an MP, especially Svend, as we shared similar views on many issues. I gained enormous respect for Alexa McDonough as our leader. She worked extraordinarily hard, and had her share of sexism and conflict thrown at her. She always looked for consensus and worked to keep the caucus together. Sticking to the party and caucus lines was not so strictly enforced then as it became in later years under Jack Layton and Thomas Mulcair. Frankly—as the third and at one point the fourth party in the House, the leader's office didn't notice so much what you were getting up to. Still, there were tough discussions in caucus. On one occasion, I was venting about the need for safe-injection sites and free heroin. My colleague Yvon Godin from New Brunswick leaned across the table in disbelief, and said, "Libby, are you crazy? No one in my community will support this and the NDP shouldn't either." In the years to come, Yvon—like most of the caucus, came to a better understanding of the issue.

These years were times of worldwide mobilization against undemocratic trade agreements and the globalization of capital, and an emerging crisis in the Persian Gulf as the US rattled its sabres against alleged weapons of mass destruction. I was still closely connected to the peace movement, and in 1998 I was approached to participate in a Citizens Weapons Inspection Team to search for weapons of mass destruction in Washington state, just south of Vancouver. The team included Peter Coombes, president of End the Arms Race, Murray Dobbin from the Council of Canadians, Ed Schmitt, chair of the Peace and Social Justice Committee of the Anglican Diocese of New Westminster, and David Morgan, president of Veterans Against Nuclear Arms.

The Bangor, Washington, submarine base was known to be home to 1,600 nuclear bombs. Definitely weapons of mass destruction. This creative action took place during the turmoil of impending military assaults against Iraq to enforce UN weapons of mass destruction inspection. Co-ordinator Steve Staples and Peter Coombs had, incredibly, secured permission from the US Navy admiral in charge of the Pacific Northwest for us to enter the Bangor base and even tour one of the submarines. We jumped at the chance. However, not surprisingly, a couple of hours later the admiral phoned back and informed our group that the Pacific Command HQ based in Hawaii had revoked the invitation.

Undeterred, we travelled down the I-5 highway from Vancouver to Bangor to announce our mission. We arrived at the base and asked to be let in. Permission denied. We unfurled a large banner that read, "This facility contains nuclear weapons." I think the navy personnel thought we were going to climb the fence or something, but as spokesperson I maintained a polite and friendly stance. That later earned me the description by local media covering the story of being a "cherubic-looking" MP. Although we were denied entry to the base itself, we'd secured the rental of a small plane that could take two people (and the pilot) for an aerial view. After driving down unknown local back roads around Bangor with Steve Staples and the videographer, we discovered the ramshackle airstrip with an interesting collection of broken-down planes. Steve remembers that the pilot informed us he hoped he had enough gas to get us up and back, and with that we sputtered into the air and flew a few hundred feet above the base, where we could clearly see the nuclear subs lined up.

This was our "visual" inspection. It was a remarkable thing to see; in today's post-9/11 world, we never would have been permitted to fly that close to the base. We later issued a full report of our inspection and felt we had helped expose the hypocrisy of the US government when it came to weapons of mass destruction. The report said, "Citizen-initiated activities are essential in ensuring accountability of government."

The NDP caucus was involved too in mobilizations against undemocratic trade deals. In 1999, Bill Blaikie, our House leader and trade critic, travelled to Seattle to protest the World Trade Organization's

At the Quebec Summit of the Americas in protest against the FTAA; NDP caucus members (*from left*) Dick Proctor, Pat Martin, Tony Martin, Bill Blaikie, Judy Wasylycia-Leis, Peter Stoffer, Wendy Lill, Libby Davies, 2001

secret negotiations. I recall being in the opposition lobby in Ottawa when Bill phoned to update us on what was going on. You could hear the excitement in his voice as he joined thousands of protesters who were out on the street to uphold democracy. Later, Alexa McDonough would lead the caucus's participation in the massive rally against the Free Trade Agreement of the Americas (FTAA) in Quebec City in 2001. The caucus travelled together by bus to Quebec City. There was a great feeling of solidarity with civil society as we helped protest the antidemocratic trade agreement, which was eventually defeated.

Back at Flora Street in Ottawa, I mostly kept to myself and avoided the gatherings and discussions floating up from downstairs. Nor did I share with my new colleagues or housemates that it had been a few months since my partner had died. Svend knew, as did Alexa, but that was it. After a year or more went by, I slowly began to emerge socially, although it was still hard. I spent my time travelling back and forth to

Vancouver each weekend, staying in close contact with Lief, who was also having a hard time.

My colleague Pat Martin moved into the Flora Street house, and I liked his easygoing manner and charming smile. He would laugh with gusto when the snow came and I stepped out with trepidation, terrified of falling, as he, a true Winnipegger, strode off toward the Hill. Pat, Kim, and I had many a fine evening at Flora Street and I felt like I was finally getting used to my new life. Kim and I had much in common—politics, human rights, books, good food, and a passion for change—and we became close friends. She told me that she'd found me withdrawn and distant at first, and when she caught me crying one March morning during that first year, I reluctantly told her about Bruce and the hard time I was having. She was quietly understanding. I helped her stuff envelopes at night for Amnesty International mailings, and she helped make my life feel much better on a personal level.

Digging In

When Prime Minister Jean Chrétien called a snap election for November 2000, we were suddenly thrown back into election mode. I was lucky that Glen Sanford came forward again to run our campaign in Vancouver East. I learned that a first re-election can be tough. You've set the bar that you can get elected, and the expectation is you will do so again. But in closely contested ridings, especially for the NDP, these things are never guaranteed. We had an added challenge in BC with the failing fortunes of Glen Clark's NDP government, as he got dogged by harsh media and one trouble after another. Door knocking was particularly illuminating during that election. I often heard, "I'm not voting for you because I don't like Glen Clark" or "I'm sending a message to Glen Clark so I can't vote for you." I did my best to explain that the provincial NDP was separate from the federal wing of the party, but voters saw us all as one indistinguishable blob. It was challenging to publicly support the government in BC and respond to the anger of voters at the same time.

We had another serious challenge in that election—a very credible Liberal candidate in the riding who presented much tougher challenges than Anna Terrana had in 1997. Mason Loh, a lawyer, was a leader in Vancouver's Chinese community and the president of the most powerful Chinese community service agency, S.U.C.C.E.S.S. The agency had access to thousands of their clients, many of whom lived on the east side, and when his election signs began to pop up like dandelions across the riding, we knew we had a battle on our hands. Glen Sanford always maintained that, to build the community's perception of momentum, you need to mark your territory with your signs in much greater quantity than your opponent. Mid-campaign it definitely looked like Loh had the upper hand. He was articulate and smooth, and though we had suspicions, we couldn't gather evidence that he was using S.U.C.C.E.S.S. membership data and possibly resources to bolster his campaign.

Glen had another worry. We learned that a crack house was located above our campaign office on East Hastings Street, and feared it could become a media story. If it did, it would be a lightning rod for my outspoken position on harm reduction, the need for a safe-injection site, and ending the criminalization of drug users. There was much fear, particularly among seniors in the Chinese community, about open drug use and crime. It was a perfect weapon for my opponent to seize upon and use to his advantage.

The November election heralded classic Vancouver weather, and as the days got wetter, my spirits took a beating. I realized we were possibly going to lose. Luckily, Glen had thought through the optics. Loh lived in Shaughnessy, one of the wealthiest neighbourhoods in Vancouver, and so we emphasized my Eastside history and activism and my commitment to the community. Who would stand up for East Van? Who would fight for people's rights? Who would take on the powers that be?

Then we had a stroke of political luck. It came to light that Loh had at some point previously joined the Reform Party of Canada—so his Liberal credibility became very much an issue. Folks in East Van had twice before elected a Liberal MP, but Reform, with its antigovernment, right-wing agenda? Loh still had tremendous loyalty in the Chinese community, but his perceived opportunism was enough to put a dent in his quest for power. By the end of that campaign, in a radio debate with me on CKNW, he was complaining that I was too aggressive. Welcome to East Van!

We won with a comfortable margin and it was back into the fray in Ottawa for a second term. I felt strengthened that even with ongoing opposition to my position on drug policy reform, I had strong backing from the community to continue to advocate for substantial change.

Many people have studied the battle for Insite—North America's first safe-injection site. It's hard to pinpoint the precise elements and ingredients that lead to a major social change taking place. But with Insite, it was organic in nature; it was about working with people who believed in each other and who trusted each other. It was also knowing that the people who had the most important message were the drug users themselves. They transformed the public discourse from one of demonization and vilification of people who use drugs to a movement to save lives and give people hope. It was up to all of us involved to help them get their message out.

I often think of Insite as a model for transformative change. What had at first seemed impossible became achievable because so many levels of engagement became powerfully intertwined. The scientists and researchers couldn't have made it happen on their own, even though they had excellent research in hand. They needed the will and strength of the voice of VANDU members to speak the truth about their lives. Similarly, VANDU needed allies in the medical and bureaucratic world to back up what they were saying about their experience. Community support was needed, from people like Liz Evans and Mark Townsend at the PHS. And political allies were essential too.

The campaign to open Insite in 2003, after many years of struggle, was a catalyst for a much bigger debate in Canada about drug policy reform and the need to end drug prohibition in favour of a health-based regulatory approach. In other words, legalization. It should not be missed that it began at a local level—in one neighbourhood—out of desperation for survival. We often think that big changes take place on the national scene, in the "halls of power." But most often the impetus is local. That's where grassroots activism for transformative change begins, although it may be overshadowed by bigger players later on. Whether it's the anti-apartheid movement, Indigenous rights, Occupy, Black Lives Matter, LGBTQ+ rights, workers' rights, farm workers' rights, or sex workers' rights, these movements began in a community where people faced daily oppression and degradation. These movements all needed allies too: people who hadn't necessarily directly experienced oppression, discrimination, and violence but were willing to put themselves on the line. That's the history of social change.

It was a constant challenge of two steps forward and one step back. On one occasion in 2002, I met with Vancouver's new chief of police, Jamie Graham. Naturally the discussion turned to Vancouver's number one issue, the drug crisis in the Downtown Eastside. I spoke about my support of opening a safe-injection site and my belief that ongoing police operations to harass and arrest users and low-level dealers were pointless and harmful. I asked him if he and the department would support a safe-injection site. I was taken aback when he told me I was full of "bullshit" and proceeded to enlighten me about his excellent relationship on law and order with Chuck Cadman, the MP representing the Canadian Alliance party in the neighbouring suburban municipality of Surrey. Graham had previously served there as head of the RCMP. I knew at that moment that, had I been one of his male buddy MPs, he never would have dismissed my point of view in such a disrespectful manner. I indignantly told him I had thirty years' experience in the Downtown Eastside and knew what I was talking about; he had been there a few months only. I left the meeting wound up and furious, and later reported on it at a VANDU meeting. They already knew what we were up against. Eventually the Vancouver Police Department neutralized its opposition to a safe-injection site and came to understand its important role in reducing harm on the streets.

A Special Committee on Non-Medical Use of Drugs was established by the House of Commons in 2002 as a result of a motion from Canadian Alliance (formerly Progressive Conservative) MP Randy White, from Abbotsford, BC. When it came to drug policy reform, he and I were on opposite ends of the spectrum. I wanted to end prohibition and see a regulatory public health approach to illicit drugs; he saw it primarily as a criminal justice issue, with some "treatment" thrown in for good measure. The special committee, chaired by Liberal MP Paddy Torsney, travelled to Vancouver for hearings. It was an eye-opener for the committee members to see first-hand what took place on the streets. I remember Dominic LeBlanc expressing his shock at what he saw on our "field trip" late at night, down some of the worst back alleys in the Downtown Eastside. That experience helped bring about an understanding that a "lock 'em up and throw away the key" approach was futile and inhumane.

Later the committee travelled to Europe to visit safe-injection sites and heroin programs in Frankfurt, Zurich, and Amsterdam. These programs were well established in Europe but still not accepted in Canada. On our minibus, I told Randy White I was personally opposed to drug use. This seemed to surprise him, as he knew I was an advocate for regulation and legalization. But I wanted him to understand that my position wasn't based on a love affair with drugs. It was based on a public policy imperative that a health-based approach and regulation was far preferable and less violent and harmful than the chaos and cost of prohibition. Like we'd experienced with alcohol, illegality did nothing to deter use; it only created risk and harm. He surprised me by saying, "I get it." And then explained the political nature of his party's stance. I got that too.

As a member of that special parliamentary committee, I sat alongside members I utterly disagreed with. That was a lesson in patience, and also in comprehending someone else's point of view. It was frustrating to see the old arguments and stereotypes trotted out, which treat people who use drugs as failures or victims who required help to "get clean," with abstinence the only measure of success. Yet again it was my relationship with groups like VANDU that kept me focused. I tried to get the committee to understand that safe-injection sites were not dens of immorality but practical places to deliver health support and prevent overdoses. Ending the war on drugs, and ending drug prohibition, became central to my work as a MP.

I've always felt my calling was to dig in deep and make myself as useful as I can. Looking back I believe my role has been to work on issues that were seen at the time as controversial and unconventional, helping to make them mainstream and acceptable. It was never a conscious decision to choose controversy or a "radical" position. It just came to be that way because I could not ignore where I was and what was going on around me. Even so, I worked on many other issues, major and minor, including fighting for antiscab legislation as NDP labour critic, as post-secondary education critic, and on childcare and immigration, to name a few. And public service to individual constituents was always a priority.

In May 2001, only a few months after the federal election, BC residents went back to the polls. Glen Clark's provincial government was thoroughly defeated, with only two NDP representatives surviving—Jenny Kwan and Joy MacPhail. Both of their provincial constituencies were within the boundaries of the federal riding of Vancouver East, and we thanked our lucky stars that the people of East Van had seen fit to make sure that at least two representatives would be in the BC legislature to take on the newly elected premier, Gordon Campbell. I recall canvassing with Joy up and down Victoria Drive prior to election day, and feeling dejected at the number of Green party signs we saw everywhere. We knocked on doors with Green signs anyway, because this election was down to the wire. We took a deep breath, went to the first door, and tried our lines. It didn't go so well. Joy was almost on her knees apologizing for the NDP. "Okay, stop apologizing," I told her. "We've got to give people the facts here—whatever screwups there have been, and no matter how mad people are at the NDP and Glen Clark, if they vote Green they will only help elect the Liberal, so we've got to get that through." "Yup," she said, and we tried again; we knocked on every door that we saw with a Green sign and talked ourselves blue in the face. Every vote does count. Joy, with her strong credibility, was re-elected by a slim margin of four hundred votes. The two East Van women went on to make history, using every ounce of their energy to hold Campbell's government to account. It was often seventy-seven votes to two.

A second national housing tour in 2001 brought me into contact with an old friend from my municipal days, Jack Layton. This housing tour ended in Toronto. We were holding a discussion at The Meeting Place on Queen Street West, when Jack came in on his bicycle looking very distressed. The date was September 11; he told us about what TV screens around the world were showing live. The meeting ended abruptly, and we stood in disbelief in small groups as Jack went back to city hall. The rest of us went to the homelessness monument at Church of the Holy Trinity next to the Eaton Centre in downtown Toronto. We held a small vigil, and I spoke a few words expressing our deep worry that if the perpetrators who blew up the World Trade Center towers in New York City were not white North Americans, it would unleash an era of fear and hatred. Little did we know what dark days would emerge. Back in Parliament the Liberal government moved swiftly to introduce sweeping antiterrorist legislation, Bill C-36. The NDP opposed this draconian legislation, which was the forerunner to Prime Minister Stephen Harper's security legislation, Bill C-51 in 2014. Both bills unnecessarily targeted civil liberties and gave authorities enormous powers to arrest and detain without due process.

Following the two housing tours across the country, I developed a private member's bill to establish housing as a human right, and calling on the federal government to work with other levels of government to introduce a national housing program. A member of Parliament can submit a bill on a topic they care about and want to see legislation enacted on. As this was my first major private member's bill, I spent months crafting the language, trying to make it as inclusive and realistic as possible. The development of the bill was enormously assisted by David Hulchanski, a housing expert and University of Toronto professor, and housing activist Michael Shapcott. We went over draft after draft, and I finally introduced Bill C-416 in Parliament on November 28, 2001. The bill was well received and, thereafter, together with my staff and allies in the community, we mounted a huge campaign to gain support across Canada as well as in Parliament. The bill nearly made it through to third and final reading, but a federal election got in the way. It can take years to succeed in getting a private member's bill voted on, and they are rarely passed by Parliament. In the case of the Housing Bill of Rights it cycled through several general elections, as I reintroduced the bill after each election. The bill still survives, most recently sponsored by Marjolaine Boutin-Sweet, the housing critic and party whip under NDP leader Jagmeet Singh.

I also developed a keen interest in what it was like for women in the political theatre in Ottawa. In my early civic days, I hadn't given these issues much thought, but as I grew older, I became more aware of the differences that gender made in politics. As I began to look more closely at the dynamics of leadership in sexist, old Parliament Hill, I noticed more and more how women were treated differently and how, in the scheme of things in Ottawa, it often seemed that we didn't really count. The NDP had a woman leader, Alexa McDonough, who took on many tough issues, and in 2002 and 2003 in the aftermath of 9/11, she led the campaign in Parliament to free Canadian Maher Arar from illegal imprisonment and torture in Syria. She never once shied away from defending Arar's human rights and she worked closely with Monia Mazigh, his determined and tireless wife, to push the Liberal government to act. The media too often sidestepped Alexa, though, and she never received proper credit for her unwavering stance against Islamophobia.

Sexism in politics is an issue that many people—well, mostly men—don't like to talk about. But it's there and it needs to be understood, and proactive change needs to be undertaken. We experience discrimination, sexism, harassment, and violence based on gender in our society, and it affects what we are able to do.

I remember following the news from Parliament when Margaret Mitchell was an MP and a staunch advocate for women's rights. When she rose in Parliament in 1982 to speak about domestic violence, she was shocked to hear laughter and heckling from male colleagues in the House. "This is no laughing matter," she challenged.

On a personal level, I sometimes faced abusive or insulting comments about my weight. How many of us struggle with that and try to bury it? It wasn't direct heckling or anything like that. As anyone who is more robustly built knows, it often manifests in underhanded ways. Like many women, I tried to dismiss the hurt and convince myself it didn't matter. But it does matter, especially when women are targeted because of the way we look and by and large men are not. The stereotypes of who we are supposed to be are so powerful that they can become debilitating.

I regret not having kept a list—which would now be very long—of each instance in which I saw or experienced sexism. Death by a thousand cuts, it seemed. So many times and so many subtle and not-so-subtle inferences, comments, and actions that clearly indicate that this shit happens. All the time. It's too easy to dismiss these incidents as a "slip" and forget the specifics. But when I think about it and talk to other women about their experiences, I have no doubt that it's not us being "too sensitive."

Too often we let it slide by, shrug our shoulders and think, oh well, maybe I heard that wrong or took it the wrong way, or think it's not that big a deal. It is a big deal. Because this is the twenty-first century and women overall are liberated, strong, articulate, and accomplished. We are leaders, but still we experience sexism, discrimination, and harassment, and are devalued because of it. While I don't have that list to refer to, let me give some general examples, in case you think it's no big deal. In caucus meetings, how many times did a female member of caucus make an excellent point, quietly and without fanfare, and with little reaction, only to see minutes later, a guy make the same point at the mic with a lot of speechifying and bravado, to a standing ovation. And then take the credit and gratification from the team. Many times.

How many times have I been told on media panels to jump in and not wait to be asked, and then later face comments from the public for being too aggressive? Ever heard of a man being called "shrill" or "strident"? Assertive and strong, yes, but not shrill.

How many times did I experience comments about my clothing, my hair, my weight, when the guy sitting next to me was wearing the same crumpled, messy-looking suit, day after day, with the same gravy-stained tie? Many times.

How many times did men dominate the convention floor, the mic, the debate, because what they had to say was "so important," even when they stated the absolute obvious and it wasn't important at all? Far too much of the time.

How many times have I received that look that makes me know I am invisible to the person who is looking straight through me? Like I don't exist. And how many times has our voice been drowned out by dominant, ego-driven men who still see women in a support role to their own sense of importance? Again—too many times.

Over the years I have talked about this to hundreds of powerful women in politics, in unions, in the media, and in the community. Sexism exists and we have experienced it—in subtle and sometimes not-so-subtle ways. Greater inequities face racialized women, whether from media portrayals and stereotypes or in the workplace and certainly in politics. No one likes to own up to it, but often words about supporting equality don't match actions. These realities don't stop us, but they do slow us down.

I would sometimes give speeches at conferences about women in politics, and it was always a juggling act. I wanted to tell all about sexism and the gendered nature of the political arena, but didn't want to come across as negative, as though there was no hope or progress being made, however slow it might be. On one occasion in 2003, I spoke at the Canadian Auto Workers (CAW) union women's conference about women in politics at Port Elgin, Ontario. I had fretted for days over what I going to say, feeling a familiar sense of inadequacy that I would not say the right thing to, in this instance, a strong group of feminists in the labour movement. Big names were speaking, like activist Judy Rebick, whose profound analysis on feminism was far better than my own. On the drive to Port Elgin, I felt tense and nervous. I wished I could go back home and not give the speech at all. I only hoped that I could rely on what had always kept me going—sharing my own experience to illuminate a bigger issue that we all faced. I wanted to focus on the issue of what leadership means in terms of gender and how we perceive power and leadership as women and men. But then I thought, maybe I have it all wrong—and it's only me who's experiencing a disconnect from the way men act as leaders compared to women.

Arriving in Port Elgin and the beautiful CAW educational centre in the woods near the lake, I drew up a quick list. It illustrated what I thought empowering leadership was about, shown more by women, compared to ego-driven leadership, too often displayed by men. The list helped me frame what I wanted to say. I read it out word for word, hoping it was a straightforward way to generate discussion to get us all thinking about different kinds of leadership.

On my good leadership list were the following characteristics:

- Compassion and thoughtfulness
- Caring about people
- Winning at any cost is not the priority—keeping sight of what you believe in is
- Taking a risk is okay
- Open up new ideas and perspectives for people
- Bring new people in
- Challenge stereotypes and biases
- Be straightforward
- Believe in *big* ideas and give hope for social change
- Act in small ways that help people
- Have a sense of humour about what you do
- Know you will make mistakes and be okay with it
- Have confidence in yourself and those around you
- See yourself as part of a team

Then I listed words and phrases that were, to me, a turnoff in political leadership and likely applicable in other spheres, including the labour movement:

- Backroom deals
- Winning at any cost
- False flattery
- Making promises that can't be delivered
- Making yourself and your actions always the centre of attention
- Craving media so much it's almost an obsession
- Diminishing others to bolster your own ego
- Driven by the need for power
- Making it clear there is an in and out group

- Inability to admit when you're wrong
- Leaving the impression you have all the answers—mansplaining

Sound familiar? I asked the women. And they nodded in agreement. So I continued:

> What do I mean by patriarchal? I mean that politics is male dominated in the sense that there are a majority of men represented in politics and leadership. But this also refers to the male way of doing things—which too often is still how we measure power and success. It's not just sexism, but a sexist way of thinking, an institutionalized sexism that pervades every level of decision making. We should recognize that patriarchal politics hurts men too, it is a way of thinking and acting that centres around male dominance.

We all experienced sexism and chauvinism in one way or another and sometimes it's shocking. Hedy Fry and I were ridiculed in a cartoon in 2003 when the parliamentary committee we were members of, studying prostitution, put in a request to travel to Europe, including Amsterdam, to investigate the issue. The cartoon showed us both, suitcases in hand, standing by a road sign pointing to Amsterdam, with a caption from a man saying, "I wouldn't give them $50." The committee's request to travel, which included male members too, was turned down. In another instance, I recall then immigration minister Judy Sgro apparently naked in a 2004 cartoon, because of a decision she had made about visa permits for exotic dancers. The cartoon was so offensive and demeaning that a number of women MPs, including me, signed a letter in protest.

The impact of the recent #MeToo movement has outed the horrific prevalence of attacks on women. I now have a glimmer of hope that female leadership is better valued and supported.

Coming Out

Who can say exactly when a friendship turns into a deeper, more intimate relationship? There's the specific moment of sexual intimacy, of course, but the drifting prelude of friendship to romance and love can be elusive until it dawns on you that it's happening. I didn't expect to fall in love again, nor did I expect to fall in love with a woman. But it happened with shock and joy and fear about what it all meant.

My friendship with Kim, from when I'd first met her at the old house on Flora Street in Ottawa, had deepened, and my feelings for her changed to something beyond friendship. We spent more and more time together and, despite our age difference, we had much in common. I found her to be thoughtful and incredibly caring, and she opened up a new world to me as I met her activist friends at Carleton University and in Montreal. In many ways our lives were very different, and I watched her poring over her master's thesis research with little understanding or empathy. For a period of time, I was the post-secondary education critic for the NDP, and it was fun to attend political events and protests at Carleton, where Kim and other students were fighting cuts. She loved social activities and visiting people, and I tagged along sometimes reluctantly, but it did me good. And just like Bruce, she had a way of pushing me to do things that I wouldn't otherwise have done. I loved the days when she'd come by Parliament Hill to meet me and we'd walk together, quite comfortable, across the green lawn, maybe to a political event or lecture.

I had never worried about conformity, but I felt deeply confused, at first, about my romantic relationship with Kim. I didn't know how to explain it; I didn't want to own it. I was torn between wanting to be with her and feeling utterly shocked that it was happening to me. At first I ran back to Vancouver feeling upside down and in strange territory.

Coming out, to myself and to others, was a very new experience that was filled with uncertainty, but a reality I had to think about. Who and when to tell. How to say it. What about family? What about public response? It was overwhelming, and I felt I'd taken on a big challenge. But Kim and I got through it day by day. I now know what it means to come out over and over again. Sometimes it's easy and sometimes it's just plain awkward. And other times, you don't want to say anything because it doesn't feel safe.

At first it was downright hard. We shared news of our relationship with only a few people, including party leader Alexa McDonough, in case she got caught with rumours. I found it hard to tell people about my new relationship with Kim, not knowing how to start a conversation that wasn't about politics and current affairs. I remember pulling Pat Martin aside in Vancouver, as we attended a political rally together, and blurting out my relationship with Kim. I wanted him to know, but it felt so weird to raise it. He smiled in his usual wonderful way and gave me a big hug. Thank goodness times have changed, and having such a conversation today is in many cases not as hard as it used to be.

Coming out in a big way, publicly, happened almost by accident. Svend had been fighting for his private member's bill on same-sex marriage for a long time. He asked if I wanted to speak to it in the House. I said sure. Never one for prepared speeches, I spoke as usual from my gut and from experience. In that speech on October 29, 2001, I wanted to make a point: people choose to be married or not, they choose to live common-law or not. And people choose who they love, same sex or not. It was not up to the state to decide this or to deny people their personal choice and right. I pointed out in my speech that I had lived in a common-law relationship for twenty-four years with a man, and that had been my choice to be not married. It was not up to the state to say I could or could not be married. And then—without really thinking about it because it was part of the debate taking place, where other MPs, too, had referred to their own relationships—I continued, and now I was in a relationship with a woman. And if people in a same-sex relationship chose to marry, surely that was their decision. End of story.

Who notices a debate on a private member's bill? Apparently Peter O'Neil, a reporter from the *Vancouver Sun*. About an hour after that speech in the House, I was called out to the foyer where media scrums take place, with word that he wanted to talk to me. I had an inkling about what. Feeling nervous, I went out on my own (probably not a good idea) and he asked me about my speech. How long, who was she, was this the first time, was I public, and so on and so on. My heart in my throat, I answered as minimally and as calmly as I could, and then suddenly, a bright light flashed to my left. By instinct I turned and realized it was the flash of a camera right in my face. Click. Click. And the interview continued.

When it was done, I jumped back into the opposition lobby, my heart beating, and a sheer terror took hold of me. What had I actually said? I couldn't remember one word I'd said to the reporter. Then my brain spun with the realization that I hadn't told Kim about the debate. And had I mentioned her by name in the interview with O'Neil afterward? I didn't think so, but I couldn't remember for sure. I immediately phoned her at Flora Street and sputtered out what I had done, including the interview. "Okay," she said, sounding surprised but not frantic.

Many of her friends did not know about us yet, and the thought of them finding out in the media first was not great. "Well, that's done then," she said. "We'll talk later."

That night was full of stress and fretting, and visions of a horrible story that would ruin me and Kim. Tossing and turning, it played out in my mind, as I tried to remember if I'd said anything ridiculous or embarrassing to the reporter. The next morning I rushed to get the paper, knowing his story was likely to be in papers across the country. Sure enough, there it was in the *Ottawa Citizen*. And in papers in Montreal, Edmonton, Halifax, and Toronto, and of course Vancouver, my hometown. I got my first taste of homophobia. The photo, a classic "gotcha by surprise" shot, went perfectly with the headline "Davies admits gay relationship." Admits? As in confessed? As in, someone found out a secret? As in, I didn't disclose it myself in my own way? I was absolutely hopping mad and for the first time felt I was a victim of sensationalized journalism.

The next day I phoned the editor of the *Vancouver Sun* and gave him a piece of my mind—something I had never done to any media in my political life. How dare they. I demanded to know why that headline had been chosen and with that photo to bolster the idea that I'd been caught out. I felt like I had been manipulated. He claimed the headline was an accident. Give me a break! An accident? I demanded they write an editorial to repair the damage and acknowledge the importance of the use of language, and how it can be used to damage and misrepresent. Okay, he said. And they did publish an editorial a few days later.

Respect: A work in progress
Vancouver Sun, November 3, 2001

.... Earlier this week, Vancouver East MP Libby Davies noted she is in a same-sex relationship, and it is evident that times have changed.

That's not to say there were no ensuing problems, but they were of a smaller nature—such as the Vancouver Sun headline "Davies admits gay relationship". The word choice was unfortunate—this newspaper has long realized that being in a gay relationship isn't something one should "admit". The word has neutral meanings, but its general use usually presumes a fault of some sort....

But rather than dwell further on a thoughtless word....

And the editorial quickly pivoted to another point, eager to get away from the paper's cheap headline.

As the story of the first out female member of Parliament did the rounds, I received wonderfully supportive messages from across the country. One email came from a woman who said she was a senior executive in a corporation and had not been able to come out for fear of discrimination. She wrote that my coming out helped her have courage to do so. It was indicative of the type of messages people wrote, sharing their personal situations. My friends in Vancouver were furious with the *Vancouver Sun* for their shoddy journalism and wrote letters to the editor in protest. A few got printed.

Various media wanted an interview about Canada's first out lesbian MP, and I had a pretty hard time with it. Not one for labels, I wasn't happy about being labelled "the lesbian." I didn't even know if I was. I loved a woman, but did this mean I was lesbian for life? It felt like it would take over my identity. Sharon Costello, my old friend, came to the rescue and we talked it through, just as we had my nomination speech. I was most fearful of an upcoming interview with the gay and lesbian paper in Vancouver, *Xtra West*. I was worried about saying the wrong thing, and fearful about putting my personal life on display for people to pick over. And how to respond to the lesbian question without alienating all the lesbians who were darn proud of their identity, and rightly so.

Sharon coached me and I did the interview with Robin Perelle at *Xtra West*. Years later, when she interviewed me again about not running in the 2015 election, I told her how terrified I had been about doing the interview with her. She said she'd felt the same way, because it was her first time doing an interview. We laughed at that one—the irony of trepidation for each of us.

Of course, I got through it all, and now I don't even think about it. Today, the questions of sexual orientation and gender identity are more open and fluid. I believe this is a good step forward toward accepting how we see ourselves and who we are. I am comfortable in my own skin and with who I am.

But the experience gave me a greater appreciation for what people face when they come out, especially in places where acceptance is difficult, isolated, and even violent. I was a well-established person, a member of Parliament, and I had support from family and friends, but even so, the whole process was challenging and nerve-racking. Kim's support and strength and our support of each other made a big difference. We operated as a team—discussing everything, including how to protect our personal space and lives outside the political arena. In the end, carrying the lesbian label didn't bother me; I was still me, and it didn't really matter what people thought anyway.

My life with Kim continued with an ongoing richness and sense of fulfillment that is extraordinary. Her academic experience and broad scope of on-the-ground activism for human rights keeps her fully engaged. Kim has a quiet way of doing things and she doesn't shout out her accomplishments, but nonetheless, she has gained a deserved reputation as a force for change and a critical thinker. Many a time when I barrel ahead on something, she will look me in the eye and ask me to think it through before I jump.

Defiance and Dignity

In the Downtown Eastside, a number of women—many of whom were sex workers—were missing and suspected to have been murdered. By 1997, the year I was first elected as an MP, there was visible fear and dread about how many women had disappeared, and posters were put up asking people to provide any information they had. Fears about a serial killer on the loose were persistent in the community, and there were ongoing calls for an inquiry into the missing women, with little police response. It was also becoming crystal clear that federal laws pertaining to prostitution were largely responsible for the high risk that sex workers faced. In particular, the 1985 communicating law, which I had fought against as a young city councillor, made it illegal to communicate for the purposes of prostitution. This provision of the Criminal Code forced sex workers into isolated and dangerous situations with their customers for fear of law enforcement.

It took many years of public pressure from the local community to get a special task force of the Vancouver Police Department and the

Red Umbrella Day in support of sex-worker safety and rights, Vancouver

RCMP established to investigate the disappearances and likely multiple murders. Not until February 2002 did the Joint Task Force begin a search of Robert Pickton's pig farm in Port Coquitlam, in the suburbs of Vancouver. It was then that the gruesome remains of women were found. Pickton was charged with twenty-six counts of first-degree murder. His trial began in January 2007, and he was convicted in December of that year. He told an undercover officer in his cell that he had murdered forty-nine women and had hoped to reach fifty.

Most shocking was that almost five years before the search, in 1997, a woman had managed to escape from Pickton's pig farm after being attacked. Pickton was charged with attempted murder at the time, but the charges were stayed and then dropped on the grounds that the woman, because she used drugs, was not a competent witness. I remember reading this news as it broke, and feeling horrified and angry that the profound prejudice against people who use drugs had allowed a killer to continue his evil acts.

As an MP, I wrote numerous letters to the minister of justice and to the media, calling for a public inquiry, and for a special parliamentary committee to be set up to look into the issue. My letter to the minister of justice, Martin Cauchon, in February 2002, gave a brief summary of the situation in the Downtown Eastside and the missing and murdered women:

> There are serious questions about the police investigations and why it took so long for a special task force to be put together. I cannot help but wonder how many of these women would not be on the missing list if their disappearances had been treated as an urgent priority earlier on....

I also called on the minister "to begin an immediate review of federal laws pertaining to soliciting that puts many of these women at risk." The letter outlined the motion I planned to introduce in Parliament "that a special committee of the House be appointed to review the solicitation laws to improve the safety of sex workers and the community overall, and to recommend changes that will reduce the exploitation and violence of sex workers." I was careful in selecting the wording for the motion, so it did not call for decriminalization of the laws pertaining to sex work, though I personally supported decriminalization. But I knew that such wording would not have been supported by a majority of MPs and would have led to the motion's certain defeat. The goal was to get the issue looked at by Parliament and get the ball rolling.

This was a strategic choice. I had to size up the political environment, and determine how far I could go to get people on board. It took almost seven months—until October 2002—to get a meeting with the minister. Notes taken by Rachel Crowder, an intern in our office who accompanied me to the meeting on October 10, describe very well what took place:

> After several cancellations and a last minute rescheduling our meeting with the Minister took place in the Government Lobby at the House of Commons. The Minister did not seem

to have much awareness regarding the situation in the DTES and Libby spent some time talking about what is happening… the impacts of the Criminal Code on sex workers in general and on street level workers in particular. Libby also impressed upon him the importance of an inquiry into the handling of the missing women investigation.

I asked the minister, "What would you do if sixty-nine women were missing and murdered in your community?" I was shocked that the minister knew so little about the issue, despite massive media coverage of the Pickton investigation. But at least he was open to listening—and in February 2003 I was able to get my motion passed in Parliament with government support. A special all-party subcommittee of the Standing Committee on Justice and Human Rights was established to hold extensive hearings across the country. We gathered testimony from expert witnesses, including from more than one hundred sex workers, who spoke with courage and honesty about their lives and the impact of the law that made their work illegal and put them at grave risk of violence and death. It was the first time sex workers had given such testimony before a parliamentary committee.

John Lowman, a criminologist from Simon Fraser University, struck a chord with the committee. For the Justice Department, Lowman had studied the impact of the anticommunicating provision in the Criminal Code brought in in 1985, and demonstrated that the communicating law "played a pivotal role in creating a social and legal milieu that facilitated these homicides, and that Canadian prostitution laws puts lower-echelon sex workers at risk." I came to trust his non-judgmental analysis. Lowman was attacked by feminists who supported the abolition of prostitution and who labelled him antifeminist because of his stance for law reform for decriminalization. Still, he never wavered in his professionalism and commitment to exposing the truth about Canada's sex laws. I also met passionate academics like

Fran Shaver from Concordia University, who had researched sex work for decades, and in presenting to the parliamentary committee also gave evidence about the harm caused by *the Criminal Code.*

I knew a few of the missing women personally, and many by name. I met Serena Abbotsway when, as a member of VANDU, she was becoming politically active. I would often run into her on the street in the Downtown Eastside, and we would chat about what was happening at VANDU. She had warm, brown eyes and a slightly crooked smile that lit up her face. I couldn't help but notice the scars on her face and skin, a visible reminder of her hard life. She was very interested to learn how things worked in Ottawa, and she told me she wanted to get involved politically in the upcoming election. "I want people to vote," she said. When Kim and I walked with her to the Chinese Cultural Centre on election day in 2000, she was excited because it was the first time she'd ever voted. True to what she had said, Serena was getting her friends to vote too, and I could see the pride in her face that she was taking charge, explaining the voting procedure and what to do if you weren't on the voters list. I saw her a few times after that and then, like so many others, Serena "disappeared." She was later to be identified as one of Pickton's victims.

The trauma and suffering in the community were shattering. You could feel it on the street—the gnawing sense of community loss. Often I would go to Main and Hastings, and hang out just outside the Carnegie Centre or a little further down the block where Insite was located. The street was always full of people; even when it was miserable, cold, and raining, they would still gather and talk. So many times people would say how worried they were because they hadn't seen a friend in a few days. The fear about more sex workers going missing was on everyone's mind. This is a community where people watch out for each other. When you have no possessions and no secure housing, and tomorrow is years away, your friends mean a lot. The Downtown

Eastside has been called a lot of things—some of it very pejorative—but in reality it's a community coping with many forms of grief and upheaval with resilience, strength, and care.

In a 2002 op-ed, I wanted to make it clear that it was public policy and the decision makers in Ottawa that had failed—not people in the local community:

> The health and safety of sex workers and injection drug users and the safety of the community as a whole continues to be put in jeopardy by government inaction. These dual crises continue to rage uninhibited in my riding of Vancouver East. So I have to ask the question, what does democracy mean to us and in whose interest is public policy being formulated? When Serena went to vote, she did so with the belief that she was entitled to the same dignity, worth and rights as any Canadian. I believe that. Being poor should not rob anyone of democratic rights nor access to resources and opportunities. Being powerless is a failure of those in power not of those who struggle at the bottom.

I also got to know Josey, who lived in the Washington Hotel at Main and Hastings. Her room was at the end of long, dark corridor overlooking the alley. As were the other single-room occupancies, the room was small and without a bathroom or cooking facility. Josey was a sex worker and a drug user. Originally from the Prince Rupert area, she was much younger than she looked. She had suffered years of unspeakable abuse as a child and had come to the Downtown Eastside to escape. We would often sit and talk, and she would laugh as her two cats, Bud and Brew, would tear around the room chasing each other. She loved those cats and once, when one of them got out and went missing, she was inconsolable. But amazingly, someone found the cat and Bud or Brew (I could never remember which was which) came home.

Josey was a fighter—tough, but with a joy for life despite her years of hardship. I met her through Lincoln Clarkes and his Heroines photo project. I was struck by the photo Lincoln took of Josey sitting on the window ledge of the Roosevelt Hotel across from the Washington, her black hair slicked back. Lincoln had captured her defiance and also her dignity. I hoped to use the photo in an annual holiday card and wanted to seek her permission first, so I went to visit her. Josey was tickled pink about the card idea. That's how we became friends.

She had my cell number and would phone me, but more often than not, we'd meet at the Washington Hotel and just talk. I learned about her daily struggles, but she never complained about her life. I bought her a microwave that she later sold—not surprising—and I would bring in a few things like food and small items to help make her room more comfortable. She wasn't ever "grateful" and my offerings weren't meant that way. Most of all Josey was funny and had an unbelievably positive attitude to life and circumstance. I had a hard time understanding that, knowing her history and life as a young Indigenous woman. But Josey was a survivor; she moved past the suffering and sought better things in life.

She thought it hilarious that my partner was a woman, and she told me about her girlfriends and the ups and downs of love. I was always aware of my privilege and her lack of it. It didn't stop us from finding something in common that that we each valued. I admired her guts and I think she liked my stories about politics and Ottawa. She also didn't mind letting it be known that her MP made house calls. Later, I was able to help move her to a better social housing situation up the street to 40 East Hastings, and things improved for a while. I was very sad when I learned, a few years ago, that Josey had died.

Knowing Serena and Josey and many other people in the Downtown Eastside allowed me to understand the harmfulness of prevalent stereotypes. Stigma, racism, poor-bashing, and classism do so much damage, and the media portrayal of the neighbourhood was harmful too.

Josey on a window ledge at
the Roosevelt Hotel, May 30,
1999; photo featured in
Lincoln Clarkes's Heroines
series

Speaking out in support of
Idle No More on the steps of
the Vancouver Art Gallery,
December 2012

In particular, the characterization of the Indigenous residents was distorted and unreal. Depictions of alcoholism, drug use, and lack of motivation are not uncommon, yet what I saw every day was something quite different. The real story was people struggling with the consequences of colonization and residential schools and the loss of language, culture, and history. People were reconnecting to their community in powerful ways, despite enormous odds.

The Aboriginal Friendship Centre, near the Downtown Eastside at East Hastings and Commercial, was a hub for connection. The gym would be full of families participating in traditional drumming on West Coast Family Night, defying stereotypes. The creativity and leadership shown, particularly by young people, was the cutting edge of transformative change, and it truly energized the community. I always felt honoured to work with the Friendship Centre, with groups like the Urban Native Youth Alliance (UNYA) and The Circle of Eagles, and with people like Jerry Adams, Lynda Grey, and Susan Tantoosh. Working with them helped me believe I could make a difference too as an ally. Mainstream media coverage on Indigenous issues often reinforces negative stereotypes, and there's precious little coverage of the groundbreaking work taking place to empower people and change decades of oppression. But that change is taking place, and non-Indigenous people can be part of it and learn from it.

Some of the ways I would challenge stereotypes are through speaking in the House and challenging the media's depiction of the Downtown Eastside:

February 9, 2002
Globe and Mail Editor

Dear Editor,
    Saturday's front-page story on the missing and murdered women of the Downtown Eastside, "BC Police Lashed Over Probe,"

Feb. 9/02, includes references to how the negative stereotyping of sex trade workers may have contributed to the negligible police resources assigned to this case over a period of years. Why then is the only space given to the actual "voices" of the people in the community reinforcing these very stereotypes?

"Prostitutes, addicts too strung out to care" (G&M Feb. 9/02) is a horrible headline, and a clear example of the negative labelling facing women in the Downtown Eastside. To further the typecasting the "informative" accompanying map headlines the "seedy side of town."

I have been involved in the Downtown Eastside for 30 years and now represent the community as Member of Parliament. I know it as a strong caring community. Josey, whom you interviewed, is a personal friend and I know she cares deeply about had happened to her friends. She is an incredibly positive person who has survived abuse and violence by the state.

If the Globe and Mail is truly interested in more than sensationalizing the desperate situation of women like Josey, then you should also write about the economic and social conditions that cause women to enter prostitution. Or what about writing on the fact that Gordon Campbell's devastating cuts are driving women into deeper poverty and despair.

Yours Sincerely,
Libby Davies
Member of Parliament
Vancouver East

That was one more letter to the editor that never got printed.

Jack Gets to Work

Icould never have predicted that one day my seatmate in Parliament would be Jack Layton, leader of the NDP, hero of Toronto, and for a brief time, the leader of the Official Opposition in Canada's Parliament. It was eminently easy to like and work with Jack. His charm and wit were irresistible. I think we were both a bit too earnest and hopeful in our politics, but heck, that's much better than being cynics!

I was not involved in his decision to run for the party leadership in 2002, save for an instance where he phoned me and said that if I was thinking of running, he wouldn't. Several activists, including Judy Rebick, had approached me to think about running for the leadership after Alexa McDonough's departure. But I doubted I had all the skills, and certainly my lack of ability to speak French was a major obstacle. I told Jack I would not be running. Svend Robinson and I discussed Jack's candidacy and felt he was the guy we could support with enthusiasm. We were the only two members of the NDP caucus to do so. Jack was still seen as an outsider; he wasn't an elected MP, though he had run federally in two previous elections. But Svend and I agreed that Jack had the energy and progressive vision that the party needed.

My decision to support Jack was partly the outcome of my involvement in a political undertaking called the New Politics Initiative (NPI) that emerged in 2001. With Svend Robinson, Judy Rebick, and Jim Stanford, an economist at the Canadian Auto Workers union, as well as author and activist Murray Dobbin, we launched the initiative to seek new ways for the NDP to work in partnership with social movements to bring about transformative, progressive change in Canada. Although Jack was not himself involved, the NPI had a strong following among party activists, and the presence of Judy Rebick—who had recently launched the online media *rabble.ca*—was a catalyst for reaching out to non-party activists across Canada who wanted a stronger political movement for change. The initiative held many consultations and discussions about a new way of approaching progressive politics in Canada. It was premised on the vision of creating a reconstituted NDP as a progressive political party, working in alliance with movements outside of the formal scope of electoral politics. With its dynamic vision and scope, the initiative caught people's imagination with the idea that a different way of doing politics was possible. We were electrified by the possibilities of change that could happen if the gulf between electoral and social movements politics was erased.

But it also was seen by some as a threat to the NDP and its established ways of doing things. At the February 2002 party convention in Winnipeg, a resolution supporting the initiative was narrowly defeated. Still, it was a powerful signal to the party that people wanted change, and they wanted a new kind of political party that went beyond electoral politics and embraced social movements outside of the electoral cycle. A meeting at the convention, chaired by Judy Rebick, was packed. This was the night before the debate on the floor at the plenary session, and there was standing room only, as person after person voiced their support to help try and get the resolution through the next day. A decision was made to have gender parity at the mics, an approach that changed the tone of the meeting as many women got up to have their say.

On the convention floor the next day, we had our speakers lined up, including Svend Robinson and Jim Stanford, who spoke out for a new way forward for the party. A young woman streaked through the room with an NPI banner positioned very nicely on her naked body. A few mouths fell open. Many people who were there will remember Bill Blaikie taking to the floor and, in his booming voice, hand raised, admonishing delegates that he was sick of people saying the NDP wasn't good enough. If there hadn't been tension before, there was now. Now we were either good party members or bad party members, and it caused a wave of unease.

In hindsight the resolution could have been better written, and we could have been better organized on the convention floor. But even so, the vote was so close that it forced a standing vote count of the delegates after a show of hands left the outcome unclear. A standing vote is not that common at NDP conventions; on this occasion, a silence fell as people craned their necks and peered around them and up and down the rows, wanting to see who had or had not voted for the resolution. Though it failed, the resolution clearly sent a message for change. Layton's leadership bid touched on some of the issues we had raised in the NPI, including better grassroots involvement of party members, outreach to social activists and movements, and seeing electoral politics as part of a bigger vision and movement for change.

Jack and his wife, Olivia Chow—a Toronto city councillor—and their team led a strong campaign for his leadership. The NDP had never seen such sophisticated campaigning before; their strategies for using data management systems were mostly new to the party. When the leadership vote took place on Sunday morning, January 24, 2003, at the Ricoh Coliseum, Exhibition Place, in Toronto, Jack had a resounding victory. I was ecstatic, along with his supporters. It felt like we had indeed moved to a new era in politics.

Jack's years of work at the municipal level in Toronto, and as president of the Federation of Canadian Municipalities, gave him a close

Enjoying Vancouver Pride with Olivia and Jack, 2004

connection to people's daily lives and struggles. His strength was always about engaging with people in a positive way. What I remember most about that leadership convention was his acceptance speech. He had the creative mind of Jamey Heath working with him on communications, both during the leadership campaign and later in Ottawa. Jack's acceptance speech was upbeat and substantive, but what stood out for me is the length of time he dedicated to speaking about his fellow leadership candidates and what they had each contributed to the overall race. It didn't come across as the usual thank-you nod, and be done with it; it was a genuine, touching tribute to each leadership candidate and the respect Jack had for them. It said something about the man when half his speech was about his fellow competitors.

About to leave the convention to go back to Ottawa, I got buttonholed by Rick Smith, who had worked on Jack's campaign. He told me Jack wanted to meet before I left. They had already set up an impromptu office in the convention centre and were busy making plans for next steps. I was happy to meet with Jack, but I had no idea what he wanted to meet about. Jack, having just pulled off what many had said was impossible, showed no self-congratulation or glee. On the contrary, he was most concerned about the NDP caucus in Ottawa and how to work constructively with the MPs who had not supported him. Most of the caucus had supported Bill Blaikie to be party leader. Bill was a very credible figure in the party and an excellent parliamentarian.

The next morning would be our regular caucus meeting in Ottawa, and the first meeting with the newly elected leader. Jack wanted to seek advice on how to approach the caucus. I told him that I thought it best that he be low-key, and that he acknowledge the enormous strength in the caucus and that he needed to learn from them. He then told me he wanted me to be his House leader. I was surprised. I said that I did not have enough experience in House procedure. He told me that wasn't the criteria, adding, "Anyway, you'll learn." He wanted someone he could trust and who would not be thrown off by the internal ups and downs that are wont to happen. He valued our common municipal experience and belief in getting things done rather than playing politics. Jack added that he would ask Bill Blaikie to be his parliamentary leader, in the House, until he was elected.

The next day in Ottawa, there was a tension in the caucus room before Jack's arrival. Many of the MPs were bruised and still in shock at Blaikie's leadership loss, and they were really not sure about this upstart new kid on the block. It would be critical how Jack handled that first meeting. He came in quietly, and by himself. He spoke respectfully and honoured the work of caucus, making it clear that he had a lot to learn and would need everyone's help. "We are in this together," he said. Jack was a superb team builder; over and over in the days and years to come, we were to witness his skill at keeping us united during difficult moments. You could feel the tension in the room dissipate, and although there were still bruised feelings, Jack had taken the first important step in bringing his new caucus together. His announcement that Bill Blaikie would be parliamentary leader was well received, and Bill also made it clear that he would help me as the new House leader.

Thus began a new role as House leader for the NDP that lasted eight and half years. I knew I had the confidence of the leader, but I wasn't so sure about the caucus. Only one other woman—unbelievable but true—had ever been a House leader for any party in the House of Commons. Suzanne Tremblay had held the position for a few weeks in 1997 for the Bloc Québécois. I was assisted in my steep learning curve by the extremely competent Rob Sutherland, who had worked on the Hill for years as well as at Queen's Park, the Ontario legislature. Rob knew the House rules well and had a peculiar hobby of taking the bible-like *House of Commons Procedure and Practice* book to his cottage on the weekend. He advised me not to worry too much about learning the rules, and I soon learned that this was good advice. I came to understand that the job was less about knowing every rule and its history—I could rely on Rob for that—it was more a question of how to apply political judgment in the face of multiple daily surprises. This was especially true in the minority parliaments that were to come.

Rob and I became a great team. We worked around the clock, often, when I was in Vancouver, on different time zones. Even when Parliament wasn't sitting, we had to be on our toes navigating the twists and turns of the other political parties. We developed a strong camaraderie, especially during the stressful times when the House was in turmoil and we had to anticipate numerous possible scenarios. The more stressful it got, the more bizarre our sense of humour would become; that seemed the only way to make it through. Joe Comartin was deputy House leader for the NDP over this period. His excellent knowledge of the House and keen legal mind were great assets for navigating the parliamentary world before us. I also worked closely with Christian Brideau from the NDP whip's office. I relied on his unfailing ability to pitch in, in tense moments, when it looked like things were going off the rails. Often, he would catch me as I rushed through the swing doors from the opposition lobby to the House and he would say, "Libby, don't forget…"

Weekly caucus meetings required the House leader to give regular reports, as well as assign daily questions for question period. Each morning caucus members would pitch their questions, and it was always challenging to stretch the few questions we were allotted between national issues of the day and local issues and needs in the ridings. The leader automatically got the first question each day in the House, so that narrowed it down even more. Complaints would mount from individual caucus members wanting to raise a question during those crucial forty-five minutes of question period each day. Never did thirty seconds count so much as in question period, when you got to ask your question of the government, even if it was to receive a non-response. It was coveted time that could put you in the national or at least local media, showing your ability to hold the government to account. Each morning the NDP director of communications—Brad Lavigne and then later, Kathleen Monk—and I would scrutinize the pitches that had come in and try to make the impossible work: balancing the questions to fit the multiple needs we had to cover off.

I developed my own style as House leader, focusing on what needed to be done rather than feeding into personal dramas and conflicts. I earned the trust of my caucus overall, as well as the trust of other House leaders, by working hard and not playing political games. I also had to stay in constant contact with the leader and his team, to develop a solid working relationship.

Most of the working day was spent in the opposition lobby immediately adjacent to the House, monitoring what was happening in the House and, with Rob's assistance, assigning our speakers on the bills

After a busy day in the opposition lobby, a chance to catch up on constituency work, Centre Block office, Parliament Hill

under debate. Often our daily work would involve informal, impromptu meetings with House leaders from other parties. We would rush back and forth in hurried conversations, negotiating on the timing of bills, length of debate, special motions, points of privilege, or upcoming votes. I worked closely with my colleague Yvon Godin, the NDP whip, as he was responsible for staging votes and ensuring our members were there. Only later at night, after the votes and House business were concluded, would I head back to my office in Centre Block to work on constituency email and any follow-up work left by my staff. There's an advantage to having a BC riding, where you can still safely make phone calls at 10 or 11 p.m. EST.

Weekly House leader meetings were rarely constructive. They were more often a venue for the government House leader of the day to bark out orders. We always had to push back on what was outrageous and to find the levers to use the House rules where possible to prevent government manoeuvres aimed at stifling debate or usurping MPs' voices. I worked with at least eight different House leaders, from Liberal and Conservative governments—all men—and learned that one-on-one communication is a crucial element to creating trust between parties. At one point none of House leaders, except me, were talking to each other, and I ended up being a go-between and minor mediator. You could argue that political differences were the cause of the rifts, but in my view it was the male egos that got in the way and prevented practical problem solving from taking place.

The biggest challenge for me, however, was not in Ottawa; it was maintaining my activism and work in the community. When Jack made me his House leader, he understood I couldn't forfeit working on the urgent issues that still needed attention, like stopping the war on drugs, sex-worker safety and rights, human rights, and housing. He was aware that some of this work was controversial, even within our caucus. Jack agreed with decriminalization of sex work, and drug policy reform, and certainly housing, on which he had led the way and written two books, and he encouraged support for my private member's bill for a national housing program. He also understood that it was helpful for maintaining connections with civil society to have an advocate out there saying and doing things he couldn't as leader.

It was a positive tension we had. He'd had some flak for his "marijuana is a beautiful substance" quote on *Pot TV* and it was made clear that the leader couldn't make those kinds of comments. Nor should he weigh in publicly on things like decriminalizing sex work, when the caucus was divided in its position. So we understood one another. I was careful about what I said and the language I used. This understanding worked very well, until several years later it almost blew us apart on the question of the Middle East.

A few weeks after Jack became leader, I was asked to participate in a second Citizens Weapons Inspection Team for weapons of mass destruction, similar to the one conducted in 1998. The action in early February 2003 was at the height of the Iraq crisis concerning weapons of mass destruction that were allegedly being built there. I asked Jack if it was okay to participate, recognizing that as his new House leader it might be seen as a problem. But he was totally up for it and even said he'd like to go too. We both knew that wasn't a good idea. The aim of the action—outside Washington, DC, at a US military research base—was to expose the fact that the United States posed more of a threat to global peace than Iraq did. George W. Bush's hypocritical stance regarding weapons of mass destruction belied the fact that the greatest stockpile of these weapons was in the United States. Donning blue look-a-like UN peacekeeper hats, we embarked on our mission to demand inspection of the weapons research facility in the US.

Media coverage was widespread, and although much of it was negative, we made our point. British MP Alan Simpson, chair of the Labour Party Anti-War Caucus (the NDP had no such caucus); Mel Watkins, learned Canadian political scientist and long-standing member of the NDP; and Steve Staples joined the action, along with other activists. It was a good learning experience on how elected representatives and social activists can work together on an action. As we entered the United States, we held a press conference to outline our mission. It was at this point that we realized that some of the younger activists with us were using provocative language to describe our mission. Alan, Mel, and I looked on in alarm, as we could see that it was creating a hostile reaction from the media. The intent of the inspection was serious, and so we set about trying to ensure that our language was diplomatic and straightforward. We learned an important activist lesson; the more audacious and radical your action, the more you need to tone down the language—the action speaks for itself.

So much has changed in a decade or more, and the control over individual parliamentarians by their own party—in every party—has increased, as has the obsession with message boxes. Today's politics has little tolerance for an activity such as the citizens weapons inspection, and you'd be reined in immediately and likely disciplined for participating.

As he grew into his job, Jack brought more discipline and control to the caucus. Under Alexa's leadership we were still a small caucus, and individual MPs had a fair amount of scope to carry out their work. Private member's bills, for example, which are submitted by individual MPs, were not scrutinized by the leader's office, nor were statements made in the House. Historically, these matters were seen as the purview of individual members to decide on.

There were exceptions to this, of course. For example, Alexa came down hard on Svend Robinson for a petition he introduced to remove a reference to God in Canada's Constitution, and later removed him as foreign affairs critic after a controversial visit to Israel and the West Bank. But mostly she focused on supporting the caucus and its work as we defined it. Jack, on the other hand, wanted to know what his caucus was up to. The leader's office took a much more proactive role in scrutinizing private member's bills and making it clear when something was considered unacceptable. He wanted a unified team with a unified voice; the notion that we were a group of individual members who happened to be New Democrats was no longer acceptable. This strategy and style of leadership became more prominent under Thomas Mulcair, who reminded us often that we were to be a party ready to govern.

Being in politics reminds me of those kaleidoscopes we used to enjoy as kids. You hold a lens to your eye and everyday images become distorted and changing. Sometimes with beautiful colours and patterns, other times, something you don't recognize at all—the patterns are fractured and nothing is what it seems. By June 2004, when my third federal election rolled around, I was much more comfortable in my role as an MP and I knew how the House worked. I had gained valuable experience as House leader and my work in the community in east Vancouver was well grounded and strong.

Even so I never took the riding for granted. The Liberals were still eager to win the riding back, and we always waited with interest to see who they would put forward as their candidate in East Van. It was a big surprise, as the 2004 election loomed, to learn that a former executive assistant to Mayor Mike Harcourt and former New Democrat, Shirley Chan, was to be appointed as the Liberal candidate by now Liberal leader and prime minister Paul Martin. Appointed? We scratched our heads at that one. Our campaign began by immediately pointing out that the leader of the NDP didn't appoint candidates—he had faith in the democratic practice of local riding associations to nominate candidates. More intriguing was the fact that Chan was generally seen as progressive and a New Democrat who, although she no longer lived in east Vancouver, had a long history in Chinatown and Strathcona.

Chan might have come closer to winning had she not made what was perceived as a politically opportunistic manoeuvre to exploit people's fears. The debate over same-sex marriage was heated in Canada, though legislation to make it legal was not to come for another year. Rather than challenging my record on issues, Chan and her campaign team conflated things to a more personal level. Playing on public sensitivities to same-sex relationships and to MP travel, she decried the fact that I was flying my "girlfriend back and forth across the country." Had I been a man and married, there is no way this travel would have been raised for cheap political shots. But the idea that a "girlfriend" was using MP travel privileges no doubt got the desired effect from some quarters.

MP travel can be a sensitive matter at the best of times. The House of Commons policy permitting a designated traveller (usually a spouse) to go between Ottawa and the riding was often the subject of media stories and claims of excessive expenditure. We knew exactly what Chan was up to: if all else fails, attack your opponent's personal integrity. She hoped to create a wedge using those who were suspicious that MPs abused their travel provisions, along with those who felt uncomfortable with same-sex relationships—or were outright homophobic. We got wind of the whisper campaign, particularly in the more socially conservative parts of the Chinese community. It backfired badly. Constituents who weren't worried about my chances for re-election became fired up and furious at such a tactic. One supporter came up to me and said, "I didn't want to see Shirley Chan win against you, but now I hate what they're doing so much I will do everything I can to see they don't win."

Our campaign didn't let the Liberal candidate's comments go by without challenge. We hit back, and at an all-candidates debate involving the five ridings in Vancouver, a voter asked respected Liberal MP Stephen Owen, running in Vancouver Quadra, if he supported the House of Commons policy regarding travel. Owen's wife often accompanied him back and forth to Ottawa. Without hesitation he voiced his support for the policy, and Ms. Chan looked deflated. Still it was a reminder that politics is that kaleidoscope where reality can be fragmented into odd pieces. In that election we pulled in more than double the vote count over Chan's campaign.

Election day across the country delivered Paul Martin as the prime minister, but with no clear majority, and Canadians experienced the first of three minority parliaments that kept everyone on their toes, inside and outside of the House. This was the first federal election that saw Jack Layton elected as the member of Parliament for Toronto–Danforth, and there was a sense of jubilation in the caucus that the party leader was finally in the House. He had also convinced a former NDP leader—tower of strength Ed Broadbent—to run in Ottawa Centre. I had never worked with Ed and had only ever seen him from afar. He had been the party leader from 1975 to 1989, years before my time on the Hill. Rob Sutherland told me Ed was so beloved in Ottawa that during the campaign, all they needed to do was park him on a visible street corner and people would come over in droves to shake his hand. His presence in our caucus was felt immediately, and his passion for proportional representation led us to take up the issue of electoral reform with vigour, hoping to convince the new Liberal government to hold hearings and a referendum. I loved being with Ed in the House during question period and other debates. He sat right behind me and I would listen to his wisecracks about what was going on across the floor on the government side. His sense of humour often kept us going.

I continued to work as House leader, now more vigilant than ever as the twists and turns of minority Parliament politics became real. Jack became more and more adept in question period, hammering out questions to Prime Minister Martin. Sitting next to Jack, I could feel his intensity and focus as he prepared himself to rise and speak. I learned his routine when he entered the chamber for question period each day: he needed a few moments of quiet to go over his questions in his mind, neatly lining up his pen at the top of the sloping desktop with its green blotting-paper cover. Often a bit later, still during question period, we would have hushed but razor-sharp mini-conversations about what was happening that day. It felt like the old-fashioned egg timer with its grains of sand, rapid time in slow motion. Jack paid very close attention to what was going on in the House and he participated in vigorous debate, surrounded by a caucus that encouraged him every step of the way.

In February 2005, the Liberal minority government introduced Bill C-38 to legalize same-sex marriage in Canada. Previous debates on the issue had been intense and fractious, with the Conservative party showing its muscle for so-called traditional values. It was an experience where the personal became political and the political, personal. Conservative MP Jason Kenney from Calgary resorted to bizarre and ridiculous arguments to bolster his position against same-sex marriage. He asserted, "The fact is homosexuals aren't banned from marrying under Canadian law. Marriage is open to everyone, as long as they're a man and a woman." He elaborated, "It doesn't say you can't marry if you're a homosexual. The fact is that homosexuals have been married and do marry." He then proceeded to the proof of his great analysis: Svend Robinson had once been married to a woman and "Libby Davies had been married to a man."

A Canadian Press story at the time also cited the latest poll on same-sex marriage, showing 42 percent of Canadians in favour and 40 percent opposed. The Conservatives were doing their best to drive division and crassly cater to conservative ethnic and religious views— indeed, Kenney's comments were made before the Punjabi Press Club in Brampton, Ontario. This strategy of exploiting faith differences to political advantage to bolster a right-wing agenda has been used many times. Kenney was good at it. He had a special role in the Conservative caucus to form relationships with communities of various ethnicities and religions in order to play up concerns about things, like same-sex marriage, that could be difficult for a particular segment of a community to understand and accept.

At the earliest opportunity, I sought Kenney out. I thought about rising in the House to demand that he publicly apologize, but decided I didn't want to further illuminate his shameful escapade. On the opposition side of the House, near the back row, where the heavy gold-coloured curtains hang and MPs enter and exit the chamber, I caught sight of him. At that moment I felt a rare, and deeply personal and intense, dislike of the man and his divisive politics. Unfortunately we would see his divisive way of working again, when he became a minister in the Conservative government of 2007. That day I spoke to him privately. I told him that, first, his facts were wrong. I had never been married. I had lived common-law with my partner, Bruce, for twenty-four years. I expressed my deep offence at his twisted comments about same-sex marriage, which used people's personal lives to score what he thought was some brilliant political point. I asked him to apologize. He only muttered about fair public debate. It felt pointless to talk further with such a person and I left.

Years later, in 2017, with Kenney now active in provincial politics in Alberta, Michael Connolly, a young NDP provincial representative in Alberta, posted a copy of the 2005 newspaper article about Kenney's ridiculous comments. He shared how as a young person, he had grown up in Kenney's Calgary riding and felt targeted and excluded by the MP's stance. It made me realize how far we had progressed for equality rights, but also how deeply personal and hurtful these issues can be for us all.

There were many times when the debate on same-sex marriage felt personal, though I wasn't myself into the idea of getting married. The debates in the House became so nasty and personal that Bill Siksay, NDP MP for Burnaby Douglas, Bloc Québécois MP Réal Ménard, and I wrote a joint letter to all four party leaders to make it clear that it was not only a political question of equal marriage under the law, it was also a deeply personal issue to thousands of LGBTQ+ Canadians and ourselves as out parliamentarians. Bill crafted the letter beautifully, making it clear how painful it was to listen to debate that was derogatory, hurtful, and homophobic. We delivered the jointly signed letter to the party leaders and hoped it would help improve the tone of debate in the House.

At its final vote in the House of Commons, Paul Martin had made it clear that the Liberal caucus were free to vote without the party whip over them. Thirty-two Liberal MPs voted against the bill. Astonishingly Jack Layton was publicly criticized for saying that in his NDP caucus there was no free vote when it came to upholding human rights and equality. I felt particularly proud to be a New Democrat that day.

The final vote on Bill C-38 happened June 28, 2005, on a hot Ottawa summer night. Many people had gathered outside the main door to

Parliament and Jack came out, with a number of us from the caucus, to greet them and give a cheer for a historic day. I remember an orange tinge to the sky (I don't think it was just my euphoria about NDP colours on such a day) and a humidity so smothering it felt like you could touch it. People had waited for hours in the heat, but still you could feel the energy and elation in the heavy air as they embraced each other with love and victory. It was a moment to reflect that the incredible work of dedicated activists over many years, from all walks of life—including parliamentarians, in particular my colleague Svend Robinson, lawyers, and the courts—had turned a page for equality and against hatred. There would be other battles for equality on many fronts ahead, but that night it was time to celebrate that something good and important had been achieved. The struggle for equal marriage in Canada is a wonderful example of how movements for social change and elected representatives can work together to achieve progress on human rights and equality.

There are also moments in Parliament when unexpected change can take place. Two months earlier, there had been high drama in the House of Commons as Paul Martin and his Liberal government faced possible defeat as a result of ongoing revelations from the Gomery Commission in Quebec into corruption involving the Liberal party and its operatives. Martin was on the brink of disaster, and he probably never thought he'd have to rely on Jack Layton for help. The Liberal government was in danger, as the Conservatives and the Bloc sought to defeat the government on a vote of confidence. In a minority Parliament, the NDP could have voted with the other two opposition parties, creating enough votes to force an election. But Jack saw an opportunity and he seized it. He went live from the foyer of the House of Commons and challenged Martin to work with the NDP to amend his own budget by eliminating the proposed corporate tax cuts and instead invest money in badly needed social investments. A desperate Martin said yes, and the ball started rolling.

It was a Friday night, and usually I would leave for Vancouver to get to my riding before a quick turnaround back to Ottawa on Sunday. But Saturday morning, still in Ottawa, I got a phone call from Jack saying, "Get to Toronto as quickly as you can, you're going to help negotiate the budget deal." I rushed to Toronto that morning and huddled in Olivia Chow's city hall office with Bob Gallagher, Jack's new chief of staff. Bob, Jack, and Olivia were long-standing teammates from their municipal days, but I had barely met his new chief of staff, let alone worked with him. Olivia did the number crunching and the ask was put together for investments in priorities like housing, post-secondary education, and public transit.

The first meeting with Paul Martin, his House leader Tony Valeri, and chief of staff Tim Murphy was at the Royal York Hotel. Jack knew the media were on the lookout at the hotel hoping for an inside scoop, so he guided us through the underground tunnel from the subway, through the kitchens and up to the meeting room floor. How did Jack know the back way? He'd been to many a fundraising dinner at the Royal York and had been through the kitchens to thank the workers there.

The Liberals looked nervous when we came in; no doubt they were wondering what the hell Layton was up to and how to outplay him. Martin politely asked us to sit down, and Jack rolled out what we were looking for in budget amendments to secure NDP support. The Liberal team didn't look too happy about it but agreed they would think it over and have the two House leaders and chiefs of staff work on it further. Subsequently, intense negotiations took place as Bob and I ferried back and forth from the hotel to Olivia's office in his tiny Miata sports car, me hanging on for dear life as he whipped around corners, shifting gears and accelerating the gas. Within a day a deal was nearly there, and when it looked like we had agreement in principle, Jack planned a press conference in Ottawa to announce it.

An optimistic person Jack was. Bob and I were still holed up in Olivia's city hall office, and I was desperately pushing Valeri on the phone to put in writing that the deal was on. At the same time, Bob was on the other phone with Jack as he walked to the podium for his big announcement. Bob was yelling in my other ear, "Get him [Valeri] to send an email now. We must have it in writing. We need it *now!*" Gallagher looked like he was going to explode. The seconds were ticking by before Jack was to speak, still waiting for the final confirmation that we had the agreement. Finally, in the nick of time, Valeri's email came through, and still on the phone with Valeri, I whispered "I got it" to Gallagher, who, on the other phone to Jack said *"Go!"* Gallagher broke into a big smile, and we let out sigh of relief.

The next morning, arriving in Ottawa for the daily caucus meeting, people clapped as Bob and I came down the hall, and it took some moments to realize it was for us and a successful outcome. The following weeks were touch and go, as we had to make absolutely sure the amendment to the Liberal budget was in order, properly worded, and passed. It meant being in constant contact with the Liberal House leader; nothing could be left to chance or allowed to screw up. The solid working relationship with Valeri had helped make it all happen. Another lesson in building trust with the people you need to work with.

Two days before the crucial vote on the Liberal budget, MP Belinda Stronach had crossed the floor from the Conservative ranks to the Liberals, giving them a needed vote to get the amended budget passed. Unfortunately that event is remembered not so much for the key vote it gave the Liberals but for the appalling language that Conservative MPs used against Stronach, likening her to "a prostitute" and "a whore" for switching sides. Funny how men can do something like cross the floor and get away with saying it's about principle, but women are viciously attacked.

In a piece written for *rabble.ca* a few days later, I shared this with readers:

In the past few weeks as the functioning of Parliament has become much more fractious, I have been sitting on the edge of my seat in the House of Commons watching insults fly like ping pong balls.... I'd really like to see a new Parliament, whatever its makeup, embody some feminist principles of working...respect, room for consensus, and cutting out the sexism and dominance. I was pretty dismayed at some of the sexist commentary in reaction to Belinda Stronach's switch to the Liberals. It's so unnecessary and demeaning to all women.

A tied vote in the House of Commons is quite rare, but in a minority Parliament anything can happen. Tradition has it that a tie is broken by the Speaker of the House, and on May 19, 2005, Peter Milliken became the first Speaker to break a tie on a confidence vote. And so, 153 to 152, the Liberal budget with the NDP budget amendment was duly passed by the House of Commons. As a result $4.6 billion was invested, including the following:

- $1.6 billion for affordable housing construction, including Aboriginal housing.
- $1.5-billion increase in transfers to provinces for tuition reduction and better training through employment insurance.
- $900 million for the environment, with one more cent of the federal gas tax going to public transit.
- $500 million for foreign aid, to bring Canada closer to its international commitment to dedicate of 0.7 percent of gross domestic product for aid.
- $100 million for a pension protection fund for workers.

Jack had demonstrated once again his ability to get things done. "Don't let them tell you it can't be done" was to become his favourite line. In fact, it is engraved on the bust his partner Olivia, a talented sculptor, made, which stands on his final resting place in Toronto.

In addition to his active engagement in Parliament, Jack paid close attention to the party. He made enormous strides in modernizing the NDP's ability to run campaigns, raise money, and hold successful conventions. He had a good team around him who worked incredibly hard, but Jack and Olivia worked harder than anyone.

Jack understood, as had the NPI, that the NDP had to be more than an efficient election machine and a hard-working caucus. The NDP needed to be part of a bigger movement for social change that involved many Canadians and civil society groups from diverse communities. It was a good sign when, soon after he became leader, Jack hired Franz Hartman to take on the new position of working more closely with civil society groups. Franz and I spent many hours discussing how this could happen in both formal and informal ways. Finally, I thought, we will pay closer attention to our partners in social movements and the labour movement, and learn how to enhance our capacity to bring about change.

Early on Jack was keen to mobilize the caucus into action teams instead of solitary critic assignments. For a period of time (though it was greeted with scepticism by some caucus members), we had weekly team meetings and were specifically mandated to reach out to our social partners. As a result of these initiatives, the party established a better relationship with civil society groups. Jack was always open to meeting people and figuring out how to work together. Franz became a liaison between the parliamentary world and the outside political world, finding out what people were anticipating and working to keep them in the loop on what the NDP was doing. This involved social policy, upcoming budgets, environmental issues, and much more. It was such a good beginning to a new way of working. But eventually limited staff resources were redirected to what were seen as more pressing needs for communications and parliamentary support work. Without dedicated staff resources, our connections to our partners became more hit and miss. We missed an ongoing opportunity to build a closer working relationship with people who believed in social justice.

Niki Ashton, the NDP's MP from Northern Manitoba, was also keenly interested in stronger connections with our political allies. When we discussed these issues recently, she told me "we need to be pushed" by our social movement partners. Niki has an instinctive understanding of the value of building genuine and sustained relationships for change—as opposed to the political opportunism of reaching out when it suits the party based on our political interest. Despite the constraints of parliamentary politics and the unrelenting deadlines, we can do a much better job of developing practices to work more inclusively with people who share common goals and outcomes, if we put our minds to it.

I often felt my views on extra-parliamentary engagement and working in a more co-ordinated and collaborative way with allies and partners weren't seen as a high priority by the caucus or the party. It wasn't that they didn't care about co-operation. But the demands of daily question period and parliamentary business, as well as the demands of the party to raise money, sign up new members, and generally focus on the next election, always took precedence. I remain convinced from my own experience in the community and in Parliament—whether in housing, the environment, or peace—that the strength of social movements and working in alliance with partners gave the party greater strength to achieve a shared agenda.

Procedures and Principles

I know it's not campaigning through a snowstorm and I shouldn't complain—but fifty-three days of straight rain heaving through grey skies, even for Vancouver, is debilitating. Especially when it's one day shy of breaking the record for rain, and you can't even boast you made it through to a new record. That was the feeling midway during the 2005–06 federal election campaign, when everything we touched was wet and soggy. Election pamphlets disintegrated when we handed them out in the early morning at public transit stops. It was still dark when people made their way to work, and the numbing dampness put them in no frame of mind to say hello and hear about election issues. It dragged on seemingly endlessly, until January 23 when I was fortunate to be re-elected to represent the people of Vancouver East for my fourth term as an MP.

We were happy that, under Jack's leadership, the NDP increased its seat count from eighteen to twenty-nine, including the election of Olivia Chow, Jack's partner. But it was also demoralizing to know that the Conservatives made significant advances, at the expense of Paul Martin's Liberals, who were reeling from the fallout of the Gomery Commission in Quebec. Many felt that the Liberals' sense of entitlement to power had done them in.

It was the beginning of minority parliaments formed in 2006 and 2008, this time with the Conservatives forming government. I had experienced both a Liberal majority during the Chrétien years, which Paul Martin briefly inherited, then Martin's Liberal minority, and now here we were—Stephen Harper in control, even if he had to rely on support from others to maintain his power. Harper was very different from Chrétien and Martin. Chrétien came across as folksy (though he was ruthless with his caucus and in keeping leader-in-waiting Paul Martin at bay). In the House Chrétien was laid-back, even dismissive, but he was tough as nails. Martin, on the other hand, seemed to lose his steam as prime minister. I used to marvel at his ease in the House when he was Chrétien's finance minister. He could reel off budget numbers and have MPs laughing their socks off. Harper, by contrast, was intense and distant, not easy to approach.

In June 2006 the Government of Canada issued an official apology to the descendants and families of Chinese head tax payers, who had suffered from a racist tax levied on Chinese immigration to Canada from 1885 to 1923. Many of the original head tax payers had worked and died building the Canadian Pacific Railway across Canada, but it took many decades for the campaign for redress to be addressed in Parliament. It was championed by MP Margaret Mitchell beginning in 1984. I followed in her footsteps, continuing the call for an apology and redress in the House of Commons. Sustained campaigns in the community both at the local and national level—led by the Chinese Canadian National Council, as well as local activists in Vancouver like Sid Chow Tan, whose grandfather had paid the head tax—kept the issue alive. Finally the government was forced to act. June 22 was a

On Parliament Hill with NDP leader Alexa McDonough supporting redress for head tax payers

proud day for New Democrats, who had never wavered in supporting the community and the call for redress.

The House of Commons is a place of minutiae—details, details, details. Yet you are at your peril if you lose sight of the bigger picture. You could get lost in the intrigue, the manoeuvrings, points of order, and political games. For the NDP, and for me as House leader, it was important to clearly establish our overall goals and what we hoped to accomplish in the House. Jack's strong commitment to getting things that would actually help people done was central to his strategy. I wholeheartedly supported it. This didn't mean we ignored the responsibility of holding the government to account. We did that every day, and it was a "prime directive. " (Yes, we were *Star Trek* fans.)

After the 2006 election, there was a lot of buzz that the budget amendment the NDP had secured with the Liberals would go down in flames with the new Conservative government. But Jack was not to be foiled. He dispatched me and Bill Blaikie to meet with the new prime minister to seek a commitment that the Conservatives would honour the NDP budget deal. I had never met with Harper formally before, and as we approached the stately Langevin Block across from Parliament Hill where his offices were located, I felt unsure about the meeting. I expected to see ornate and richly furnished offices—I mean, heck, this is where the prime minister of Canada hangs out. But it was drab, even shabby, and somewhat in disrepair. Our meeting was cordial and Harper was polite. We got quickly to the point; no small talk here.

Harper assured us that the budget amendment would hold and the dollars earmarked for housing, transit, pensions, and education would go ahead. We left satisfied, but it was my ongoing job as House leader to keep tabs on the money to make sure it was not redirected for other purposes. Following federal money through to provincial coffers, and then making sure the provinces didn't redirect the funds to their own pet projects, is no easy task. And I came to understand the loosey-goosey nature of our federation. The public is not served well by the lack of transparency and follow-through on agreements for federal funds.

In minority parliaments almost anything could happen. Things can go extraordinarily well or extraordinarily badly. We had to pay attention. In March 2008 the Liberals, in opposition in the Conservative minority Parliament, moved a motion of non-confidence in the government, that if passed would trigger an election. The NDP supported the motion, but in a typical parliamentary manoeuvre, a preceding motion was also put that needed to be voted on before the main motion was put. Parliamentary procedure is such that not all motions are automatically voted on individually by MPs, and it was usual to "force the vote" in these situations by having five MPs stand up when the Speaker called for the vote. (Still with me?) In this instance the Liberals who were present in the House at the time forgot to force the vote, and we would have lost the main motion to bring down the government. But

NDP members instead jumped up and forced the vote with five members, thus making sure a vote would indeed take place.

On another occasion, during debate on a Conservative budget, the Speaker, seeing no other speakers rise in the House, moved on, and the budget was adopted at that stage of debate without objection from the opposition. We messed up on that one. It was challenging to be the House leader during these minority Parliaments—but also exciting and fascinating. I feel fortunate to have experienced all the ups and downs. It was a balancing act, knowing that at any time the government could fall on a vote of confidence. That meant we had to be in a perpetual state of election readiness. Jack would sometimes joke at caucus meetings that the campaign airplane was waiting on the tarmac. Except sometimes, it wasn't a joke.

Jack constantly peppered us to be ready for an election and urged us to use our mailing privileges as MPs to frequently send out what were referred to as "10 percenters" to our constituents. These mailings on parliamentary business could be sent to 10 percent of your riding at any time. It was also possible at that time to send mailings into other ridings held by another party (something the Conservatives excelled at); the rules were changed in later years to prevent that practice. Jack was very enthusiastic about 10 percenter constituent mailings, and he would distribute charts at Wednesday caucus meetings showing which MPs were doing well and which were falling behind. In my riding, I was lucky to have a secret weapon named Sam Moncton, who designed our popular and readable mailings, which rarely got negative feedback. Sam was so good that Jack ended up securing her services for his own mailings in Toronto–Danforth.

Of course politics is by nature a partisan affair, especially in the Canadian parliamentary system (which follows the UK model), where the party is held up as supreme. Jack was partisan like all leaders, and he went to bat for his brand and his party. But what I liked about his style is that he had a keen awareness that we were in Parliament for the Canadian people—to make things better for them. So while he was fiercely protective of the NDP, he also knew he had a bigger role to play in Canadian politics that was good for all people. He would often speak about his father, Bob Layton, who had been caucus chair in Brian Mulroney's Progressive Conservative government. It was very clear to us in the NDP caucus that Jack believed you could get above partisan stances for the greater good.

In 2008 the government issued a formal Statement of Apology to Former Students of Indian Residential Schools. This apology was in recognition of the immeasurable suffering caused by residential schools that were sanctioned by numerous governments over many decades. Leading up to the apology, there was a standstill on how to ensure that Indigenous leaders could be heard following the statement from Prime Minister Harper. The procedural rules made it impossible for Indigenous leaders to speak from the floor of the House of Commons itself. Ian Capstick, a young communications staffer in the NDP leader's office, suggested that by a simple motion after the speeches of the prime minister and other party leaders, unanimous consent could be sought from members present to invite the Indigenous leaders to speak on the floor of the House of Commons. It was a simple solution, but no one had thought if it. Jack made it happen.

It may seem like a mere symbolic gesture, but on such a historic day it meant a lot. Moreover, Jack's speech that day was strong as he acknowledged the importance of the government apology concerning a dark period in Canada's history, and then demanded that the government take concrete and long overdue action to forge a nation-to-nation partnership with First Nations, beginning with support of the *United Nations Declaration on the Rights of Indigenous Peoples.* Jack had shown that, despite leading the third party in the House, he was able to influence what needed to be done. Representing a riding with strong

Indigenous communities, I heard from many people how proud they were that the NDP had stood up and fought for their rights.

My work continued too on the missing and murdered women and the risks facing sex workers. The parliamentary subcommittee I had secured in 2003 continued its work, despite two intervening elections, and a report was tabled in the House of Commons in December 2006. The report had no consensus for the decriminalization of the laws pertaining to sex work, but there was consensus that the current laws were harmful to sex workers and their safety. Sex workers were terribly disappointed that the report didn't go far enough. Nevertheless, it was a historic report that fully outlined the issues of sex work in Canada and the need for change. The NDP caucus itself was divided on the issue, with agreement only that the current laws were harmful. On issues like this, the caucus ended up with an uneasy truce, with agreement on how much (or little) could be said and more importantly on what couldn't be said.

Having a parliamentary committee report in hand was not by any means the end of the struggle to change Canada's harmful laws and practices as they pertain to sex workers. I used as many opportunities as possible to raise the issue in the House of Commons, the media, and the community. This wasn't always easy; it wasn't popular to talk about sex-worker rights in Parliament, in the caucus, and even in the community at large. And it didn't only mean holding governments to account; it was also calling the media out when they reinforced harmful stereotypes.

In a press release in December 2007, at the conclusion of the Pickton trial, I drew attention to the need for concrete action:

> I am deeply concerned that with the conclusion of this trial, nothing will change. Sex workers will remain at risk without the minimum of their basic human rights being met. Harmful laws will continue to be enforced against sex workers and con-

ditions of poverty, discrimination, racism, and violence will continue as well.... Needed changes must include law reform, improved police training and the security of human rights for housing, a living income, social supports and an end to violence.

These were tough years to advance these issues in the public realm, especially under Conservative governments. We were battling not only against commonly held prejudices and stereotypes about drug users, sex workers, and homeless people, but also against a government that had no interest in evidence-based decision making. The Conservatives were hell-bent on an ideological approach and the politics of fear that pitted people against each other, creating false scenarios of good people and bad people. They did it to bolster support among their base of supporters, and it was very effective until they went too far.

So many times the House would have to debate boutique private member's bills from Conservative backbenchers, who felt confident they could rip apart the Criminal Code of Canada and insert nasty barbs like tougher sentencing provisions for punishment, to underscore their dogma that everyone in jail was a bad human being. There were draconian government bills too, on law and order—so many that it was sometimes overwhelming for our justice critic, Joe Comartin, to keep up. These bills were like armaments for battle, containing provisions like striking down the "faint-hope" clause for murder, changing the age of consent, and removing discretion for judges within the justice system.

Our caucus had many tough debates, to decide whether to vote for or against a Conservative bill that brought in harsh provisions, including mandatory minimum sentencing. Sometimes the caucus was divided between those of us who wanted to battle against the Conservative crime bills, and others who worried about the impact locally, where the Conservative mantra of the NDP being "soft on crime" was taking root. Some caucus members supported certain provisions of the crime bills, and on occasion we would seek to have a bill passed "on division," to avoid having a formal member-by-member vote in the House. Bill Siksay in particular was a strong advocate against the Conservative law-and-order agenda. To me he was an unsung hero of our caucus. Many a time I looked silently at Bill and thanked my lucky stars he was there.

These caucus sessions could be exhausting. They sometimes felt like doing battle with your friends, and I worried that we were becoming too cautious about speaking out. It's not that I was always right and others wrong—it's not that simple. There were numerous considerations in play. What were our political opponents doing on the issue? How will they use it against us? Is this the hill to die on? I heard that one many a time—or that it "wasn't the right time" to speak out on a certain matter because we'd get clobbered. Sometimes I could be persuaded by my colleagues—they were all intelligent and thoughtful people—but at other times I felt we diminished our values and history. It's hard to sort out these dilemmas, and partly that's what makes politics so fascinating and dynamic. Timing and strategy count, but so do principles and guts.

I believe my strength is an ability to work with people and find a way forward. Being part of a team of New Democrats was like being in a big family, and as in any family, there are squabbles and siblings can become competitive and downright nasty, but they are also loving and will go to the wall for you. I experienced all of that. There were times I felt lost, bewildered, and frustrated. Driven by the issues I was working on, I couldn't understand why it was so hard to convince my colleagues of my point of view. In hindsight I know they gave me lots of space and put up with my regular entreaties to support the issues I brought forward.

$\sim$

Back in my Vancouver office, my two trusted constituency assistants, Janet Woo and Phyllis Loke, earned stellar reputations for their work in the community. We worked as a close-knit team, no matter the time zones and distance between Ottawa and Vancouver. Neither of them had backgrounds in the NDP, and I think it was one of the best decisions I made to hire folks who saw their role more as community advocates and not party insiders. Born, raised, and living in east Vancouver, Janet had been a social planner in West Vancouver. When I interviewed her in 1997, I was impressed with her thorough knowledge about my civic history. She made it clear she didn't know a lot about politics, but I had a hunch she had all the right qualities to work in a busy office handling difficult issues. "I won't let you down," she promised, and she was right. For eighteen plus years until I retired, she gave it her all and was key to our political success. Phyllis, who had worked previously at the Chinese Cultural Centre, had an uncanny political mind that could nose out what was happening in the local community. She was extremely capable in undertaking complex immigration casework, and she gave our office enormous credibility and professionalism. They both stood by me through every up and down, and I know that, even when they sometimes doubted the ventures I would take on, they had as much faith and trust in me as I had in them.

On Saturdays we would often set up what we called our Travelling Community Offices. We'd advertise in advance our presence at local community centres, neighbourhood houses, libraries, and even the mall. If ever the goings-on and political intrigue in Ottawa started to cloud my mind, it was these community sessions that kept me grounded and real. Sometimes only a few people would show up—just to say hello and chat about their concerns. I got loads of feedback that let me understand what people were thinking and feeling. But most of the time we'd have lineups and hear heartbreaking stories of what people were up against, and we'd rack our brains on how we could help. Hearing about people's hardships and misery, Janet and I would often be close to tears. Like the old pensioner who'd worked his whole life in low-paid jobs, and because of a small error in reporting to the Canada Revenue Agency years earlier, found out he owed more than ten thousand dollars in penalties. He had no hope of paying anything, and he was distraught and afraid he'd be hauled off to jail. We got to work. Janet's excellent relationship with public service staff, and our reputation for due diligence and competency, helped work out a solution.

We met many constituents who were on the brink of disaster, or homeless, destitute, or fighting addiction, or worst of all, terribly alone and fearful about their future. Rodney Watson is a courageous young man who in 2009 refused to return to the US army and the war on Iraq. For almost eight years we fought for his bid to stay in Canada. It was one of the most difficult individual cases I worked on, due to the political mindset of the government in power, particularly when the Conservatives were in power. Rodney lived in sanctuary at First United Church. He could not set foot outside the building during this time, for fear of being arrested and deported by the Canada Border Services Agency. The war resisters support group never gave up on their advocacy. It was years later, after I left Parliament in 2015, that Rodney Watson emailed to let me know that he had been freed.

Situations like these made my work in Ottawa very real. I absolutely knew what I was there to fight for. I would often be asked what kept me going; it was the people of East Van and their resilience to keep going against unbelievable odds that kept me going too. Sometimes late at night, I would read emails from constituents and hear their stories. One constituent in particular often wrote me gut-wrenching handwritten letters, sharing his deep anger about the so-called residential school settlement that he felt he had been coerced into. I would phone him, because it was too difficult to write a short note back, and we would talk for hours as he voiced his grief and anger about the lack of understanding of reconciliation. He had been horribly abused at residential school and later became an abuser himself.

The tragic guilt and sorrow he carried into his senior years was a reflection of Canada's colonial and racist history. Often I couldn't think of the words to respond adequately, and so I would listen and make sure his letters were sent on to the minister in Ottawa.

Of course we saw the quirkier side of community life too. There were regular visits from folks who were convinced of conspiracy theories or visiting aliens. We would listen respectfully, keeping an eye on how restless the lineup was getting. We also got mixed up in the conspiracy theory of "chemtrails." Julius Fisher, who continued to produce TV reports for me on cable TV, inadvertently listed something on the subject after one of my reports. From then on and forever, it seemed, I was thought of as an advocate and would receive copious emails asking me to speak out on these mysterious cloud trails in the skies that were allegedly created by the US military for nefarious purposes. We developed a standard response to make it clear I did not believe in chemtrails, nor was I following up the entreaties to take action on them.

We interacted with many people suffering from mental illness. Janet and Phyllis took special courses at the Justice Institute to better understand how to respond to situations that were tense and sometimes violent, and on rare occasions, even to death threats. We sometimes had to call the police—but mostly we got by, by listening calmly and knowing how to de-escalate things. I once had a Conservative MP tell me that I was perfect for my riding, and I was too taken aback to ask him what he meant.

I felt very bad one time when Phyllis and I were at one of our community sessions and not a single person showed up. This had never happened before, or since. Five minutes before we were due to close up shop, I said to Phyllis, "Okay, no one's coming—let's leave." On Monday morning, a very elderly woman phoned our community office and in a quavering voice said she had walked a long way to get to the Saturday Travelling Community Office to see us. "I came just before

3:30 p.m.," she said, "but the door was locked and I had to go all the way back home." We were mortified that we hadn't stayed the last five minutes, and never again left early.

The strength of the community was rich and powerful, and I attended as many community events as I could every weekend that I was back from Ottawa or during the weeks Parliament was not in session. A wonderful and funky two-act musical drama, *Bruce: The Musical*, was created by Theatre In the Raw. Lyrics and writing were by Bob Sarti (a veteran *Vancouver Sun* reporter); Bill Sample and Earle Peach created the music; and it was produced and directed by Jay Hamburger. Premiered in November 2008, *Bruce* chronicled the life and times of the vibrant battle to save the Carnegie Centre at Main and Hastings and the campaign to stop rooming-house fires and beer parlour violations.

Lief and I, Kim, and my mum attended the show, and we got swept up in the wonderful history of the early days at DERA in the Downtown Eastside. The characters of Bruce, Libby, and Jean were magically recreated, and with singing too! The musical captured beautifully the story of the fight for the Carnegie Centre, and fights we'd had with the city over bylaw enforcement to keep people safe. It was surreal to see actors portray our early escapades, and it gave me insight into the intensity of what we had gotten up to. It seemed like we were always breathless with anticipation for the next battle, and with a zeal that was a bit scary. Maybe it's always like that when we look back on our lives; the highlights become compacted into bite-sized memories that take moments to relive. I would never have imagined those early struggles portrayed through a musical, but somehow it worked and made the history of the times come alive through songs, like this one:

Hastings Street Rumble

Oh, marching arm in arm down Hastings Street
Snaking back and forth on Hastings Street

Staring down the cops on Hastings Street
We've got it beat on Hastings Street

We got a cause and it ain't just hay
We want real work and at decent pay
We're mad as hell and won't take it any more
Whoever don't like it, we'll show them the door.

Oh, marching arm in arm down Hastings Street,
Yes, snaking back and forth on Hastings Street
Staring down the cops on Hastings Street
We've got it beat on Hastings Street

Marching past Woodward's we're quite a sight
Blocking traffic, don't stop for the light
Stay in formation and heads up high
Not waiting for the sweet by-and-by.

We call it the snake dance and we really do move
The cops on the sidelines, they don't approve
They can't stop us, we got nothing to lose
They're afraid to act, cuz we've found our groove.

Unlikely Allies

Jack was known for his big ideas and desire for progressive change. And he always believed that you didn't have to be "in power" to be a catalyst. He was willing to take risks when he saw an opportunity to do something good. I loved him for that.

Who could forget the coalition we almost had in 2008–09? Jack saw an opportunity, in this case to defeat the Conservative minority government. The government was in denial about the economic recession, and even before a budget was brought in, their fiscal update fell far short of any expectation of what was needed to mitigate the impact of a global recession in Canada. Jack went to work and set about negotiating a coalition arrangement with the Liberals, now under Stéphane Dion's leadership, with the Bloc Québécois in support. My colleague Dawn Black, our defence critic at the time, was part of the NDP negotiating team. I recall her clear, informative updates to our caucus executive as the agreement took shape. It was a bold move and Harper countered by shutting down Parliament—his third prorogation over his short time in power, a response that was thoroughly unpopular and antidemocratic.

Huddling in the opposition lobby to study the speech from the throne, November 2008 (*left to right*) Libby Davies, Yvon Godin, Jack Layton, Charlie Angus

When I returned to BC at the end of the parliamentary session in December, although Harper and his gang had hit the airwaves hard, trying to frame it as "an attempted coup," there was an excited buzz in the community. A progressive coalition government could be coming to Ottawa. The arrangement later failed when the new Liberal leader, Michael Ignatieff, announced in January 2009 he would have nothing to do with the coalition. I always thought it was a mistake on his part, and his loss too. It likely would have rebuilt the credibility of the Liberals, long before Justin Trudeau emerged as leader four years later.

Jack's bold proposition for the coalition agreement was focused on a parliamentary response. The impetus for the agreement was our dismay at the Conservatives' failure to meaningfully address the recession. But we also had an opportunity to work with civil society and progressive forces to give a deep, authentic analysis about the recession and the failure of global capitalism. People were hungry to understand how

Media panel, foyer of the House of Commons, with Ralph Goodale, Liberal House leader, and Jay Hill, Conservative House leader, November 2008

screwed up our international financial system was and what could be done about it. I wish we had also been able to foster greater public dialogue about the economic recession itself. It was a unique historic opportunity to speak truth to power and call for a substantive new approach in financing, bailouts, and the regulation of capital.

I raised the opportunity in caucus, but we shied away from it and were content to call for more "investments" that even the Conservatives ended up embracing. It's very possible that, had we taken on the recession more broadly and called for radical changes, we would have lost support and become more politically marginalized. It's also possible that masses of people would have eagerly joined a dynamic debate about macroeconomic policies and the state's failure to control obscene wealth at the expense of middle class and poor people. By not engaging with these questions, we became not much different in our response

View of Yes/Oui coalition rally on Parliament Hill, from Libby's fifth-floor office, December 3, 2008

Libby Davies, Rob Sutherland, and Ross Sutherland at the Yes/Oui coalition rally, December 2008

from any other party. Certainly the global crisis of capital and climate change was complex; it would have required enormous capacity and heft to change direction.

I sometimes felt I led a dual life. I was a community activist and organizer at heart, someone who wanted to push further in a more radical way. But I was also a parliamentarian, and NDP house leader and deputy leader, roles where rules and tradition were restrictive. I tried to navigate these two paths and reconcile them. One of my core beliefs was that by being a parliamentarian in the House of Commons, as well as an activist, I could help bridge the gap between these two very different worlds to bring about change.

For example, in June 2008 I was requested to help American peace activists get into Canada to attend a Vancouver conference on women war resisters. The women had on other occasions been denied access to cross the Canadian border because of arrests for peaceful non-violent action in the US. The sharing of databases between the US and Canada was emerging as a civil liberties issue. The activists attempted to cross at the Peace Arch crossing in BC by vehicle. We had worked out logistics to get through the border in advance. I crossed into Blaine, Washington, so that I could travel in the same vehicle as Medea Benjamin of Code Pink (a women's peace initiative) and Ann Wright, a retired US Reserves colonel. I was to cross the border into Canada with them, to vouch for their peaceful intentions to speak at the conference. We waited in the car lineup and I repeated my lines in my head, keeping in mind the need to stick to the point of getting the women into the conference. After three hours of questions, phone calls, and waiting at the Canadian border offices, the two women were finally issued permission to enter Canada, Medea with a twenty-four-hour visitor permit and Ann with an "exception" to her earlier exclusion order. It was an affirmation that thought, planning, and exerting some parliamentary muscle could sometimes get around bad rules. It seemed ludicrous that these wonderful, brave women would be deemed any kind of threat to Canadian security—but such is the sinister makeup of security databases.

I had no hesitation in vouching for both women, having worked with them on other occasions, including participating in antiwar actions outside the White House in Washington, DC. Helping them cross the Canadian border and supporting them in their work seemed the least I could do. It was part of my dual life, switching from House leader mode in Ottawa to on-the-ground activism where an MP could help people in a bind.

Being House leader for the NDP taught me a lot about the insider's game in politics. It can be nasty and intense, but it is always riveting. Personalities and egos become inflamed. Staying calm and focusing on the issue at hand, even when your adversaries are acting like fools or bullies, is a good way to survive. Treating people, including your opponents, with respect is more likely to lead to resolution than fighting it out in a way that can easily become personal and demeaning. I watched many a time as other House leaders duked it out, shouting matches and all. It seemed to me a traditional male way of doing things, and I rejected it. The easiest thing in the world is to sink to that level. Soon enough there's no room to manoeuvre. It fascinated and disappointed me that hurling insults and making ridiculous challenges, like boys in a sandbox, was considered a mature way of resolving differences. But on Parliament Hill it was the big boys who did it all the time. And the nastier they were, the higher opinion they usually had of themselves.

Oddly enough, the most interesting House leader I got to work with was Conservative John Baird, during his tenure as House leader for his party in 2010–11. Though we were miles apart on just about everything, we got on surprisingly well. John was always good on his word, and he treated the NDP in a reasonably fair way. He would often call out during votes, as we sat on opposite sides of the House, and make a joke or ask when we were getting together. The view that Canadians have about MPs' relationship to each other is usually based on what they see in question period—aggressiveness, hostility, and a lack of camaraderie. And certainly John Baird earned that reputation, snarling away as the government's favourite pit bull. But that was just question period. Most often he was funny, warm, and very human.

We once took a selfie together at the Ottawa airport, and we both tweeted it out. Most people seemed to think it was cool. But each of us got angry responses too, saying, how *could* you take a photo with him/her! In reality MPs from different parties are very social, and they can not only like each other, but also work together on commonly supported issues. In 2014, I worked with Steven Fletcher, a Conservative MP from Winnipeg, to support his Dying with Dignity private member's bill. We co-hosted a meeting in Calgary in July to speak about the need for Parliament to legalize physician-assisted death. Numerous multi-party groups and friendship associations can also be a rich source of constructive work, both nationally and internationally.

Despite the personal and working relationships between MPs of different parties, the overall big-*P* politics in the House could be nasty, hurtful, and exhausting. I don't regret having experienced it, but there were many times when I faced my demons of not feeling good enough to be in that game or even know how to play. Over time I developed my own version of the game. I knew if I stood aside and watched the fireworks for a while, I could find a moment to intervene, literally lower my voice, and express my view in measured tones. Even so, I worried too much about what others thought of me, and I knew I was still a minority in the men's room. I remember raising the issue of sexual harassment and harassment generally on Parliament Hill, at the Board of Internal Economy (BOIE)—the governing board of the House of Commons, where I represented the NDP—and being told that it wasn't a matter for the board to deal with; it was up to each party to clean up its own mess if they so chose. Only years later, in 2014–15 and beyond, as highly publicized cases of sexual harassment came to light, did the BOIE realize it had no choice. On other occasions, at our caucus meetings, I would catch myself feeling insecure as I watched the guys strut to the microphone with such confidence that what they had to say was new and terribly important. Then I would stop and think: Hang on, I know exactly what we need to do and I know how to do it.

Ottawa felt like a place where I was good at my job—and I saw it as a job, because it is a very structured place, with rules and practices. But it was in the community back in east Vancouver, or working with other communities across the country, that my passion for change surfaced and directed me forward. Parliament was in great measure a vehicle for that change, but it was driven by outside forces that I was intensely connected to. Sometimes I would arrive home from Ottawa after a long plane ride feeling utterly exhausted by the numerous antics that had taken up so much time and energy. And for what? Some minor point or victory. But after a few hours of being home, talking to people, getting the real scoop, hearing the stories, and generally digging into whatever was going on, I would feel reinvigorated to my purpose. The energy and compelling drive would return to get me going.

In any successful movement for change, you'll usually come across, by accident or design, unlikely allies whom you wouldn't otherwise normally work with. I love discovering that some person or group outside your usual practice is deeply connected to what you are working for. It's like parallel universes that actually do cross paths; you find a whole new way of acting together.

In the case of drug policy reform, working with groups like VANDU and the PHS, it was totally unexpected to cross paths with middle-class parents from Kerrisdale whose kids were suffering and dying from drug overdoses. The likelihood of parents from this well-established community getting together to collaborate with Downtown Eastside advocates for people who use drugs was not very high, but it happened. At a meeting at St. Mary's Church in the heart of Kerrisdale, Bud Osborn and I met a number of parents and talked about the difficulties of convincing the provincial and federal governments to change their harmful views on illegal drug policy and treatment. From Grief to Action is a brave and outspoken group of parents who are advocates for a sensible drug policy, not only for their own community and children, but for the Downtown Eastside too. They would show up at public events and speak out, and although VANDU's base was very different in location and experience, support the network's work. They became trusted allies who helped foster other alliances with students and professional groups. When such alliances take place, new ways of working are needed that are transparent and collaborative. Not always an easy thing to do. But as I've seen over and over, working together is also transformative. It becomes much tougher for those in power who try to isolate and divide those seeking change, or to write them off as having no political clout.

Creative action—well timed—is a key ingredient to the process of change. I'd first learned this in my early days as an organizer at DERA, where we dreamed up impossible actions that raised our causes' visibility. It was the same in the battle for Insite, not only the battle to get it established, prior to 2003, but also later, the battle to stay in operation. The formation of two Conservative governments, in the minority parliaments resulting from the 2006 and 2008 federal elections, led to a tenuous situation for Insite's continued operation. Insite relied on special federal exemptions under the *Controlled Drugs and Substances Act*. The Conservatives were vigorously opposed to Insite itself, and to its challenge to the status quo of viewing illegal drug use as a criminal justice issue.

Every time the permit came due for a further exemption to allow Insite to continue, another battle would ensue. On many occasions, I and others in the community asked Stephen Harper to visit the facility and see for himself what was going on. We believed, naively, that evidence would change the Conservatives' political mindset. It hadn't quite sunk in yet that being against harm reduction and safe-injection sites wasn't a matter of evidence for the Conservatives. It was a matter of ideology and a tool for creating a powerful wedge from which to wage a politically motivated war on drugs and poor people.

In February 2010, a day after the federal government announced it would go to the Supreme Court of Canada to oppose Insite's operation, Harper's planned visit with seniors at the Chinese Cultural Centre a few blocks away garnered a "welcome" from Friends of Insite. The group demanded that Harper, on tour leading up to the 2010 Vancouver Olympics, stop his government's latest attack on Insite and at least pay a visit to see it for himself. Friends of Insite placed yellow tape around the perimeter of the premises, and I watched, supporting my constituents who were drawing attention to the prime minister's rare visit to the neighbourhood.

The next thing I knew, my BlackBerry was buzzing like crazy and Karl Bélanger, Layton's press attaché, was frantically asking me what's going on. Then a message from Mitchel Raphael from *Maclean's*, saying, "Libby, do you know what they are saying about you?" Finally a message from Jack himself: "Is there anything I need to know about?" Unbeknownst to me, Dimitri Soudas, the prime minister's director of communications, had put out a message to the media that the MP for Vancouver East was responsible for blocking the exit of seniors who were meeting with the prime minister. What? Of course, this simply wasn't the case. But that didn't matter to the Conservatives, as long it could be used to motivate their base for political gain:

Protesters chain doors of centre ahead of PM visit
Canwest News Service, February 10, 2010

VANCOUVER—A Vancouver protest against the federal government's latest bid to shut down a safe-injection drug treatment site turned into a political donnybrook Wednesday after protesters chained and barred the doors of a Chinese cultural centre.

Prime Minister Stephen Harper was scheduled to attend the dress rehearsal of the Vancouver Chinatown Spring Festival Celebration Parade in Vancouver Wednesday afternoon. Seizing an opportunity, about 150 protesters attended to attack Harper's decision to launch an appeal of a B.C. Court of Appeal decision that ruled Insite, North America's only supervised injection site, can remain open.

Dimitri Soudas, Harper's press secretary, said that the protesters delayed the prime minister's visit to the cultural centre by taping the door shut, which trapped seniors, veterans and children inside.

"The protesters definitely crossed the line," he said in an interview.

Earlier in the day, Soudas sent several notes to reporters in Ottawa reporting the protesters sealed off the building where the dress rehearsal was taking place.

"Veterans, seniors and young children are currently being prevented from exiting or entering the Chinese Cultural Centre of Greater Vancouver because the Libby Davies 'welcoming committee' has taped all exits shut," Soudas wrote. "This is a lack of respect for seniors, veterans, Canadians of Chinese origin and the young kids inside the building. The situation has created a security risk for all the people currently in the building.

"Some doors have been chained or taped shut while people were preparing for a Chinese New Year rehearsal."

Poppycock, said Davies, the New Democrat MP for Vancouver East. She said the rally, which she attended in support of Insite, was "low-key" and quite peaceful.

"It's outrageous for him to suggest that I organized this or somehow I put people's lives in danger," she said. "The whole point of the rally is about saving people's lives with Insite. That's what Insite does."

Vancouver police officials confirmed Wednesday that Harper was not in the building while the protest was taking place.

They said officers attended the protest and removed the chains from the doors.

"There were no injuries and no arrests," said the police media release. "The protest was allowed to safely continue without further incident. The Vancouver police respect the right to protest safely and the right to assemble safely. However, in this case, the protesters infringed upon the rights and safety of others. Minimal steps were taken to ensure those locked inside the building were able to leave safely."

Soudas suggested the protest could have ended in disaster for the people inside.

"Of the 250 Chinese Canadians, 50 are uniformed veterans, 50 are young children who have come to showcase their culture to the [prime minister] and media," he wrote. "In the horrible event of fire or emergency, all those good willed people would be prevented from exiting.

"Is Libby Davies proud of this?"

The NDP issued a press release demanding an apology from the prime minister for his spokesperson's false and misleading statements. In a follow-up story in the *Globe and Mail*, February 11, I stated, "I was there as I have been at many rallies in support of Insite, and I'll continue to do that because I am outraged the Conservative government is continuing to challenge Insite's operation."

As the 2010 Olympics approached, there was intense public debate about the impact of Olympic venues and visitors on vulnerable populations and scarce housing in Vancouver. There were fears and anger about the loss of civil liberties and the right to protest, and

Annual Valentine's Day Women's Memorial March brings out thousands of supporters during Vancouver Winter Olympics, 2010

the possibility that homeless and low-income people would be evicted and driven from the streets to make way for Olympic participants and visitors. Yet again the lack of affordable housing was top of mind—it seemed to forever cloud the beauty of the city. Something so basic was beyond the reach of growing numbers of people, and it defied logic that it was still a crisis that no government or initiative would solve.

Am Johal, a local organizer in the community and chair of the Impact on Communities Coalition, organized a seventy-six-week rolling hunger strike called the Homelessness Hunger Strike Relay. Begun in 2009 in the lead-up to the Olympics, it invited people to participate in a hunger strike to raise awareness about housing issues and homelessness. I became the fifty-fifth participant in January 2010, and accepted the ceremonial wooden spoon from Amy Walker, co-publisher of *Momentum Magazine*, next to the Olympic countdown clock near the Vancouver Art Gallery. It felt a bit funny to stand next to the larger-than-life Olympic clock and accept a long-handled wooden spoon for such an unusual kind of relay.

For the next week, during my fast, I hung out at Main and Hastings in front of the Carnegie Centre with a flip chart, asking people to write their comments about the housing situation. I thought they would think it too flaky to write anything down, but page after page kept turning as people poured out their guts and anger about what they were facing. The week flew by, despite cold and wet weather, as people stopped to chat and tell me stories. This intersection is teeming with people on the move; it was like a fast-flowing river of humanity with countless cars and buses passing by on the side. I gathered pages and pages of

Downtown Eastside community residents add comments onto a flip chart, Homelessness Hunger Strike Relay prior to Vancouver Winter Olympics, January 2010

extraordinary, powerful testimony. We later transcribed the comments and I read them in Parliament, yet again calling for the federal government to invest in social housing for people.

Later in June, Am Johal also organized the On to Ottawa Housing Trek—in memory of the seventy-fifth anniversary of the famous On to Ottawa Trek of the unemployed during the Depression of the 1930s. The housing activists arrived in Ottawa via train, determined to raise their concerns about the shrinking affordable housing supply across Canada and in support for Bill C-304, my Housing Bill of Rights. We all went out for pizza in the ByWard Market, close to Parliament Hill, and I heard the stories of the train ride across Canada. For some it was their first visit to the nation's capital. It felt very special to host such a great group of activists who had travelled far to make their voices heard. It was tough going on this issue; the Conservative government kept housing at the bottom of their list. We all needed to keep pushing—like pushing a boulder uphill—firm in the belief that such actions kept up the pressure for such a basic human right.

◦◦

That year, 2010, Jack also faced some tough challenges in his caucus, reconciling the NDP position on the national long-gun registry. The registry had been brought in by the Liberals in 1995 at enormous financial cost. Harper's Conservatives were determined to not only dismantle it but also use it to create havoc in Parliament. A Conservative private member's bill had passed at second reading in November 2009 with twelve NDP members voting with the government in favour of ending the long-gun registry. The NDP was about to get hammered. Conservative material flooded into NDP ridings where the registry was a sensitive issue. Gun control advocates, aghast that some NDP members were offside, mounted pressure on the leader to bring his members into line.

Historically, votes on private member's bills are free votes, in which MPs can vote how they wish without fear of reprisal from the party whip. Indeed, some of our members from rural and northern ridings had run for office with full disclosure to the leader that they could not support the registry, which they believed was onerous, bureaucratic, and an infringement on a rural way of life. Several felt on principle they could not vote to maintain the registry as it was. Jack had a difficult conundrum: how to defeat the Conservative bill without forcing the vote of his caucus. Jack had a strong reputation as an advocate for gun control and ending violence against women, so his personal integrity was on the line.

Numerous caucus meetings and discussions took place over the months the bill was under consideration. Joe Comartin, the loyal NDP justice critic, was charged with helping to find solutions to the political dilemma. It was further complicated by the Conservatives' delay of the final vote on the bill. They were waiting for an opportune time to pounce, while pouring propaganda into susceptible ridings that could do damage to the NDP.

In September 2010 things came to a head. The Liberals introduced a motion to defeat the Conservative's Bill C-391, and at the NDP caucus meeting held in Regina just prior to the opening of a new parliamentary session, a critical decision had to be made. Jean Crowder, the chair of our caucus at the time, recalls the extraordinary scene in a hotel meeting room as Jack suspended the meeting to speak one-on-one with individual MPs who were likely going to vote against the Liberal motion, thus setting up a future vote where the Conservative bill could still be approved. Things were very tense, as it became clear that half a dozen or more NDP members needed to reverse their opposition to the registry. Some had already done so, and there was a feeling that the leader was manipulating the caucus to achieve the political result he needed, without actually ordering anyone to change their mind. "Someone's got to give," Jack said, in a rare display of anger.

I doubt many leaders could have done what Jack did—painstakingly build his case as one by one the members in question stepped out to the balcony with him to have a conversation. The rest of us sat watching and waiting, and as Rob Sutherland noted later, with gallows humour, we were counting how many went out and how many came back. Meanwhile, Charlie Angus played "Kumbaya" on his guitar, and we didn't know whether to laugh or cry.

Bill Siksay, a staunch gun registry supporter, says he began to feel sympathy for his colleagues in caucus who were under pressure to change their position. In the end, the Liberal motion passed 153 to 151 (thus defeating the Conservative bill), with six NDP members who changed their position from previously voting to eliminate the registry. Very close. But a victory for Jack, both in the vote and in his ability to bring about a result that didn't bust apart his caucus and didn't defeat the registry. As Jean Crowder noted, "We came out of it united."

A Rocky Road

Hater's Test
Ottawa Citizen (editorial), June 11, 2010

It is profoundly disturbing to realize that a prominent Canadian politician has crossed that line. Libby Davies, deputy leader of the New Democratic Party, was recently captured on video saying that, in her view, Israel's illegal "occupation" began in 1948, the year of Jewish independence. The year 1948 was, of course, before the 1967 Arab-Israeli war that left Israel stuck with the Arab territories of Gaza and the West Bank. Davies is saying that the Jewish state was illegitimate from the moment of birth—that Israel is by definition an abomination, no matter what the borders. NDP Leader Jack Layton needs to say publicly whether disgust for Jewish self-determination is official party policy.

Not what you want to read about yourself. But there it was, a horrifying editorial that branded me as antisemitic and accused me of things that were as loathsome to me as they would be to any decent person. It was a shocking turn of events. Within minutes there was an email from Jack on my BlackBerry: "You have to apologize."

A few days earlier I had attended a rally in Vancouver calling for Israel to end its blockade of Gaza. I had attended many such rallies over the years, as a city councillor, a peace activist, and an MP. I often spoke at the rallies because of my deep concern about the situation in Palestine. It wasn't unusual to have someone stick a tape recorder in my face, as they incoherently introduced themselves over the din of the rally, as a freelance "journalist" with a publication no one had ever heard of. I never worried about such off-the-cuff interviews; they were a common occurrence in the activist world, where people had learned to use social media in an effective way.

With this particular interview, however, it became obvious quickly that the interviewer was not a journalist, nor sympathetic to Palestine at all, but had another agenda. He demanded to know when the occupation by Israel had started, and interrupted me in a hostile way. I ended the interview quickly, realizing he was an angry young Zionist who was only interested in his own view of history.

A video of the interview surfaced a few days later. Jack told me Thomas Mulcair, also a deputy leader of the NDP, had raised it with him and was upset with my comments. I sent Jack a link to the video so he could see it for himself. It had less than dozen views at that point. He wrote back saying, "I can see how you were caught in this, and tried to pull it back. Don't worry, it's happened to all of us—I'll talk with Mulcair." I was still worried but felt assured that Jack had absolutely understood the circumstance of the interview. But hours later that day, after question period, the *National Post* wanted to do an interview in the foyer outside the House of Commons. The video had mysteriously been handed to the media. I declined comment, knowing that whatever I said would be torqued to suit a nasty political story that was already written. The same decision was not made by Tom, who spoke to the reporter. The story instantly had legs.

One deputy leader of the NDP going after the other in public is not a good thing. I knew we were in for a rough ride. The next day the Liberals jumped on it. Marc Garneau made a statement in the House condemning me as antisemitic and calling for my resignation. This brought cheers and a standing ovation from many of the Liberals and Conservatives. And one New Democrat: Thomas Mulcair. The Bloc Québécois remained seated. I learned later from a Bloc MP that their leader, Gilles Duceppe, had instructed his members not to attack me.

I sat firmly and quietly in my seat in the front row of the New Democrat benches, keeping my best British poker face on. Of course, things escalated. For two days, when Jack rose during question period, Harper gleefully jumped on him, asking why he wasn't firing his House leader and deputy leader, the member from Vancouver East. What had been a dumb video interview became a national news event. The gloves were off. The truth is, though, I believe it was never about me and the Middle East per se. But I had inadvertently created an opportunity for a political attack from within and without.

On Saturday morning, back in Vancouver, I got a phone call from Anne McGrath, Jack's trusted chief of staff. I'm sure it was a call she didn't particularly want to make, but she took her duty seriously. She told me Jack wanted me to resign my position as House leader after the parliamentary session ended, only a few days away. This was to be done to maintain peace within the caucus, while attracting minimal attention once the House had recessed. It was clear to me that the pressure was coming from Tom and that he wanted Jack to free himself of me. Something in me revolted. I told Anne I couldn't accept Jack's request and needed to talk to him. As respectful as I was of Anne I was upset that Jack hadn't spoken to me personally.

By Sunday night I had returned to Ottawa. That evening a few of us got together to discuss the situation, including Joe Comartin and

Chris Charlton, who both came straight from the airport. These were people I trusted, as I did the learned Rob Sutherland, from my office, and Kim. Chris remembers it was the first time she had been to our little row house on Bell Street North, and the shrimp and pasta dinner was the first she'd tasted made by Kim. There was agreement in this group that it would be a mistake for me to voluntarily resign as House leader.

The next morning, I met with Jack. I could see how distressed he was. He and I went way back; we were friends and we had a crisis on our hands. For the first time in my life, I pushed back for myself rather than taking one for the team. I was so used to advocating for other people and issues, but not for myself. But this day I had to defend myself and my own sense of integrity. It was one of the hardest things to do. I knew I was putting Jack in a difficult position. We both had tears. I told him I could not voluntarily resign and quietly leave my position as though it were my personal decision (you know, saying it was for the family or my health). I made it clear that if as leader he no longer had confidence in me, then that was a different matter and his decision to make. But I refused to resign voluntarily from my leadership position within the caucus.

Over the next two days discussions continued; I was not privy to what discussion took place with Tom. Joe told me he said to Jack that if I was forced out, he too would resign as deputy House leader. Other caucus members also said that they would not support my "resignation." I later learned that a number of labour leaders, some of whom phoned me, also contacted the leader to say they would publicly oppose my departure as House leader. And then the thousands of emails came flooding in, to me, to Jack, and to the party. The majority were very supportive, but some were hateful. An article in *rabble.ca* by well-known political author Murray Dobbin came to my defence and blasted any notion that I might be fired. In all this time I refused to speak to the media, knowing it would only fuel the story.

For the next few days, Leanne Holt, who worked as a legislative assistant in my office, and Kim went everywhere with me on the Hill, on the lookout for media. Both of them remained incredibly calm and supportive as the pressure mounted for me to say something publicly. Leanne and Anthony Salloum, an NDP staffer on the Hill, and Ian Capstick, communications consultant and former NDP staffer, stood by me, helping me out along with Kim, Joe, Chris, and Rob. The support from each of them was personal and unwavering. I am grateful for how they jumped in and helped manage my worst political crisis. Joe and Chris also talked to other caucus members quietly and gauged that I had strong support in the caucus. It's times like this that you know who your friends are. Sticking with me, even if they weren't comfortable with the issue, and in effect going up against the leader and Tom, was courageous on their part and not without political risk. Rob changed his Facebook cover page, as did others, to "I am Libby Davies." I felt deeply thankful for all the support shown.

By Wednesday morning, at the regular weekly meeting, the leader gave his report before a grim-looking caucus. Jack laid down the law that no one but himself, and the foreign affairs critic, Paul Dewar, would speak to the media on the Middle East. It was out of bounds. He was stern and clearly aimed his fire in my direction. I left the meeting feeling beat up. As I met with Rob in an adjoining room to go over House business that was coming up that day, someone popped their head in the door and said, watch out, there's a ton of media waiting for you in the hallway. There was only one way out—slap-bang through the media. I could see Tom in the room across from me, standing with Anne McGrath and others. He and I had not spoken once during the whole matter. Thinking quickly, I took a deep breath and, knowing he couldn't brush me aside if others were there, approached him. I said, "Tom, there's a lot of media waiting to jump on us out there. I think we should walk out together, to show unity, and not give any comment." Anne nodded her head in agreement. And so Tom and I left together—

in silence, and walked through a mass of shouting reporters who desperately wanted comments and acrimony to embellish the story. It didn't happen.

Tom and I never spoke of the matter, and it took months for us to reconcile. It wasn't the first time that he and I had clashed on the issue. Earlier that year, he was so mad at me for responses I had sent out to emails I'd received about the Middle East that he refused to attend meetings if I was present. Kim believed the whole affair wasn't about me, nor Palestine and the Middle East; it was an effort by Tom to pressure Jack and assert his own power within the party and caucus. Whatever it was, it was nasty and a rough time. I agonized over the impact I was causing Jack personally, as he was beginning to publicly grapple with prostate cancer. Yet I could not in good conscience walk away and accept being a scapegoat by resigning as he wanted. In the end, I stayed in my position and my work continued.

The whole affair left me shaken. At times it felt like I was on the edge of a political precipice—about to go over, or worse, be pushed over. It taught me some new lessons about political survival: Act quickly. Don't escalate. Seek out your allies, stick to the truth, and gather your strength.

In August I went to Toronto. Jack and I met in a small coffee shop near his house on Huron Street. Neither of us could stand the idea that we remain estranged in any way over the matter. We talked about what had happened during the controversy. I told him I had felt betrayed because he had been willing to throw me under the bus, to solve the political challenge he faced. He listened carefully, as he always did, and described the real pressures he'd had to deal with on a very contentious issue. I knew he'd wanted me to take one for the team and to see it as upholding the greater good. It wasn't an easy conversation. We both felt bruised and hurt. But our long-standing friendship, political maturity, and lack of malice got us through it. It was another example to me of how the strength of a solid relationship can see you through the most difficult of times.

This episode remains a sensitive and sad part of my political experience. I hurt people I loved, and I experienced what it felt like to be under serious political attack, from within and from without. At one point I spoke to a lawyer who handled libel cases, as to whether a series of absurd and false statements from Bob Rae, foreign affairs critic for the Liberals at the time, could be acted upon as libel. One is titled "Why Jack Layton has to fire Libby Davies" published June 22, 2010, on *MarkNews.com.* The article accused me of calling for "violence"—"an intifada"—and said that all my "rhetoric is the Hamas line":

> She must know that, and her recent protests are just disingenuous. Calling for a renewed intifada is calling for more violence, more suicide bombing, more death, more destruction.

It could, the lawyer thought, but then explained that it would involve spending tens of thousands of dollars and likely end with a judgment that put it all down to politicians slagging one another in public, a part of public discourse, as vile as it was. But I also learned that I had precious friends and allies, and a partner who stood by me.

Curiously, researching material for this book years later, I could find no trace on the internet of either the *Ottawa Citizen* editorial or Bob Rae's opinion piece on *MarkNews*. Every link I found, including on my own website, led to a blank page. Even a link on MP Carolyn Bennett's website to the Rae statement ended in a dead end. I spent hours trying to find the two pieces, becoming more and more puzzled. Nothing. Kim looked too and concluded, "It's been scrubbed." What does that mean, I asked her. She explained that it was possible for someone who knew what they were doing to "scrub" any trace of something on the internet. Like it never existed. I was astonished. Even an editorial in a major Canadian paper? Apparently, it's that easy to revise or erase online history. I then turned to the sixty boxes of archival material I had deposited in the national archives, hoping I might find a hard copy of the editorial and Rae's piece. And there it was for the historical record, my own neatly filed hard copies of what they wanted buried. Had they worried in the end that what had been written was indeed libellous?

6⁓

I was never the foreign affairs critic—and therefore never an official NDP spokesperson on the Middle East or any other international issue. I can hear rumblings in the back of my head: Well, what the hell were you doing when it wasn't your job? Then I say to myself, what happens when we are silent? What exactly is an MP to do? Are we not elected to speak out, even when it creates discomfort? There are limits, of course, and in a caucus, you have to reasonably assign duties and responsibilities to various critics. I know all this and understand the rationale behind it. Better to have smooth waters than the rough waters of people freelancing everywhere. But the image of a docile Parliament, and parliamentarians who are afraid to speak out, is intolerable to me.

My years as a peace activist drew me to speak out and see myself as part of a global movement against war and the violation of human rights. It's been part of my political nature for a very long time. My involvement in the issue of the occupation of Palestine began with my father. Before I was born, he was a young British soldier in Palestine during the 1948 British Mandate. And in his later years, he became a strong proponent for justice for Palestinians—working with the Middle East Council of Churches, and living in Cyprus and then Jerusalem with his second wife, Mary Davies. His memories of the Nakba left an impression on me too. From my earliest political days, I felt strongly about the plight of the people who had been forced from their land, and also suffer still under illegal occupation in the West Bank and Gaza.

In 1991 both my father and I contributed chapters to *Peacemaking in the 1990s* edited by Thomas L. Perry, a wonderful man educated at Harvard and Oxford as a Rhodes scholar. He was driven to Canada by McCarthyism in 1962, and his peace work and books on peace and disarmament contributed vastly to Vancouver's prominence as the "peace capital of North America." Rereading his books today gives a marvellous overview of Vancouver's activism for peace during the 1980s and 1990s, including the proceedings of the 1986 Vancouver Centennial Peace and Disarmament Symposium. It featured internationally renowned peace activists like Rear Admiral Eugene J. Carroll, Jr. (retired), economist John Kenneth Galbraith, Brazilian bishop Dom Hélder Câmara, Petra Kelly, founder of the German Green Party, Canadian diplomat Stephen Lewis, and anti-nuclear activist Dr. Helen Caldicott.

Peter Davies's contribution to the book is a fascinating read to me now, decades later. I can appreciate how his life as a soldier and then peace and justice activist influenced me and my work. In his concluding passage, he wrote:

> Throughout history, injustice has been the fundamental affliction of humanity. I have now come to believe that in the fight against this foe, Peace is neither the goal nor the reward for victory. Only Justice can be that. In the Middle East today, injustice corrodes the foundations of national life and permeates the structures of society. Peace is but a mirage, an illusion, a distant object turned upside down that simmers through "the dust of death" churned up by tanks moving into battle positions. The arms manufacturing sites of the world that equip the armies of the Middle East rulers, attempt to use the hope of peace as a tool to control events in the region. When the tool fails them (which is when their client states fail to do their bidding), the presidents and prime ministers give the order, "let loose the dogs of war."
>
> Justice will continue to be defined imperfectly and with barely concealed self-interests and self-delusions. Like truth, it will always be just beyond our grasp. Yet we must strain to reach it. In the name of peace, of Shalom, of As-Salaam-Alaikum, Justice must not be sacrificed.

The shadow of cynicism in his writing, based on his experience as a soldier "keeping the peace" in war-torn countries, is evident. But so is his idealism and his belief that justice is paramount to our human future.

As an MP I travelled twice to the Middle East to see the situation for myself. These were life-changing experiences. My first visit to the West Bank and Gaza was in May 2002, the result of a multi-party parliamentary delegation led by Carolyn Parrish, an outspoken Liberal MP from Mississauga. It was hosted and paid for by that community's Palestine House. The mission wasn't without controversy, but it was a great initiative by the community to involve MPs in a hands-on experience. For years the Canada Israel Committee had offered free trips to MPs and staff—a practice that continues—but it was rare to have a delegation hosted by a Palestinian organization. The highlight of the trip was a meeting with Yasser Arafat, head of the PLO. Originally scheduled for thirty minutes, it turned into a fascinating hour-plus meeting where Arafat spoke openly and with great clarity about the twists and turns for the peace he sought for his people. What was remarkable to me was his lack of rancour and bitterness, as a leader imprisoned in his own compound in Ramallah, with the Israeli Defense Forces (IDF) monitoring his every move.

Later that same year, Svend Robinson, Judy Rebick, and I were invited by the Concordia Student Union in Montreal to speak on campus at an event on Peace and Justice in the Middle East. The university had earlier cancelled a speech by Benjamin Netanyahu, then Israel's foreign affairs minister, due to protests, and instituted a moratorium on events concerning the issue. The university sought an injunction to prevent the three of us from speaking, and the Quebec Superior Court granted one for ten days. The Student Union vowed to go ahead with the event nonetheless, and we moved onto the street, standing on tables to be heard by hundreds of gathered students. It was the first time I'd faced an injunction for wanting to speak out publicly, and it reinforced the volatility of what it meant to be seen as supporting Palestine.

In August 2009, I returned to the area on a trip Kim organized with help from contacts she made with Code Pink. I cannot forget Kim and I rising before dawn in Gaza city, a city full of rubble and destruction, to meet the fishermen coming in with their small boats and paltry catch. The fish were small because the fishermen could not go far from shore, for fear of the IDF boats that would send warning shots across their bow. A small boy waited patiently on the dock as his father hauled in his meagre catch. As we talked to the fishermen, one of them said, "You will forget us when you leave. We live this every day." The sky was a glorious pink, streaked with light across the blue Mediterranean—yet the water was polluted by raw sewage as a result of the sewage system being destroyed by the IDF during Operation Cast Lead. Though he had little in life, the young boy looked at his father with great love. It was heartbreaking to know that thousands of children were without fathers and mothers and without a future because of the unrelenting bombing and destruction that had taken place during Operation Cast Lead earlier that year.

They call Gaza the largest open-air prison in the world, its 1.8 million inhabitants denied their human rights of life, liberty, and livelihood. When we visited, families were still living on the beach in UN tents, and block after block of apartment buildings—even the parliament building—were destroyed or severely damaged. My colleague Richard Nadeau, a wonderful, passionate MP from the Bloc, played with the kids on the beach who were attending a summer camp run by UNRWA (United Nations Relief and Works Agency for Palestine Refugees in the Near East)—a week's respite from debilitating living conditions and lack of basic provisions. While we had begun our visit in the West Bank, we were refused consular support or permission to enter Gaza. We gained access to Gaza through Egypt at the Rafah crossing, after driving from Cairo through multiple military checkpoints, spending a night in el-Arish, and waiting hours to have our papers processed, not knowing if we would be allowed in. It was a brief visit, but the intensity of what we heard became part of our report to Parliament when we returned. It seemed cruel that Canada's Conservative government would refuse to support the humanitarian work of UNRWA—a UN mandated agency—and portray them as Hamas sympathizers, when there was so much that needed to be done to provide basic relief.

We met with Dr. Eyad El-Sarraj, a well-known Palestinian psychiatrist who would pass away in 2013. In his back garden, we heard Dr. Sarraj describe the deep psychological damage that was a now an intergenerational trauma in the Palestinian community. As we sat there, we heard rumbling gunfire; he smiled and told us not to worry too much—it was the IDF making its presence known. We visited the illegal underground tunnels, used for transporting goods during the blockade, and spoke with businessmen who told us of the industrial district that had been systematically destroyed, flattening every enterprise to the ground. It was a shocking environment to witness and feel the sense of despair that was so much a part of the community.

Our trip included Jase Tanner, an independent filmmaker from Vancouver; Liberal MP Borys Wrzesnewskyj; Sarah Marois, who had been on a previous Code Pink trip with Kim; Ehab Lotayef, an activist from Montreal and our interpreter; as well as Richard Nadeau, Kim, and me. We all paid our own way. Unfortunately, Borys was only able to be with us as we visited parts of the West Bank including Ramallah, Bil'in, Hebron, and Jerusalem. The Liberal party, with Bob Rae as its interim leader, had refused to allow him to go to Gaza. In East Jerusalem we met with incredible Israeli activists, including Jeff Halper and Danny Seidemann. Their dedication to uphold international law and human rights was inspiring. We visited a site in Area C—an administrative division of the West Bank, where the Palestinian Authority is responsible for medical and educational services, though infrastructure construction is controlled by Israel. We saw a Palestinian house that had been demolished (one of thousands of demolitions under Israeli policy), and a Spanish youth peace brigade energetically engaged in building a new home by hand. We also met Dr. Mustafa Barghouti, an outspoken Palestinian parliamentarian who urged us to reach out to Canadian parliamentarians to pressure our government to call for an end to the occupation and bring peace and justice to the region.

We did indeed try to do that and upon our return to Canada—with the help of Ellie Russell, a terrific young intern from the UK working in my office—we produced a report with unequivocal recommendations. Ironically, many of our recommendations upheld the existing official policy of the Department of Foreign Affairs and International Trade (DFAIT) to halt illegal settlements, oppose the Separation Barrier, also known as the Wall, and to fund UNRWA. But the Conservative government under Harper had ideologically aligned itself as a non-critical "best friend" of Israel. We also called for an end to the cruel blockade of Gaza, which is still a humanitarian disaster today. I presented our modest and factual report in Parliament as part of a statement in November 26, 2009—wanting the report to be on the public record:

> Mr. Speaker, I am honoured that the report of the parliamentary delegation to the West Bank and Gaza this past August has been presented.
>
> It was a significant and compelling experience, and I am committed to raising awareness about the worsening humanitarian disaster in Gaza and the need to end the blockade, normalize borders and end the occupation of Palestinian lands.
>
> I am deeply concerned that the Conservative government has so politicized the situation in the Middle East and has gone so far as to attack MPs and organizations who criticize the actions of Israel as being anti-Semitic. Let us be clear. Antisemitism has no place in Canada.

Visiting a Palestinian refugee camp on the beach in Gaza, with filmmaker Jase Tanner and interpreter Ehab Lotayef, August 2009

Libby and Kim on the beach in Gaza City, August 2009

The Conservative attacks are reminiscent of McCarthyism and also have no place in Canadian society.

Rather than trying to silence and denigrate legitimate public debate, including its contempt of the Goldstone Report, the Conservative government must stand up for international law, human rights and the fourth Geneva Convention.

I hope all Members will consider this report and ensure that Canada affirms its commitment to peace and justice for Palestinians and for a lasting [peace].

Not surprisingly, a few days later James Lunney and other Conservative members challenged the legitimacy of the report and our right to present it, charging that we were violating House rules. Lunney asked the Speaker, Peter Milliken, to rule against us. So I gave a response to the Speaker, in the House and in writing, to make it clear that we had done nothing irregular and that it was nothing more than a scurrilous political tactic by the Conservatives to silence us. Speaker Milliken ruled in our favour.

The ongoing attacks, sometimes vicious ones, to silence any criticism of Israeli policies, became a sophisticated and successful tool for Conservatives and their allies to deploy. In earlier years, I had attended and hosted many events on the Hill concerning the situation in the Middle East and Palestine, by organizations such as the Canadian-Palestinian Educational Exchange (CEPAL) and the Middle East Discussion Group. Kim and other activists, including Hala Al Madi, Maysa Jalbout, Nader Hashemi, and Mohamad Barakat, consistently engaged with parliamentarians and the government. Dozens of MPs would attend to show their support. But the fearmongering by the Conservatives and their skill at labelling any criticism of Israel with charges of antisemitism had a chilling effect on the comfort of MPs to speak out. I encountered this many times; many MPs told me privately they were sympathetic to the issue, but they dared not say anything for fear of being branded. This type of political environment is reminiscent of the McCarthyism that had been so successful in the US during the Cold War.

Fear is a powerful weapon. I felt deeply saddened to see our Canadian Parliament succumb to it. The predominant perception in the parliamentary world was that the Jewish community was of one mind when it came to supporting the policies of Israel and its occupation of Palestinian land, and that no opposing view could be tolerated. Of course, this isn't true. Groups like Independent Jewish Voices are very outspoken in opposition to the occupation and the violation of human rights and international law. But still the big chill and self-imposed censorship took a toll on Parliament Hill and elsewhere.

The distance between the political world and what's really going on in the community can be wide and empty. Many campuses and student organizations have embraced the Boycott, Divestment, and Sanctions movement (BDS), and the United Church of Canada bravely supported economic action in regard to the occupied territories. Many Canadians support these positions too. But they have never translated well into the political arena—and still today the fear of being branded as antisemitic or anti-Israeli overpowers any debate. In February 2016 the Conservatives, now the Official Opposition, brought forward a motion "to reject the BDS movement" and calling for the government to "condemn any and all attempts by Canadian organizations . . . to promote the BDS movement, both here at home and abroad." Unfortunately, the new Liberal government voted for the motion, while trying to explain that they had no other option in the current political environment. I'm glad to say that the NDP, under Thomas Mulcair, did not.

There is a lot of work to be done on educating parliamentarians that it is okay to stand up for a decent Canadian policy on Israel and the Middle East that respects international law, and to defend it publicly without fear of reprisal. It may sound too simple, but our elected representatives need to know that they will have visible support in the community, and in their constituency, if they face McCarthyist tactics when they speak out and are charged with being anti-Israel or pro-terrorist. It's another example of the disconnect between electoral politics and social movement politics, and the need to engage in supportive and collaborative strategies.

It's incredibly frustrating, because many activists think, Why should I bother to educate and support these politicians? The reason is simple. If we want change, we need our elected representatives to be on board; we need them to oppose bad policies and fight for progressive change. So we need to figure out where our political allies are at, and what real or perceived barriers they face that prevent change from taking place. Groups like Canadians for Justice and Peace in the Middle East (CJPME), based in Montreal, and Independent Jewish Voices have valiantly striven to keep an open dialogue with parliamentarians about the Middle East. I applaud their work to bring forward factual briefings and discussion for MPs to consider. I only hope that more MPs respond and support the work being done in the community, sometimes at great personal cost.

I have no regrets about my work with Palestinians and the growing community that supports their cause for justice. I feel honoured to have made lifelong friendships and connections, over many years, with Jewish and Palestinian activists for peace and justice, in Canada, Israel, Palestine and in other parts of the world. I only loathe the toxicity of the politics surrounding the issue. Few other issues summon such a visceral and hateful response in politics from people who should and do know better.

The Closer You Get

S ometimes the most significant moments are when you lose. Maybe it's the effort of trying, of giving it your all against impossible odds. Or maybe it's the people who are there with you, who also know the odds are impossible but keep going anyway. That's what it felt like during the forty-eight-hour debate on back-to-work legislation against locked-out postal workers in June 2011. For the new Official Opposition—the NDP—it was nearly impossible to beat down the bill. But it galvanized the 103-member strong NDP caucus.

That battle brought back memories for me: as a new member in 1997, I also saw postal workers legislated back to work, though at that time by a Liberal government. I'd gotten my knuckles rapped because, in the wee hours of the morning, I had followed a passionate speech from a Bloc member and congratulated the member for such a fine speech—saying we were in this together to protect labour rights. Apparently, we weren't in this together, and I was criticized by an NDP staffer for being too sympathetic with the sovereigntist party. We voted against the back-to-work legislation in 1997, while supporting some nimble footwork by Pat Martin, who quietly and quickly negotiated an acceptable amendment.

In 2011 it was like magic to watch the new young members of the NDP caucus from Quebec sitting in the opposition lobby in the early hours of the morning. Sucking on coffee and tapping on laptops, they frantically wrote speeches for an important milestone—standing up to the ideologically powerful Conservatives and using the power of debate to show our strength and conviction about labour rights. Many of the new young MPs had been slagged in the media, told by cynical commentators that they were too young, too inexperienced, or too whatever else. It made me furious: the hypocrisy of constantly talking up the need for young people to be involved in politics and decrying the fact they don't vote, and then here they were—elected and about to change the way Parliament worked, yet belittled by people who said they shouldn't be there. It was a breath of fresh air to have the marble halls of Parliament Hill filled with young voices and new ideas. It felt like the maudlin politics of aged white men was finally being shaken up.

The 2011 election, weeks earlier, had been full of opportunity and even surprises, not only for the Orange Wave in Quebec, but also for the national outpouring of support for Jack who, despite his cancer, kept up an energetic and gruelling campaign pace. We all worried terribly about Jack and his health. But his walking stick, waved in the air at every rally, became a symbol of strength and defiance. None of the incumbent MPs who were running in 2011 had forgotten the tough caucus phone call we had, just prior to his press conference on February 5, 2010, announcing that he had prostate cancer. We had seen him soldier on, undertaking treatments, but also back in the House doing his duty. I think, in that 2011 election, we all had a grim determination to dig in. It would turn out to be the last one for Jack, though at the time none of us could imagine it. Our strength of party organization had never been better. There was a resolve to be the best we possibly could be, to defeat the Conservatives and their divisive, harmful agenda.

Volunteer Sheila Poznikofa helps me get out the vote on election day, 2011

On Jack's frequent visits to BC, he was enthusiastically greeted at large gatherings, welcomed almost as a hero. I took my mother, Margaret, then ninety-one years old, to the rally near the end of the campaign in a movie production hanger in Burnaby. You could barely make your way in, it was so packed with happy, energetic people. I found a seat for my mum, and she smiled broadly, so happy to see all the hoopla and eventually Jack, who came on stage with his cane. Everyone was buzzing about what was going on in Quebec, and we were following the campaign news closely, hardly believing our eyes and ears.

In Vancouver East the sense of excitement was palpable. We ran a great campaign, led by Janet Woo, our campaign office full of volunteers who wanted to see Harper gone and the NDP in the strongest position possible. I campaigned like I always did—up and down the streets, knocking on doors, getting prominent signs up, and meeting everyone I could. I even had time to attend a local poetry slam event;

An image from our 2011 campaign, managed by long-time staffer Janet Woo; I spent many a day in campaign offices in thirty-one years as an elected representative

I made my debut performance reading a poem I had hastily written at the campaign office as the phones were ringing off the hook.

Ode to East Van

The Drive is awash
people, skateboards,
Brother can you spare a dime
Smell the fair trade,
I mean coffee, washing over
Until we're soaking aroma

Brother can you spare a dime
I mean toonie

Dogs gotta eat
Homeless and community meet

Brother can you spare a dime
Million dollar houses
Shine
Shine till the blossoms fall
Don't forget the roots
Working class for all
Solidarity forever
May Day, Queer Day, Car Free Day
Peddle your feet

Brother can you spare a dime
Is an election a feat
Or fate or a crime
To some who see an imposition
What's your position?

Say No to Harper, Barker, Darker,
Prorogation doesn't work for the Nation

East Van alive, The Drive, thrive
I'm running to know
What do YOU know
May second, May 2
May after May Day

May we all
Go with courage to support
Our community
Unity

When news started to make its way from east to west, on the night of May 2, 2011, it felt like we could see over the Rocky Mountains, right into every seat that was turning orange in Quebec. We celebrated. But we also mourned. It was a bittersweet moment. Stephen Harper had won a majority in Parliament, and to put it bluntly, that meant some really bad shit was going to happen. Then came the realization that the NDP was, for the first time in history, the Official Opposition. We had a big job to do.

So on June 23, 2011, as the new Official Opposition went into debate around the clock, the new caucus was on fire. No doubt it's been forgotten now—just one of many, many debates. But I remember it as a night of renewal within our ranks. Anticipation of what lay ahead, and the possibility that one day we might actually be the government. Pride. And eagerness to take on the job as Official Opposition with strength and toughness, and hold the new government to account.

Though we all knew the legislation would pass, it was a good night. It bound us together with unity and purpose. I sent out tweets and Facebook messages, knowing that folks in BC were likely still up and watching—and indeed they were. Jack, despite his poor health and the pain he was in, gave a moving speech. Sitting next to him, I could hear Jack wince in pain every time he stood up to speak. I'd worked with Jack for years, but many of the new young members had barely met him, and some not at all until they were elected. Like many Canadians, they were inspired by Jack and what he stood for.

Two months later Jack was gone. I don't think many people, or the political pundits, really understood how hard it was for us. We were a family—and we had lost our best after having done our best. It was very hard to cope with. For the new MPs in particular, it was a time of deep loss mixed with the excitement of new beginnings and new experience. It was during this time that the caucus, new and old, showed what we were made of. We showed that we could continue with conviction and determination. We supported each other every day, and especially supported the new young members of Parliament who were still learning the ropes. We showed ourselves to be competent and worthy of the title Official Opposition.

At the last caucus meeting at the end of June before the House recessed for the summer, we gathered in Centre Block and Jack spoke to us via video conferencing from Toronto. We couldn't ignore how sick he looked or how weak his voice was. The stillness in the room as he spoke was disturbed only by our tears. He told us how proud he was and that we should be strong. He said he would be back.

I was able to see Olivia and Jack briefly before he died, on my way to the Canadian Medical Association conference in St. John's, Newfoundland. Two days later on the opening morning of the conference at about 8 a.m., August 22, a reporter came up to me and said, "Libby, we're getting information that Jack has died. Can you confirm this?" I could not. I immediately went into a nearby washroom—the only place I could escape to quickly—and phoned Anne McGrath. On a toilet seat with my voice echoing in the tiled bathroom, I whispered on the phone what the media were saying in the hallway. I sat silently as she confirmed he had died just hours earlier, and I knew I had to go back out and face the media. I mustered my resolve for calmness when it felt like my heart was breaking. I wanted to convey how important this man was in Canadian politics, and especially to all of us in the NDP. As I came from the washroom back into the hallway, the assembled media immediately gathered around and looked at me expectantly, waiting for comments. I did many interviews that day and was even asked to read his beautiful letter to Canadians out loud on the radio. That was hard to do.

To young Canadians: All my life I have worked to make things better. Hope and optimism have defined my political career, and I continue to be hopeful and optimistic about Canada. Young people have been a great source of inspiration for me.

Thomas Mulcair, Libby Davies, and Kim Elliott pay their respects to Jack Layton on Parliament Hill, August 2011

I have met and talked with so many of you about your dreams, your frustrations, and your ideas for change. More and more, you are engaging in politics because you want to change things for the better....

My friends, love is better than anger. Hope is better than fear. Optimism is better than despair. So let us be loving, hopeful and optimistic. And we'll change the world.

I phoned Kim, who was out hiking the steep trail on Signal Hill in St. John's, to let her know of Jack's death. As I spoke to her, she watched a feather fall from the sky. She brought it back to the hotel for me. We returned to Ottawa two days later, and as his casket left Parliament Hill on August 25, 2011, the driveway was lined with so many people from all walks of life. It felt like the end of a very sad chapter—but as he would want, in a book that still had a big story to tell.

I left Ottawa that day with Kim and went straight to a speaking engagement outside of Toronto for the National Union of Public and General Employees (NUPGE) leadership retreat. It might have been a good idea to beg off the event, and the union would absolutely have understood, but we went anyway. I did what I had done with Bruce, burying my feelings of loss and grief. It took me a long time to come to terms with Jack's death.

The day of the state funeral for Jack, we visited Nathan Phillips Square at Toronto city hall. It was surreal to walk among so many people, quietly lighting candles, pointing to the thousands of chalk sayings on the walls and ground, and speaking in soft voices about what Jack Layton meant to them.

After the funeral, a few of us had dinner together. Being good New Democrats, we embraced each other with buckets of tears and moved into intense discussion about what was next. Who would run, who should run for the leadership? This might seem a crass thing to do, the same day as the funeral. But it was part of our political nature and our closeness to Jack and each other to have such a discussion. Jack's leadership was a big part of our lives, and so was the question of what would follow. It was anticipated that Thomas Mulcair would run. Ed Broadbent sat at the head of the table and, after several bottles of wine, there was some discussion that Brian Topp should think about running. He knew the party well, had deep roots, was from Quebec, was fluently bilingual, and had experience working in NDP governments. No one worried too much that he'd never been elected.

When Parliament resumed in September, I would sit in the House and think, Where's Jack? Why isn't he here? I missed the rapid conversations we had. And I missed hearing him whistle in the hallway on the fourth floor of Centre Block. I missed him at caucus meetings, where his wise counsel had made everyone feel cared for and part of his family.

We worried about Olivia and the toll on her as, without Jack by her side, she went flat out with her MP work in Ottawa and the riding. I understood what she was going through: losing your beloved partner and political mate. We marvelled at her strength, and in the caucus, she kept everyone else going, never lightening her own burden or commitment.

Jack has many legacies; in many ways he changed the culture of the party and insisted that we become in practice a truly national, bilingual party reflecting both the official languages of Canada. Certainly, the purchase of a property for national party offices in downtown Ottawa was a huge accomplishment, with Jack personally raising much of the funds needed. My former colleague Chris Charlton noted that he brought about a much stronger style of management after the 2011 election when he became leader of the Official Opposition for a few short months before he died. There were, for example, more formal rehearsal sessions for daily question period and you could see MPs walking about the Official Opposition offices, intensely practising their questions. Up until about 2008 MPs mostly wrote their own questions, but now communications staff hammered out the questions of the day. Freelancing your own question was frowned apron. Likely Jack's most important legacy for the NDP was the intense debate and adoption of the Sherbrooke Declaration outlining the NDP's social democratic vision and relationship to Quebec. Creatively crafted by Pierre Ducasse, a party activist and contender in the 2003 leadership race, the declaration firmly committed the NDP to the notion of asymmetrical federalism and recognition of the people of Quebec's right to self-determination. After Jack's death, Canada's Official Opposition soldiered on under the committed leadership of interim leader Nycole Turmel. She had a very difficult job to do, holding the caucus together as we stood our ground in Parliament while waiting for a new leader to be elected by the party members. Nycole was tough and determined, and when Stephen Harper mocked her in question period, she would carry on undeterred.

⌒

I didn't support Thomas Mulcair for leader. It wasn't because I bore him any ill will from our fractured history on the Middle East. My decision had more to do with where the candidates stood on the issues. I liked the strength of Brian Topp, who was focusing on income inequality in his campaign.

Leadership campaigns (notably, I think, in the NDP) are odd affairs. You want to appeal to your base without seeming to attack your opponents—because it's their base too. Nevertheless, there can be nasty moments, and the 2012 leadership campaign was no exception. There was suspicion about the political direction Tom, as a former Quebec Liberal, would take the NDP, and whispers about Brian's lack of election experience. By the time we got to Toronto for the convention, things were tense. Leadership candidates Nathan Cullen, Peggy Nash, Niki Ashton, and Paul Dewar had all run good campaigns. Tom was clearly a very strong and capable candidate who had deep support in Quebec and elsewhere too. Still, those of us supporting Brian were hopeful.

Tom won on the fourth ballot. Olivia Chow and I were both asked by his team to be on stage when the new leader came forward to make his acceptance speech. Neither of us hesitated; we knew it was important to support the new leader immediately and wholeheartedly. And we did. He had the members fully with him, including me as his deputy leader, and a new day began for the NDP.

Many things have been written about Thomas Mulcair, and he's had many tags hung on him, including "angry Tom." But my overriding sense of the man is that he has strong convictions—and he's a secret stand-up comic! So often in question period he would quietly mimic government members and launch into brilliantly accurate Monty

Python voices that would crack me up. His reaction time was like lightning, and when he struck you knew it. I would describe him overall as complicated. At times incredibly confident and strong, staring Stephen Harper down like Perry Mason and leading caucus in the fight against the "Unfair" Elections Act or Bill C-51, which quashed civil rights in the name of security. But other times he seemed oblivious to what was going on around him in the caucus, and a few of us on his Planning and Priorities Committee would spell it out to no effect.

Tom set his sights on forming government and he wanted his caucus to be ready. He brought about discipline, knowledge, and determination. But there were flaws too. Jack was a party builder, and he was on the road constantly, setting a gruelling pace both in Parliament and outside. He stayed in close daily contact with people across the country and had an uncanny ability to make people believe they were his unique eyes and ears in their community. Tom was more focused on Ottawa, and at the beginning of his leadership, we all encouraged him to get out and about and build the base. He did some of this, but it wasn't his strength. His forte was in the House, where he excelled. But unfortunately most Canadians aren't glued to question period and its long, drawn-out debates. I think it's fair to say that under his leadership, the party shifted and we lost some of our activist base.

There's a seemingly never-ending debate within the NDP—and among progressives outside the party—about whether we are truly a left party or we are moving to the centre. Sometimes the pundits in Ottawa like to cast their eye to this question too and pontificate about NDP fortunes in the political spectrum. But the question can't be answered adequately without looking at the overall progression of Canadian politics. The rise of right-wing populism—most recently beginning with the Reform Party in the early 1990s—caused a massive shift. The formation of three Conservative governments under Harper dragged the political agenda more to the right, as did global forces of neoliberalism and undemocratic trade deals. That's not to say there wasn't massive resistance and some victories along the way—but in the electoral arena, politics moved overall to the right of the political spectrum.

Joe Comartin pointed out to me that under Chrétien there was an increase in control and centralization, as all parties responded to new technologies in getting their message out. More centralization and control at the top meant less independence for individual MPs. Less freelancing and less open contact with the public at large. Things inevitably became more conservative, even while claiming to be more innovative.

Successive leaders of all parties have played on the notion of modernization. It always seems to be a code for ushering in more central controls while moving closer to the mainstream arena of Canadian politics. Maybe some of that will change as we see grassroots movements gain strength and strong campaigns from people like Jeremy Corbyn in the UK and Bernie Sanders in the US gain a huge following among young people. I remain optimistic that left and even radical politics is going to find its place and grow in Canada.

Thomas Mulcair had my total loyalty—even when I disagreed with what we were doing. Our past under Jack was in the past. I simply let go of any sense of hurt and betrayal, choosing to focus on what was needed right now. I always felt that as leader he respected my opinions and was open to hearing a different point of view—but at the end of the day Tom would make his decisions, and many of us wondered who he really listened to. I have a lot of respect for Tom as leader. He had a difficult job to follow in the footsteps of Jack Layton and to show he was a loyal New Democrat. His style was at times harsh and at other times thoughtful and brave, showing his political smarts. He had a very loyal caucus, even though there was a storm gathering on the horizon about our readiness for the upcoming election in 2015.

We were a strong Official Opposition under both Jack Layton and Thomas Mulcair. The party had good front-bench strength of experienced

MPs and dynamic new members who learned with vigour and enthusiasm. Our MPs and staff worked hard and Tom showed his immense capabilities in the House. We had a few defections along the way—who doesn't?—but by and large we were a solid and united group. A group resolved to carry on the legacy of Jack Layton for the people of Canada.

The Long Haul

O f all the issues I worked on both as a city councillor and member of Parliament, the issue of sex work was the hardest. It was divisive and full of conflict. Like John Loman—the criminologist at Simon Fraser University, who did years of painstaking research to demonstrate that federal laws were killing sex workers—and like others who supported decriminalization, I was attacked by people who advocated an abolitionist approach. I was told I was supporting the slavery of women and condemning women to exploitation and violence.

As a feminist myself, this was hard to take. Having spoken to many sex workers, and having seen the evidence gathered by the parliamentary committee in 2003 and its report of 2006, as well as Loman's analysis, I knew beyond a shadow of a doubt that the current laws were harmful and had to go. I believed, and still do, that the state should not criminalize consenting adult sexual activities, whether or not money is involved. The law does need to focus on exploitation, coercion, violence, and harm—as is the case for any sexual assault, domestic violence, or exploitation. But making consenting sex work, and sex workers and their customers, illegal at all times, is not only unrealistic but also horribly harmful.

In the NDP caucus it was a touchy subject. During my early days of being an MP, my colleagues just didn't see it as an issue worth raising and felt it was too controversial. Many a time I felt frustrated at the subtle and sometimes not-so-subtle hints that I was overdoing it, and I knew that many of my colleagues thought I had become obsessed with the issue. They were probably right. I couldn't let it go, because it was obvious (at least to me) what needed to be done. It was only bad laws and lack of political courage that obstructed a better outcome.

In 2013, Katrina Pacey from Pivot—a legal advocacy organization based in the Downtown Eastside that worked with sex workers—approached me to ask what I thought about trying to advance a clear resolution on decriminalization of sex work through the NDP, so that at least one party would be clearly in favour of decriminalization. Having co-operated with Katrina over many years, I greatly admired her work and bravery. Pivot's groundbreaking documentation of the precarious life of sex workers, which was aided and abetted by archaic laws, helped transform the debate on these controversial issues. It ensured that the people directly affected were heard on the national stage. Pivot worked from evidence-based research and demanded public policy based on evidence. Katrina, a brilliant young lawyer, was also one of the intervenors in the historic case, *Bedford v. Canada*, that was then before the Supreme Court of Canada.

Although the NDP had spoken out against the current laws that criminalized sex workers, the party's official position did not go as far as supporting decriminalization. I knew it was going to be one of those tough issues where there would be internal opposition to taking a clear stand, but I agreed with Katrina that we should try. She drew up a resolution and we submitted it through the Vancouver East NDP riding association for the upcoming NDP convention in Montreal. I spoke with a few of my colleagues in Ottawa who were supportive on the issue, and a small group of us—MPs Craig Scott, Megan Leslie, Randall Garrison, and Niki Ashton—spent weeks strategizing an approach for getting such a resolution through at the convention. We worked closely with allies in the sex-worker community, including Jenn Clamen, a sex-worker rights activist and national co-ordinator of the Canadian Alliance for Sex Work Law Reform. We were also delighted to learn that two activists in the sex-worker community—Émilie Laliberté and Anna-Aude—had joined the NDP and wanted to help get the resolution passed.

The first hurdle was to get the resolution prioritized for debate, which meant attending an in camera panel session to make sure it got voted as one of the top three or four resolutions. Only then would the resolution make it through to the main plenary session for an open debate and a vote. Having tried unsuccessfully at previous conventions to get resolutions through on sex-worker rights, I knew we were in for an uphill battle. Members of the NDP weren't by and large against decriminalization, but party officials and the leader's office saw it as a divisive and a non-strategic election issue. To me—having seen so many sex workers harmed and killed as a result of the current laws—it was an urgent matter.

I really wanted my party to be brave and to speak out—despite the controversy surrounding the issue and the abolitionist argument that full decriminalization was exploitation. I wanted the NDP to be the first national party to be clear on where it stood. The first panel where our resolution was to come up was a packed room of delegates. You could feel the anticipation; people knew it was going to be a big debate. We were fortunate that party president Rebecca Blaikie chaired the discussion. She guided the meeting with skill and fairness. Some of our high-profile MPs were not happy with the resolution that was presented; they thought it went too far and would only create division. But we pushed on, and Niki Ashton made an impassioned plea for sex-worker rights. She got a great response. We left the room feeling very upbeat that we had successfully gotten the resolution high enough on the list to ensure debate at the plenary session.

It was no surprise to learn that opposition to the resolution was also mounting. We heard that the leader's office was now expressing its concern, and there were MPs ready to hit the plenary floor to speak against the resolution. No one in our small group wanted polarization, and we certainly didn't want the setback of a defeated resolution. So we had a very strategic decision to make: fight it through and quite possibly lose the resolution on the convention floor, or seek a referral back to federal council to work on the wording some more. We huddled in the hallways trying to decide on the best course. After much anguish and weighing of the pros and cons, we opted for a referral back to federal council, but only if we could be assured of specific instructions on a timeline to ensure the resolution wasn't mothballed. We also negotiated an agreement with convention organizers that we would make the motion for the referral ourselves, and set the tone by speaking to it briefly on the convention floor.

It was not easy to explain these tactical decisions to our sex-worker allies, who, in good faith, had come to convention to see the full resolution debated. They felt very let down. It reinforced for me how "inside" a game political parties and conventions are, and how used we were to adapting to changing political dynamics around us. For someone not used to that environment, it can look convoluted, unprincipled, and messy. Conventions can be contrived and manipulated, but they can also be wonderful examples of grassroots member democracy at work.

We agreed that I would speak to the referral motion and explain why we were taking this course. We also agreed that Émilie and Anna-Aude would speak to make it clear how important the issue was—for them, it was a matter of life and death. That was a pivotal moment at the convention. Never before had sex workers addressed a national political convention, and they received a standing ovation. It was a victory even though the resolution was not passed that day. We knew we had successfully navigated a tricky situation. Later, Craig Scott put his legal mind to work and crafted the new wording:

Resolution on sex worker rights

WHEREAS Canadian values include respect for human and labour rights of all persons, including the right to life, liberty, security, equality and freedom of expression and association as set out in the Canadian Charter of Rights and Freedoms;

WHEREAS an unacceptable number of sex workers in Canada have experienced extreme violence, murder or have become missing persons;

WHEREAS the current legal framework has caused many Canadian communities and neighbourhoods to experience tensions, conflicts and disruptions often pitting neighbour against neighbour;

WHEREAS adult sex workers have the right to live and work in conditions that are safe, healthy and free from violence and discrimination;

WHEREAS social science and public health research in Canada has found that criminalization of adult sex work endangers sex workers and deprives them of the means of preventing coercion and violence, as well as constituting a barrier to sex workers' ability to protect their safety and health;

WHEREAS Canadian courts, the Parliamentary Subcommittee on Solicitation Laws and the Missing Women Commission of Inquiry each concluded that criminalization of sex workers increases the violence perpetrated against them.

THEREFORE BE IT RESOLVED THAT the federal NDP will:

- Advocate for the rights and safety of sex workers;
- Work with all stakeholders to end exploitation and violence;
- Condemn the countless number of assaults, murders and missing-persons disappearances continuing to be perpetrated on Canadian sex workers;
- Recognize that the current legal framework places sex workers in unacceptably dangerous situations;
- Within the above framework, oppose the enactment of legislation that prohibits the purchase or sale of adult sexual services given that evidence shows such laws increase the risk of violence and other harms to sex workers;
- Work, in consultation with sex workers, affected communities, police, justice officials and other stakeholders to identify and repeal those sections of the Criminal Code of Canada pertaining to adult activities involving sex work that undermine the rights to life, liberty, security, health, equality and freedom of expression and association of sex workers; and carry out this work through an evidenced-based, human rights, and labour rights approach;
- Call for a federal strategy that encompasses prevention, education, harm reduction, and safety for sex workers and affected local communities, including safe exit strategies, addressing critical issues that affect the freedom to choose one's work, including conditions of poverty, discrimination, inequality, poor housing and under/un-employment;
- Take note of the Supreme Court Decision of *Bedford v. Canada* pertaining to this issue.

That October I attended the federal council meeting on behalf of our MP group and spoke to the revised wording we had submitted. The federal council approved it unanimously. To me, and I think to the four other MPs who championed the issue, it was a positive example of the political process at work. Trying to keep everyone on the same page, not piss off too many people, and keep principles and integrity front and centre—but to be smart about it. And most of all, to engage constructively with activists, in this case sex workers, who never thought they'd be in the spotlight at a political convention.

On December 20 of that year, the Supreme Court of Canada handed down its historic ruling, *Bedford v. Canada*, throwing out the harmful laws. Of course, it never ends there—a party resolution, and even a Supreme Court of Canada ruling, is only one part of it. What happens afterwards is just as significant.

We had a difficult time getting attention that the resolution had been passed and that the NDP had taken a strong position. There were still party members who wanted the resolution conveniently forgotten. But we did our best to make it known in the community, and I felt overall my party had done okay. In Parliament it was another matter. The court ruling gave Parliament a deadline to change the laws—but of course the Conservatives mashed it up, and after lengthy and contentious summer hearings by the Justice Committee, Bill C-36, the *Protection of Communities and Exploited Persons Act*, was passed in November 2014. In the sex-worker community, a strong consensus emerged that the new law was harmful and certainly did not embody a decriminalization position. And so, the work continues. For me and many others it was movement forward, only to be blocked again by the Conservatives' harshly partisan agenda.

A decision by the Supreme Court of Canada brought things to a head in the face of Conservative attempts to lower the boom on Insite as well. It had taken about six years of slogging work by many us from many different walks of life to see North America's first safe-injection

Responding to the Supreme Court of Canada ruling on Insite, Ottawa, September 2011, with Dean Wilson and Nathan Allen

site, Insite, successfully up and running by 2003. The Vancouver facility had been able to maintain its operation, despite many twists and turns in the political world to stop it. In September 2011 the Supreme Court had mandated the legitimacy of Insite's operation and life-saving measures. As was the case with sex work, the court gave the federal government a window to comply with its ruling.

In October 2013 the Conservatives introduced Bill C-2, the so-called *Respect for Communities Act*, in response to the Supreme Court's ruling. The bill was predicated on such onerous and, frankly, ridiculous criteria to establish a safe-injection site, that it was clear it had been written so as to make it nearly impossible for any application—including

Celebrating Insite's tenth anniversary on East Hastings Street with Earl Crowe (*left*) and Bud Osborn, 2013

a renewal application from Insite—to be approved by the minister of health. For years the Conservatives had battled Insite and tried to cast it as an evil, harmful service. They ignored the dozens of scientific reports that showed its value, and they campaigned against it at every opportunity. But now, even up against a Supreme Court ruling, they were determined to eliminate any possibility for such life-saving health services in Canada.

The day they introduced the legislation in the House of Commons, the Conservatives simultaneously launched a party fundraising appeal to exploit fears about drugs, drug use, and criminals. It was a shameful manoeuvre and so transparently a self-serving political one that it was almost laughable. Except that they were playing with people's lives and real need for health care.

When speaking in the House for the NDP, I felt such anger and disgust about the bill and the government that created it. I have no

March to stop the war on drugs, Washington, DC, while attending the International AIDS Conference, 2012

problem with honestly held disagreements and differing positions in politics—that's part of public discourse. But when a government deliberately engages in deceit and fear for its own political purpose, contrary to the public interest, it's easy to understand how people get so turned off from politics. The NDP held up the bill as long as we could, using every tactic available, to delay its passage through the House of Commons and on to the Senate. It was one of the last bills the Conservative government pushed through before the federal election of 2015, and it took us backward not forward.

The fight against Bill C-2 was ultimately a losing one, with a Conservative majority government, but even so the spirit in the community was resilient and strong. Especially in the case of Bud Osborn, who continued with many others to speak out against the criminalization of people who use drugs and the impact of the war on drugs on their lives. Bud's 2009 book *Raise Shit*, with Donald MacPherson and Susan C. Boyd, had given a vibrant account of what had taken place in the Downtown Eastside to establish rights and dignity for people who use drugs. The passage of Bill C-2 could not stop Bud's continued activism or the powerful movement to end the war on drugs.

Recently, in October 2017, Donald MacPherson, Vancouver's first drug policy co-ordinator and now executive director of the Canadian Drug Policy Coalition, gave a lecture after winning the Nora and Ted Sterling Prize from Simon Fraser University. Called "Heroin at Your Corner Store," it argued for the need to move from prohibition and a corporate model of drug distribution (as we are now seeing with legalized marijuana) by creating a "drug supply through public health distribution." The drug crisis is far from over. The staggering number of overdose deaths across the country demands bold solutions—most critically a safe supply of drugs, so people are not captive to a poisonous drug market. In the face of a growing crisis of overdose deaths, debate and action in Vancouver continue to lead the way.

Around the time the Conservatives' *Respect for Communities Act* was being debated in Ottawa, things were heating up at home too. The PHS Community Services Society was under intense public scrutiny as a result of an audit that questioned the organization's expenditures and ethics. It wasn't the first time an organization in the Downtown Eastside had been raked through media fires for its practices, but in this instance, the anger was staggering about how the PHS spent money. Many in the community defended the organization because they knew first-hand— as I did—that it provided critical housing and services to the most marginalized people. And for many years, it had influenced changing attitudes about people who use drugs. The PHS had also run Insite in an exemplary way, despite all the opposition waged against its operation from the powers that be in Ottawa. Controversial spending decisions—even though many did not involve use of public funds—provided a fertile ground for a political gang-up on the PHS by the BC Liberal government, and the media dribbled out information day by day to shock the public.

I knew it was inevitable that I would be asked to comment. This didn't bother me; it was part of my job to respond to issues in the media. But I have to say that the interview with Stephen Quinn on CBC, March 25, 2014, was one of the worst interviews I ever did. I was told in the pre-brief that the interview wasn't going to focus on the expenditure scandal but rather on the importance of the work that the PHS did in the community. I should have known that it would focus, anyway, on the highly publicized expenditures on hotels, trips, and personal items. Quinn hammered away at me, demanding to know if I condemned such expenditures as outrageous for an organization that worked in the Downtown Eastside. It felt like that famous loaded question to a witness in court: When did you stop beating your wife? I absolutely didn't want to be part of the gang-up on the PHS. And as Quinn wrote a few days later in his *Globe and Mail* column, I "was going around in circles" in my defence of them. He was also taken aback, he said, at the tweets and reaction he received from people who were mad about the interview and his harshness regarding the PHS.

On my end, I felt like I had indeed gone around in nonsensical circles, trying to do the impossible: defend a great organization while neither condoning nor condemning their budgetary expenditures. Such is live media. And you have to live with it. I've always had great respect for individual journalists, even when I knew they were out to get me. That's the nature of politics and the relationship with the media. They are your friend but also your enemy. By and large I could handle myself well, even in difficult situations—but there were days I wished I could turn it off or press a different replay button.

In May of that year, the community grieved the loss of Bud Osborn. The last time I saw him was in hospital, a few days before he was discharged. He died at home shortly afterward. I counted him not only as one of my closest friends but also as someone who taught me about the real impact of the American-style war on drugs and how it destroyed people's lives. Bud was a very special person in the Downtown Eastside community, but his reach went far beyond the core of Main and Hastings. His influence, as he spoke out against the criminalization of people who use drugs, became national and international in scope. He inspired many and lifted the voices of people who were forgotten to national prominence.

Bud would talk often about the demonization of people who use drugs, and his poetry spoke to us in a way that is simply unforgettable. He was creative, politically astute, and a leader. His life experience as a drug user, including several attempts to take his own life, and his tenuous relationship with society made him unique. He spoke like no one else could to the drug crisis in the community, and people listened to him—from the most humble people on the street to the most powerful people in office. A small circle of us did our best to support him throughout his tumultuous life in the Downtown Eastside; Liz Evans, Dave Diewert (who took extraordinary care of Bud), Jean Swanson, Donald MacPherson, and Ann Livingston showed what friendship really means.

These issues had a global dimension too. Svend Robinson, no longer an MP and working for the Global Fund to Fight AIDS, Tuberculosis and Malaria, recommended me in about 2010 to chair an advisory committee of MPs for the Inter-Parliamentary Union (IPU) on HIV/AIDS, sex work, and criminalization of drug users. The IPU was a long-standing non-governmental organization (NGO) made up of individual parliamentarians, sort of like the UN but for members of parliaments. It was an excellent venue to engage with parliamentarians from member countries and connect to work being done by UNAIDS, the World Health

Organization, and the Global Fund (where Svend was senior parliamentary liaison). The IPU allowed us to work together on issues including development, human rights, health, international affairs, and peace. Collaborating with MPs from Africa, South America, Europe, and Asia was informative and rewarding, and it broadened my understanding of the global nature of HIV/AIDS and its impact on marginalized populations.

As an advisory committee, we urged MPs to speak out on these issues and not abandon their constituents who were in desperate need of health care and support. We wanted to show that as elected representatives we could both be successful in politics and advocate to stop the criminalization of people who were marginalized and ignored. Especially in countries where drug users, sex workers, and people infected with HIV, as well as men who have sex with men, were vilified, jailed, and at grave risk of violence and death. On these issues, I was inspired by the leadership of Svend and his work with parliamentarians around the globe through the Geneva-based Global Fund. I felt part of a connected global effort of like-minded parliamentarians, as small a group as we were, to effect change.

Svend and I have always been close political buddies and friends. He was the first person I turned to the day after I was elected in 1997; a few days later we had lunch at Paul's restaurant on East Hastings Street in Burnaby, not far from his constituency office. I peppered him with questions about Parliament and the NDP, and he patiently answered all my queries and gave me advice. We were political allies on many issues, and I learned from Svend the importance of never forgetting the needs of your constituents and riding. On occasion we would hit a rough spot, usually around tactics, and his demanding expectations of what needed to be done would challenge me to the core.

In 2014 we attended the World AIDS Conference in Melbourne and shared a hotel room to minimize costs. We have a great camaraderie and a deep personal connection. Things were going swimmingly until

With Svend Robinson at Vancouver APEC protest, 1997

the sensitive subject of the bombing of Gaza came up. We had worked together on many occasions on the Middle East and justice for Palestinians, and Svend expressed his view that I needed to speak out publicly to counter the NDP's near silence. He knew I wasn't the party's spokesperson on foreign affairs. I had already organized an internal letter, signed by a number of MPs, to the leader and foreign affairs spokesperson to signify our deep concern that the party was not speaking out boldly enough to condemn yet another attack on Gaza. "That's not good enough," Svend said. He went further to say that were he still in caucus, he couldn't tolerate such a poor stance from the NDP and would resign from his post.

There it was, the ultimate political dilemma: Do you resign in protest because your party has failed on a critical matter, or do you stay and push where you can? We had a fearful row. I argued that my resignation from my duties wouldn't help the Palestinians at all. It would only divide the NDP and allow the media yet again to use me as fodder to attack the leader and undermine all the decent things we stood for. It was the last day of the conference, and I moped around thinking about what he had said, full of doubt. Maybe he was right and I needed to speak out and oppose the party publicly, and then resign from my position, despite the damage it would do to the party and the caucus of elected MPs.

Even today, I think of these dilemmas that arose over the years, where I felt offside with the stance of the party and the caucus. My nature was to battle on—inside the party—and do what I felt I could publicly without undermining my colleagues and the team overall. Maybe I'm right, maybe I'm wrong, but it's a dilemma you have to play out issue by issue and instance by instance. It has to be one of the toughest elements of political life to navigate. And the closer you are to the centre of leadership, the harder it is to be offside. When do you cross that line and say everyone else is wrong and you're right?

Being in Ottawa can be a lonely affair—your family thousands of miles away and a gruelling daily routine. But you get used to it and it somehow becomes "normal." Of course, there are times when there's just no semblance of normal. The rush of the House takes over everything, from overnight debates, hours of voting standing row by row, and days of filibusters at parliamentary committees. I considered myself extremely fortunate to have my partner Kim in Ottawa, and I was always happy to return to my second home each night, even if it was close to midnight, down the hidden laneway off Bell Street in Chinatown. I was never happier to get home than October 22, 2014, the day a lone gunman killed a young soldier at the national monument and then set his sights on Parliament Hill.

The NDP caucus room at the time was just off the main hallway in Centre Block. It was a regular Wednesday caucus morning, until we heard multiple gunshots ring out, right outside our closed door. We hit the floor with no idea of what might come bursting through. Lying next to me, my fellow MP Peter Stoffer whispered, "Are you okay, Libby?" and I nodded my head, feeling quite calm and empty of emotion of any sort, as the seconds ticked by like hours. It's hard to imagine that MPs came that close to disaster. I always wondered if the gunman knew he was just a few feet and a doorway away from the government caucus on one side of the hallway and the Official Opposition on the other. Much has been written about the incident, and it was disturbing to see how volatile some of the analysis was, playing into fear about terrorism.

We spent the rest of that day lying under tables in East Block, adjacent to the main building of Parliament. We had been taken through the underground tunnel, still not fully knowing what was transpiring. Sometimes we whispered back and forth under the tables, legs and arms at all angles; at other times there was utter silence as we heard security personnel outside the door on their walkie-talkies. Our treasured BlackBerry devices had mostly run down, and if they were still on, they were jammed because of an overload on the parliamentary server. We were allowed to use the washroom once in groups of three and four; we crept silently from one hallway to another with armed personnel, in full assault gear, on guard to make sure our path was clear.

Was this for real? echoed in my brain. A female officer stood guard in the washroom, as we did our business as fast as possible. East Block houses many offices for senators, and on the ground floor, we raided the small cafeteria kitchen, grabbing anything we could find. Including the best tuna sandwich I have ever eaten. We were finally allowed to leave at about 7 p.m., when we were sent in the small green parliamentary buses to the Lester B. Pearson Building to be debriefed. It wasn't much of a debriefing—officials only wanted to know if we had seen anything. It took ages to get a taxi from there, as hundreds of MPs were let out into the night, all in a rush to leave.

I was lucky that I got to go home and not to an empty hotel room. I treasured Kim's welcoming presence as she opened the door to me and our neighbours, MPs Chris Charlton and Jean Crowder, who lived down the lane. Kim had made a wonderful vegetarian chili, and the four of us huddled for hours talking about the day's events. Kim, too, had been caught in the lockdown and had spent most of the day in Ian Capstick's office, MediaStyle, on Bank Street, where she had been for a meeting. To be able to debrief with family and friends made such a difference—what a relief to be at home with people I was close to. When I first met Kim in that old house on Flora Street I worried about the parties she mentioned. But now they are a part of my life that is beautiful and social because they symbolize Kim's joy of giving to people. We had many dinners over the years with Chris and Jean, and other MPs who came to visit; it made my life in Ottawa feel balanced even when extraordinary things happened. Most of all though, it was Kim who kept me balanced in my personal life. Her caring and generosity is boundless, to me and to her many friends. She works tirelessly to maintain independent media at the non-profit *rabble.ca*, but I love that she still finds the time to take extraordinary photographs of the places we experience.

After the 2011 election I became the party's health critic, and it became my task to update our policy and program on health care. Jack said he wanted me to go across the country and expand our vision for Canada's public health care system, which was suffering from neglect and lack of federal leadership. I travelled the country seeking input and holding town hall meetings to gain insight and fresh ideas to strengthen medicare, which was always under threat from privatization.

In late October 2014, MP Murray Rankin approached me and said he'd heard from an old friend that thalidomide survivors in Canada were going to make a big public push to demand government compensation. The "thalidomiders" are people whose mothers had been prescribed the drug thalidomide in the late 1950s and early 1960s for morning sickness during pregnancy. The drug caused congenital malformations. They desperately needed compensation for serious health issues that had been ignored by many governments over many decades. I contacted the public relations people who were helping the association pro bono, and suggested we might be able to help by getting a motion passed in Parliament calling for compensation. They were very open to the idea, and eventually I met the extraordinary Mercedes Benegbi, from Montreal, head of the Thalidomide Victims Association. I told her the NDP would do everything it could to help get compensation, and I immediately set to work on wording for a motion. We needed government support for the motion, so the wording was key. It would have been be easy to fire off a quick motion condemning the government for its inaction, and that would have been it—a one-day alarm bell, resulting in a defeated motion. That was the last thing the thalidomide survivors needed.

It was here that my years of parliamentary experience came to my aid. To get something concrete accomplished, I first needed to convince the leader's office—and the leader himself—that we should use one of our valuable opposition day motions on the issue of thalidomide compensation. Second, I had to convince them that the aim was to get a substantive motion passed in Parliament, not just to score political points, as often happens on opposition day motions. When I made my pitch to Tom, he was very supportive, and so, with Murray Rankin's support, I submitted wording for the motion.

Usually in such circumstances the opposition doesn't divulge to the government, in advance, the issue and wording of its planned motion to be debated in the House. The element of surprise is part of the game plan. But in this case, if we were to be successful, I knew it was absolutely necessary to get the support of the minister of health, Rona Ambrose, and the Conservative government in advance. One day after question period, I walked across the aisle and told her what I was up to and that, if she was in favour, I would show her the wording. After some discussion the minister said she was. For the next couple of days, we went back and forth adjusting the wording to meet government concerns while keeping the substance intact. I made sure to let the survivors association know how things were going, and also talked to the Liberals and the Green party to seek their support, which they readily gave.

The Thalidomide Victims Association itself did incredible work, lobbying MPs and holding press conferences urging Parliament to act. For many thalidomiders it was their first experience on Parliament Hill, and maybe even in the political world. Their courage to share deeply personal information about their lives and what it was like to cope with severe physical limitations and obstacles was unparalleled. It could not be ignored. You could see the emotional toll on each person as they navigated an unknown place with dignity and determination.

The night of the vote, December 1, 2014, was emotionally charged. Thalidomide survivors cheered and wept in the public gallery as they witnessed the 256 MPs present vote solemnly in favour of the motion for full support for the nearly a hundred thalidomide survivors in Canada. There were zero MPs opposed.

Some months later a negotiated compensation package was announced by the government and the association. It was a positive example that we can put aside partisan attacks and mudslinging and just do the right thing. Parliamentarians can work together on occasion, and it doesn't have to be a rare thing, when there is good faith and trust.

It was soon after that that I announced I wasn't seeking re-election in the upcoming 2015 federal election. It felt like I had done my job with as much fortitude as I could muster, and it was time to leave.

Back to Third

Many things have been written about the 2015 federal election, which sent the NDP back to third place with a Liberal majority government in power. Having retired from political office prior to the election, I nevertheless helped with the national campaign in BC. What the NDP did or didn't do—or should have done—has been the subject of much debate. What I think about is our drift... like a lifeboat cast from the mothership.

The common analysis is that the NDP abandoned some of its traditional social democratic principles and Thomas Mulcair took the party to the centre, in the hope that we would attract more centre-minded voters, particularly when it came to supporting balanced budgets. But it's a lot more complicated than that. I think we lost the imagination of the voters because we thought being an efficient and pragmatic electoral machine would do the job. It didn't begin with Tom; it began earlier as attention focused on "winning"—not at any cost, but by drifting at the margins.

What I dwell on is thinking that said, it's what's happening in Parliament that Canadians pay attention to and determines how they will vote in an election. That thinking bolstered our hope that we could win in 2015. Certainly, what happens in Parliament is enormously important. The terrible legislation passed by Harper's government, his disregard for democracy, his secrecy, arrogance, and elitism, it was all part of a decade of darkness. Fighting the government in Parliament was our job, and we did it well. But somewhere along the way we lost our bigger vision and connection with people, including some of our base, as we became focused on winning. We forgot how to be creative and bold outside of Parliament and bring people with us.

One example involved the legalization of marijuana. I cannot fathom why we didn't clearly take a stand. Instead we let the Liberals walk all over us with their pronouncements on marijuana. For years the NDP had led the way on drug policy reform; we had been the first federal party in 1971 to call for the decriminalization of marijuana before legalization was even raised. The need for a regulatory and legalized approach is obvious—just as it was during the prohibition of alcohol. But somehow, despite excellent resolutions crafted by NDP marijuana activist Dana Larsen calling for such an approach from more recent NDP provincial and national conventions, we couldn't say it clearly and unambiguously. We wrapped ourselves in a blanket that we were protecting ourselves from Conservative attacks and that it was a niche issue that only a few people cared about. I fought tooth and nail, along with Dave Christopherson in caucus, to get us on the right track. And many in the caucus supported a position of being bold and outspoken on the issue. In the end, we settled on lines that were so nuanced that they just missed the point. New Liberal leader Justin Trudeau was on the issue and we looked like tag-alongs, showing up after the fact.

The report of a parliamentary committee studying marijuana gave me the opportunity to table the NDP position in the House on June 15, 2015. Having worked closely with Steve Moran, the NDP's head of parliamentary affairs and deputy chief of staff, I hoped the statement would make our policy clear—despite avoiding the term "legalization." In part the statement read: "An NDP government would: Establish an independent commission with a broad mandate, including safety and public health, to consult Canadians on all aspects of the non-medical use of marijuana and to provide guidance to Parliament on the institution of an appropriate regulatory regime to govern such use." Unfortunately our position was either ignored, or criticized by pro-legalization groups who thought the NDP had not gone far enough.

Of course that issue didn't lose us the election. But it's a nagging example of the mindset we got ourselves into. We acted cautiously and too late. The same with climate change, and natural resource management, including pipelines. We started on the right path and then somewhere along the way let ourselves limp along—becoming cautious and careful when people wanted boldness. As often happens in federal politics, we became focused on "managing" what was perceived as a difficult issue, particularly as it impacted various provincial party interests, rather than simply doing the right thing. No political party is exempt from this kind of game plan; maybe it's an inevitable outcome of our federation and its complexity of federal/provincial/territorial relations. But there are moments when it is necessary to speak truth to power. I think of the history of the NDP and its opposition to the *War Measures Act* during the 1970 October Crisis or the original anti-terrorism legislation in 2001, or earlier, speaking out against the internment of Japanese Canadians during the Second World War—these were historic moments that displayed courage and integrity.

All of this to say, I am an optimist by nature and proud of so much of what the NDP does and stands for. I know we face formidable double standards in the mainstream media. Regardless of how well we do, they would still find a way to trash or ignore us. On that I am cynical. All the more reason for us to be smarter than all of them, and find new ways to do politics with people who have a passion for social justice and a better world.

In these political times, the NDP is needed more than ever. The rise of right-wing populism even here in Canada and the underwhelming position of Trudeau's Liberal government on crucial issues such as climate change, democratic electoral reform, income inequality, and more make it crucial for the federal NDP to stand tall and unwavering in its commitment to a boldly progressive agenda. We must embrace a post-fossil-fuel economy and lead the way on an economic and social transition to it, and demonstrate that retraining, good jobs, and social advances create a healthier economy and healthier society overall. We have nothing to lose and everything to gain when we stand by what we believe in and learn from the historical roots that are our foundation. Tommy Douglas brought public health care that we couldn't now not imagine. Jack Layton brought hope and optimism that a different kind of politics and country is possible. I know we have the ability and capacity to realize a vision with Canadians where people live their lives to the fullest potential without destroying the environment around us.

I've been fascinated by this question of how progressive elected representatives, political parties, and social activists work together, and why it is such a challenge for us when we believe in many of the same values. The intersection between the political world of social activists and the world of people in elected office—who are progressive, and on the left—can create misunderstanding and a tense relationship. Social activists can act more freely to achieve their goals for change, and they don't face the same demands and constraints as those in or running for elected office. Activists see their job as primarily putting pressure on the people in power to make change happen. Their motivation is to win on an issue.

Here you find the dilemma of social movement actors backing the political party that supports—and can implement—the issue they are advocating for. (And this, of course, is not always seen as the NDP.) Activists are not necessarily as aware of what other pressures those in political parties or elected office might face from a hostile media, unrelenting conservative forces, or the political games of other parties. Players on the electoral side of things may come to see social activists or "pressure groups" as another element to be managed as they endeavour to carry out their political mandate, even though both sides may share commonly held values and beliefs about what needs to be done. These are two very different political arenas, each with its own culture, its own way of operating, different constraints, and quite different roles in the overall movement for change. So in many ways, it's not surprising that a lack of understanding and mistrust develops.

It has been mind-boggling to watch these two worlds unfold and sometimes collide. At times it was like watching a political Shakespearean drama with self-important stars, misunderstood actions and counteractions, puzzlement, and strange manoeuvres. There are so many conflicting variables at play. Activists both within and outside the party become turned off and cynical when, as electoral success comes within reach, they see their party compromise on a key issue or become more interested in raising money for an election. People in the activist community and the labour movement recoil from the highly partisan nature of politics, believing it conflicts with opportunities for achieving overall change, beyond the agenda of any one political party. You need to look no further than the 2015 federal election to see this scenario in play.

Many activists and progressive movements wanted more than anything else to defeat Harper after ten years in office as prime minister. And many engaged in various forms of strategic campaigning and voting to achieve that, often to the detriment of the NDP. There was also frustration from NDP members and supporters that the party sacrificed a stand on fiscal policy in favour of balanced budgets, even though the platform overall was strong and progressive. It's a tough conundrum—being seen as too partisan by some and not principled enough by others. It's not difficult to understand how the party felt, as though it was dogged by people's uncompromising expectations or expected to take a back seat, leaving little room to manoeuvre in a complex political environment. I very much like what Karl Nerenberg, parliamentary reporter for *rabble.ca*, had to say on the question of strategic voting: be careful it doesn't backfire on you. At the end of the day, he said, it's better to vote for the person in your community who best represents you and whom you believe in. An electoral system based on proportional representation—something the NDP has long advocated for—would help eliminate the dynamics that play into strategic voting. Under proportional representation every vote counts.

The party worked hard to respond to complaints that it beat up on the Liberals too much when the real enemy was Harper. Sometimes I felt conflicted myself. The NDP had every right, I believed, to assert its partisan agenda and push back as hard as it could against any other party, including the Liberals. The Liberals themselves certainly never had any problem doing that and never faced criticism for it. But I also understood the concerns of activists who thought the NDP was playing politics in the small world of Ottawa. I would read the emails from party activists who felt the party had abandoned important positions on foreign policy, taxation, or the environment. At times it seemed that we could never satisfy anyone no matter how hard we tried.

The political right has historically had a good record of keeping itself united while in power and maintaining a connection to its base. They have learned to be disciplined and focused. Although there are limits, and when the base of support is alienated, as we saw in Harper's dying days in the 2015 federal election, defeat is around the corner. On the left, we are held together by a fragile and fractured unity that threatens to break apart. People who see themselves on the left of the political spectrum have powerful ideals, and when differences occur it's easy to slide fiercely and destructively into internal divisions. I saw this happen at the municipal level, and I saw it on occasion at the federal level too. It's a political environment that creates tension within and outside the party.

However you look at it, progressives—elected or not—have a pattern of behaviour that plays out over and over. There's a lack of understanding about how to work together coupled with mistrust, poor communication, and a lack of transparency. But it is possible to have successful working relationships and unity with allies and like-minded activists outside the party working for change. It can be exciting and inspiring, and for me it always produced the best experience in politics and led to the best outcomes. The answer, I believe, lies in building genuine, strong relationships between these two worlds of politics. You can only begin at the ground level and build connections and trust and establish lines of communication, so that when things do go wrong, as they will, you have a political infrastructure both inside and outside the party to help guide you through the conflict. It takes debate, practice, and consensus about how the left works together internally and with its allies. If we are honest with our allies and share real information about the political obstacles and challenges we face (whether as a political party or an NGO or a union), it is amazing how much time and space people will give you to work it out.

There are ways to work together successfully, and there are many ways for people to get involved in the political process for change. As an MP, I conducted many workshops on community lobbying, because I was surprised how little people in the community knew about how to engage in the political arena and influence the political agenda. Often people didn't know who their elected representatives were, let alone how to effectively lobby for change, even though they were deeply involved in their issue. I've had countless encounters with people over the years, young activists and others, who would say, I want to get involved but I don't know how. The desire for change is enormously strong, but the know-how is not always there. For a robust participatory democracy, we need to deconstruct the political process and clarify how it can better work for people. Whether for seeking a nomination, running for office, working on an issue, or working in alliance with others for change, we must loosen things up and strive to make politics more accessible.

I developed a simple framework for workshops on lobbying based on outlining a group's objective for change and the means to attain it. This involved exercises to understand that lobbying is as much about influencing the political agenda as it is about empowering your base to know they have a voice that can influence what is happening. Lobbying is a small but vital component of working for change. It's not mutually exclusive to mass organizing, rallies, public demonstration, and direct action. But we must engage directly with elected representatives (and not just what people see as "government").

When Gordon Campbell was the premier of BC (2001–11) and it was impossible to get through to him, I would say: Forget about the premier and the cabinet ministers who are so far removed from you. Go after the backbench representatives who have to go home to their ridings every week. They are the ones we need to get to. They are the ones who will put pressure on the government at their caucus meetings because they've been inundated with petitions, letters, meetings, and local actions. I would also tell people to use the opposition. Build alliances, find champions in the caucus to raise your issues, and plan joint strategies. Even if the government in power is seen as generally friendly, it can help maintain the government's accountability to keep the opposition party in the loop, if they have some affinity to your cause. Community lobbying is about intelligence gathering and laying out a detailed plan to connect with decision makers using every means possible. It's systematic and doable, but most folks I worked with felt overwhelmed by it and didn't know where to begin.

In the workshops I conducted, I often used the firefighters' union as an example of successful lobbying for change. Most people looked surprised when they heard "firefighters"; that isn't a constituency that naturally comes to mind when thinking about political change. But in my years of being lobbied as an MP, I rate their work highly. It had the hallmarks of a successful lobby: achievable goals, grassroots participation by the union members, real local connections, and excellent follow-up. So many times, being lobbied by so many different groups, I wanted to reach across the table and say, "You're doing this all wrong." Most groups would dump a ton of material on you and erroneously assume you knew their issue, which they, of course, had worked on forever.

The firefighters' union, by contrast, would present minimal information. It was concise and could be read easily and quickly. They never assumed you knew it all, and the discussion would mostly focus on how the issue could be followed up by the MP. They would propose realistic actions for follow-up that would be hard for an MP not to agree to. The goal is to develop a relationship for ongoing work with individual elected representatives. Don't expect to "win" your issue in a single first meeting, if you even get a meeting. It's the long-term relationship that counts, so that ongoing, frank communication can take place to attain your goals. Initially just getting an elected representative to commit to something simple like writing a letter to a minister or raising the issue in their caucus is perfectly adequate. It's the ongoing follow-up and emerging relationship that leads to figuring out how change can take place. If you are organized, methodical, strategic, and willing to follow through, you can absolutely influence the political direction or stance of a party, a government, and even Parliament as a whole.

Legislators and political parties are not exempt from better learning either. They make a mistake when they write off the work of social movements and activists as lopsided or single-issue oriented and therefore unrealistic and unattainable. If they only took the time to figure out what was being asked for and engaged in serious discussion, they would be able to sort out a way forward that satisfies both sides.

Canadian Students for a Sensible Drug Policy led successful lobbies on Parliament Hill starting in about 2000, speaking truth to power about the abysmal failure of Canada's policy on "illegal" drugs as it impacted young people. They won over many MPs with their honest, forthright approach—even Conservatives who were in an ideological lockdown on the issue in their party. The students were eager to participate in warm-up sessions that we had on the Hill and learn the basics about community lobbying for change.

Being an activist, working for transformative change, and interacting successfully with political parties and elected representatives to bring about that change isn't a recipe for disaster. Nor does it mean you have to forfeit your principles or political soul. It is a futile waste of time to get mad and stay mad, or say all politicians are the same. Change happens when activists work at all levels, including with legislators of the same mind or even with opposing views.

Politics is a dynamic process of power and change, and it's in constant flux (even if it doesn't seem so at the time), reacting to forces all the time. It's not a static, immovable object. If it were, human rights would never have been won, unions would not exist, and women would never have gotten the vote. Not to say that these issues were won because government "gave" people their rights. Success is about the struggle and how we take it on. The central element is trust: within your movement and with the people you work with. It's about valuing and accepting each other's unique position, circumstances, and vulnerabilities. It doesn't mean you have to be bought off or concede your own agenda. There will be disagreements and even impasses that can be successfully managed.

And for the political party, or elected person, learning how to trust allies and social movement partners, and understanding what can be done together, fosters transparency and dialogue about the real challenges and making progress together. This trust can certainly be seen as a risk if confidential information is leaked or ends up in the wrong hands because a group is also working with other political interests. When I worked with organizations that I trusted on issues such as drug policy reform, I acted as openly as I could to strategize on a way forward. It often involved sensitivity around timing of when something was going to happen, and it was important to spell out the need for discretion and trust. I never once felt betrayed or taken advantage of in any situation. On the contrary I found working with activists and social movement groups helped create the space to advance a more radical agenda within the more formal political arena.

When activists and social movements comprehend the power they have to make change by activating their own members and the broader community, there's no limit to what can happen. Even when those in power appear opposed to what you are trying to accomplish, mobilization and organizing can shift public opinion and the position of the powerful. The key ingredient is sustained action at every level possible. It may take weeks, months, and even decades, but if mobilization happens locally, nationally, in the streets, in the halls of power, by lobbying or engaging with the political process—things can and do change. And the broader the movement, the greater the chance of making change happen.

In the lead-up to the war on Iraq in 2003, there was big question mark about whether Canada would join the invasion as demanded by the US and other allies. It was the work in Parliament, day after day in question period challenging Prime Minister Jean Chrétien; it was the constant contact from assertive constituents with their individual MPs; it was the petitions, letters, and undoubtedly the massive rallies and demonstrations against Canada's involvement that compelled the Chrétien government to reject the call for military intervention. (Though they undertook other questionable involvement.) This success took the co-operation of many diverse groups who stood their ground, and, despite disagreements on tactics and approaches, worked together.

Of course it's not a one-way street. There are powerful forces at work to prevent progressive change from taking place. In the case of drug policy reform, we learned that taking on prohibition meant taking on law enforcement agencies, the criminal justice system, the judiciary, and hardest of all, the entrenched stereotypes and prejudices that saw people who use drugs as subhuman. (That is, if they were poor and visible on the street.) Layered on top of that was a right-wing political agenda to create fear and division. But we found cracks, allies, strength, and evidence, and worked at every level.

The ongoing struggle for environmental protection and to meet climate change goals is similar. It involves powerful forces that have a vested interest in maintaining the status quo and loads of money and resources to make their case behind closed doors. As we've seen with Standing Rock and the Keystone XL and Trans Mountain pipelines, it takes enormous energy and creativity to mobilize and sustain people's involvement. But that's what transformative change is about; it's lifelong work—I've never yet seen the quick fix.

The mainstream media, too, can play both a positive and negative role in how change takes place. Most civil society groups that can afford it have full-time communications positions to connect with the media. Back in my old community organizing days, there was no such thing. We relied on Bruce's sheer will to connect personally with the media. There was no plan or strategy, only an instinctive imperative that guided us day by day. To build awareness for an issue or campaign, you need to get your message out into the media. And you need to build strong working relationships with the media too.

The media can also present a negative picture of politics that makes people feel cynical and uninvolved. It's stupefying when politics and politicians are continually portrayed as underhanded. When the media continually harps on the negatives, it leaves a sour taste that politics is bad no matter what. How many times have you heard that, or even said that? It becomes part of a worrisome social construct that we can't change anything anyway, so why even try. It plays into a narrative that keeps the elites in power. They don't exactly want a fired-up population making waves of change, do they?

I never believed the mainstream media is unbiased and neutral. There are many good reporters, but they too have become stifled as media concentration limits their scope. The advent of social media and independent progressive media is a good counter to this disempowerment. The importance of independent, progressive media is especially close to my heart, as I have witnessed Kim's committed work as publisher of *rabble.ca* since 2006. When you think about powerful movements like Idle No More or Black Lives Matter, the role of independent and progressive media has been crucial to successful mobilization and organizing. Although, as we see in the current crisis of "fake news," right-wing forces can undermine the power of the direct connections to people these mediums are built on. The editor of *Huffington Post*, Lydia Polgreen, commented in a 2018 *Variety* article: "Open platforms that once seemed radically democratizing now threaten, with the tsunami of false information we all face daily, to undermine democracy." I can't begin to imagine what new forms of communication/marketing/information will come in the future—but I do know that we need to remain ever vigilant.

The way political parties operate also affects the movement for change. Parties can be strange institutions, full of hierarchy, hidden rules, and initiation that is never acknowledged as such. For most people they are mysterious, closed, insider entities. A political party needs to be open and inclusive. That requires critical self-analysis—sometimes they are so immersed in their hierarchical and discriminatory practices that they don't know that what they are doing is alienating and marginalizes people.

Often over the years, people approached me because they were interested in running for a nomination; they were sincere about getting involved and becoming an agent for change. They wanted to know how it's done and had difficulty finding out. While each party has basic rules, it can be a cut-throat process with backroom deals and power plays. This is the side of politics that can be perilous and disturbing. The closer a riding is to winning a seat, the nastier it can get. Sometimes it erupts in the media, as potential candidates slag it out. The best bet to win a nomination is to focus on your potential support, line it up as firmly as possible, and make sure you have a team that knows the rules and the inner workings of the party. I wouldn't have survived my first nomination if I hadn't had that going for me.

Many potential candidates, particularly women, have asked me about the difficulties of balancing family and political life and asked about my experience. I fear I was never a good role model for striking that balance. Lief told me a few years ago how hard it was for him as a small boy when he went out with his parents hoping to have a good time. We might be doing something as simple as shopping for groceries, and people would buttonhole us at length to raise some issue or to complain about something at city hall. Lief would be left standing there, waiting patiently till they were done. He told me this without any rancour, but I felt pretty bad. I know it happened constantly; there were precious few boundaries between family life and political public life. This is something I regret; potential candidates need to think about those boundaries.

All political parties have double speak on this issue. We claim to be family friendly, yet demand an enormous amount of time and energy no matter what the hour or day. When Rona Ambrose became interim leader of the Conservative party after Stephen Harper's defeat, she made this an issue with her new caucus, saying she wanted them to strive to have better work/family life balance. Easier said than done, for sure, but openly discussing the question is a necessary start. Nevertheless, we should be hopeful not despairing. How amazing, now, to see more women in the House of Commons, especially young women and babies too. Gone are the days when there were no women's washrooms near the chamber of the House because they weren't considered necessary.

Strategizing at a federal NDP convention with Rebecca Blaikie and Itrath Syed

The federal NDP developed solid affirmative action policies over the years, to be more inclusive and ensure fairness for underrepresented groups. Change requires a proactive stance to ensure that barriers to women, Indigenous people, people from visible minorities, people with disabilities, and the LGBTQ+ community are removed. It requires constant vigilance and accountability to ensure that equity is achieved both within the party and in society at large.

Sexism, like racism, is a learned systemic practice in our culture—and as with any anti-oppression training, it has to be unlearned and understood. White people, and in particular men, grow up with entitlement. So to all my dear male colleagues, some of whom are aware of sexism and racism, but to the ones who are blind to it: look at your behaviour and be aware of it. When you next feel compelled to jump up to say your piece, look around and think about others in the room and literally give space for people to be heard. Talk to your female and racialized friends about sexism and racism and ask them what they have experienced.

I'm no academic expert on the question of gender, power, and leadership, but I know my own experience and that is irrefutable. For too long I felt like I didn't belong or I was an outsider—even having reached the position of deputy leader of the NDP. It took an illuminating conversation with Itrath Syed, a feminist scholar and one-time candidate for the NDP, and Kim, my partner, both of whom struggled with PhDs, to explain to me the "imposter syndrome." I had no idea that so many of us experience the socially constructed culture of being an outsider in the face of white male privilege.

Looking back, I realize that many of my mentors were strong male figures. My father, Harry, Bruce, Bud, and Jack were leaders who influenced my political development. Over the years I developed my own style of leadership. I never wanted to clobber anyone personally or see someone reduced to shame and pain. It was always about fighting for the issues and making progress.

Strong women have influenced me too: from Joy MacPhail, the gutsy and colourful leader of the British Columbia NDP whose fighting spirit took on Gordon Campbell, and Darlene Marzari before her, to my former colleagues in Ottawa—the tireless Olivia Chow, the sharp and witty whip Chris Charlton, and Jean Crowder, a stellar critic and liaison with Indigenous communities and NDP caucus chair under Jack Layton. Dawn Black, Judy Wasylycia-Leis, and Megan Leslie were three formidable members of the NDP caucus as well as young women, like Niki Ashton, who shows courage and stamina. And I think back to feminist pioneers before us: Alexa McDonough, Audrey McLaughlin, Margaret Mitchell, Rosemary Brown, Grace MacInnes, and as far back as the first female MP, Agnes Macphail, elected in 1921 from the Progressive Party of Canada, which became the Co-operative Commonwealth Federation (CCF), the forerunner of the NDP. All these women and more give us tremendous strength to move forward, to not be outsiders but to be agents for change.

A few years ago, I would never have contemplated mentioning the merits of women in other parties, especially conservatives. But distance and perspective can change things. Rona Ambrose was a very effective leader of the Conservative party caucus. She breathed new life into them after Stephen Harper's departure and did her job with class and integrity. And I remember the likes of Bonnie Brown, Paddy Torsney, and Sue Barnes, terrific MPs in the Liberal caucus, or senators Salma Ataullahjan and Mobina Jaffer.

I'd like to say progress has been made, but the trappings of sexism, discrimination. and male domination are still evident. I know this from many of my young female colleagues elected in 2011, as part of the Orange Wave. They experienced sexism and harassment in all kinds of inappropriate ways, and they suffered embarrassment, hurt, and harm.

Thankfully the vast majority of my experience and interactions has been positive and incredibly inspiring, the times I came up against misogynist hatred, particularly on social media, were always surpassed by positive responses and support. But still it's shocking to see the venom that can be spewed out on Twitter and Facebook—as though people have lost all semblance of decency and the civil act of disagreement. This was evident in the attacks on Ruth Ellen Brosseau, the NDP member on the receiving end of Justin Trudeau's "elbowgate" in May 2016, as he took the unacceptable unilateral action to push for a vote that was delayed by mere seconds. He apologized for roughly elbowing Brosseau out of the way as he pushed through MPs—rightly so. But the ongoing misogynist and partisan attacks heaped on Ruth Ellen and Niki Ashton through social media were so out of line, and so hateful, that it would cause any woman to wonder why on earth she would enter politics.

It's those days that make you wonder, where does all the hate comes from and how does it become so personalized? I like social media and I use it—it's a great outreach tool to comment, get feedback, and find out what's going on. But it also gives licence to cowardly trolls who stalk and pursue and attack. They are most often men, and I always wonder if they have partners and kids at home and how they reconcile their weaselly existence as haters. I can only say, let's stand up to it— the violence, the fearmongering, misogyny, xenophobia, homophobia, and hatred—and seek ways for society to have respectful, open discourse that is not based on hate.

Younger generations do not tolerate this behaviour any longer. Treating women or any group in an inferior, racist, hateful, or discriminatory way is just not on. All of us must call it out, whenever and wherever it happens, and support the important work we have to do as equal players in our society.

A Vision for
Transformative Change

On Sunday morning, April 11, 2016, the NDP took a Leap for the future, for ourselves, and for our planet. The NDP convention in Edmonton will be remembered for many things, not the least of which is the leadership review vote for Thomas Mulcair, following the 2015 election. It took many by surprise that only 48 percent of delegates didn't want a leadership review, not anywhere close enough for him to stay on. It's hard to see a leader take an exit, because it's a thankless job in many ways that takes a toll—and in the NDP, we're not always good at saying thank you.

This particular convention had many vibes to it. Being in Alberta, NDP premier Rachel Notley's hometown, gave it a special twist. She gave an outstanding speech at the convention, followed a little later by NDP icon Stephen Lewis, whose wisdom and passion captured people's hearts. Two months earlier, officially retired as an MP, I had started to work with Avi Lewis and Janet Solberg from Toronto on a resolution to be submitted to the convention on the Leap Manifesto. The manifesto was a significant collaborative body of work from many organizations in Canada outlining a way forward for a society based on income equality and climate justice.

Avi had contacted me in January and asked if I would motivate a resolution through Vancouver East. I immediately responded yes. We chatted back and forth about wording, and he and Janet drafted what eventually became the core of the resolution delegates passed. By coincidence Craig Scott (former MP for Toronto–Danforth) was also submitting a resolution about the Leap Manifesto linked to improving internal party democracy. We put our heads together and, along with Megan Leslie (former MP for Halifax), embarked on a lively long-distance conversation on the best way to combine the Vancouver East and Toronto–Danforth resolutions for a successful outcome at the convention. It might have been a bit unusual for a group of former MPs to collaborate, but it was indicative of our interest and commitment to continue working on issues concerning social justice and climate change justice.

Having been closely involved with the New Politics Initiative resolution that went to an NDP convention fifteen years earlier, I now had a much better understanding of how best to go about it. The NPI approach had been very grassroots in nature. We had done extensive outreach both within the party and outside to engage people in reinventing the NDP to become more activist-based and more closely connected to the work of social movements. But we had done little to explain our approach and the initiative's motivation to the party leadership. Nothing was hidden, but neither did we go out of our way to try to get the leadership of the party, including leader Alexa McDonough, to understand what we were up to and why. It wasn't a consciously chosen strategy, as I remember it; it just happened that way. I had one meeting with Alexa in the lead-up to the convention, but it was already set up as a firm divide, with the resolution being seen as a direct challenge.

With the Leap resolution, we wanted to clearly lay out what the resolution called for: support of the manifesto in principle, and for debate at the riding level to take place, so that party members could consider further how the manifesto's ideals could be incorporated into a policy process for the NDP leading up to the 2019 federal election. The combined resolution from Vancouver East and Toronto–Danforth read as follows:

(1) The NDP recognizes and supports the Leap Manifesto as a high-level statement of principles that speaks to the aspirations, history, and values of the party. We recognize and embrace the opportunity to confront the twin crises of inequality and climate change with an inspiring and positive agenda—to transform society as we transition to an economy beyond fossil fuels. The specific policies in the manifesto can and should be debated and modified on their own merits and according to the needs of various communities and all parts of the country, but the goal of transforming our country according to the vision in the manifesto is entirely in harmony with the core beliefs and tradition

(2) THEREFORE, BE IT RESOLVED THAT the New Democratic Party looks forward to meaningful opportunity to debate [the Leap Manifesto] in riding associations across the country

(3) AND BE IT FURTHER RESOLVED THAT these discussions be part of a pre-convention policy process leading up to 2018.

Those of us working on the resolution felt it was important to make sure the leader's office was aware of the resolution and open to its consideration by the convention. Resolutions submitted by a number of local riding associations proposed outright adoption of the manifesto, which we believed would be undesirable. Outright adoption left no room for open discussion and debate, and presupposed that the manifesto as written was exactly what the NDP should take on. We wanted to make it clear that it was the high-level principles of the document that mattered, and that adopting the resolution from Vancouver East and Toronto–Danforth demonstrated a positive commitment to work within the party as well as with broadly based movements outside. As a result, we had numerous conversations with the leader's office including an understanding that the resolution would be acceptable to the Alberta NDP. Indeed, on the Friday morning of the convention, staffers helped on the floor of the prioritization panel meeting to ensure the resolution was high enough up the list that it would be debated by the convention as a whole.

It all went smoothly until it didn't. At the time it felt like a good example of how to work effectively in a convention setting, keeping everyone in the loop for something that could be deemed controversial by the media. I studiously avoided media comment, knowing that it was a convenient segue for reporters wanting comment on the leadership review. I figured we did everything right. But even so, the manifesto became a polarizing issue. Many Albertan delegates (especially labour) felt that the resolution was an attack on Alberta and its oil-based economy. Opponents charged that it was mucking things up for the Alberta NDP on a sensitive issue, and why on earth would we bring forward such a resolution in Alberta? I had heard this type of argument so many times in the past; "now is not the right time" was a familiar refrain. If that attitude prevails, it's never the right time. There's always something in the way or an optic that isn't quite right.

As with the NPI initiative in 2002, the motivation of the resolution got lost in the drama. Both initiatives were about working beyond the traditional way of doing things by engaging with people outside the party for a strong vision of the future. I felt like I'd come full circle; it was the same question for me. How do we do our politics differently?

How do we engage with people in a way that is part of a bigger movement for social change? How can the process of electoral politics and a progressive political party work successfully and democratically outside of itself for transformative change?

It's more about the *how* than about the *what*. It's about harnessing our power together and figuring out that we can support each other in attaining transformative change. The Leap Manifesto authors had already done incredible groundwork across the country to bring people together for a vision and hope for the future. How could the NDP be part of that vision, of that movement for change? What do we have to do to engage our own members and the broader community?

The NDP did not need to own the Leap Manifesto—the manifesto has its own independent path to create. The issue was to work cooperatively and democratically with people who want transformative change to produce a better and more equal world. We can't wait a decade to move forward. There will never be a "right time"; there is only now, and there is also too late. So yes, needed change is about pipelines and priorities for public investment, it's about closing the gap between extreme wealth and extreme poverty, and it's about upholding international law and human rights. Fundamentally the change we need is about participatory democracy. Some folks went home from that convention feeling burned and others disillusioned. I felt neither. I'd rather have a convention where things are happening and real debate is taking place than a smoothly managed show. The members at that convention spoke out, as they should, and a good resolution helped us move forward.

Approval of the resolution on the Leap submitted by Vancouver East / Toronto–Danforth forced the party to follow up and consult with riding associations across the country, although it remains to be seen if meaningful policy change will follow. The Leap resolution also helped motivate other initiatives within and outside the party, including NDP4LEAP at a local riding level, and an independent left alliance,

Courage, that seeks to influence the NDP "to align the party with the will of the members and the energy of movements [to] make it a more effective force for change." Both of these initiatives demonstrate the ongoing desire for party members and activists to work together. I feel confident that it's a vision that won't go away.

This was also the first party convention after the 2015 federal election, and there was an undercurrent of discussion and opinion about what had happened during that election. Members had been terribly disappointed in the 2015 election result for the NDP. We had hoped to form government or at least maintain Official Opposition status. The campaign itself had not met the expectations of many members and supporters. New Democrats always have robust opinions and ideas, and this convention was especially full of buzz—not only concerning the leadership review, but also on where the NDP was headed in the future.

Party president Rebecca Blaikie had done an incredible job of travelling the country post-election to listen to members. She'd heard their angst, fears, hopes, and ideals. Her speech at the convention captured people's mood and reminded us who New Democrats really are:

> New Democrats are called, particularly in times of danger, or crisis, or war, to keep our perspective and not succumb to jingoistic views, or the temptation to scapegoat. New Democrats are those who aren't afraid to lay blame where blame is appropriate, but who also are not afraid to ask how we and those whom we count as our allies and friends could have done things differently to create a world less likely to breed the problems we face.
>
> New Democrats are not afraid to talk about root causes, because it is only in getting to the root of problems that we can solve them.

Supporting the next generation of political activism; Joel Harden campaign launch in Ottawa Centre, 2018

Over my years in elected office, I've been in many political battles. I've taken strong positions and stuck to my beliefs. I've seen the destruction that happens when people take their strongly held beliefs and use them to bludgeon the other side—or worse, their own side, no matter who gets annihilated in the process. If I had success moving forward on issues, it was because I did my best to avoid this kind of winner-take-all approach. I've seen too much harm and grief when people do horrible things to each other to win. Politics can be a merciless game, and any public admission of doubt or failure is seen as weakness. In reality, there are ups and downs, failures and mistakes. Politics is much like any other job. And we can do the job better. We can do politics differently. We can hold on to our core beliefs and principles, and still be civil to people on the opposing side. It is not mutually exclusive to be respectful and strong.

I've learned so much of what I know from the people of east Vancouver who supported me in six federal elections. The community gave me lots of space to pursue political action that some would describe as unorthodox. I did my best to represent a multitude of issues and concerns. Our busy community office on Main Street was always humming with activity. I was blessed to have incredible staff over the years, both in Vancouver and Ottawa—they went the distance too and never shied away from the difficult cases and the slogging work. No MP can honestly claim any success without recognizing the support of trusted staff.

East Vancouver is a place of great diversity and many needs, but it's also the heartland of groundbreaking activism and community power. It always inspired me to know that I am a part of a bigger thing. The memory of Bruce and his work kept me going—so often I would think of our old organizing days, or being on City Council together, and the lessons I learned would help me through difficult situations. He had a deep impact on me and on the city of Vancouver. The experience at DERA and working with Bruce in the Downtown Eastside was pivotal to the development of my political voice. It was a foundation that helped me work inside the political system for change. Eventually it felt as comfortable at city hall, and later Parliament Hill, as it did at Main and Hastings. The goal—transformative change for social justice—was a constant.

Looking back on those early experiences, I am struck by how, even if we didn't know it at the time, we learned to work both within and outside the established system. We knew it wasn't enough to demonstrate and protest—though that often helped us gain attention. We also understood the value of using every tool we had, every ally we had, every opportunity we had to fight for people's rights. At the time I didn't realize what an impact the work of DERA had on civic politics and the city overall. Certainly DERA's work has been studied and written about in numerous publications over the years. Nathan Edelson, a

Continuing the work to address the drug overdose crisis, supporting Kennedy
Stewart's mayoral campaign, Vancouver, September 2018

retired city planner and good friend, told me about a chapter he is
writing in an upcoming book, where he addresses DERA's profound
impact on the city and on the issues we worked on. The emergence of
the Downtown Eastside changed the scope and outlook of civic politics
and the city forever. And it changed the national level too.

In 2011, celebrating the City of Vancouver's 125th anniversary, the
Vancouver Sun's John Atkin and the *Globe and Mail*'s Rod Mickleburgh
published stories noting ten influential people in the city's history.
Bruce Eriksen was included in both. Mickleburgh wrote of Bruce:

> He was as crusty as they come, but few did more for an area
> of Vancouver than Mr. Eriksen did for the downtrodden
> Downtown Eastside in the 1970s. He awakened the city's con-
> science to the plight of its poorest residents, spearheading
> campaigns for the Carnegie Centre, making it harder to get
> booze, and, most life-saving of all, mandatory sprinkling systems
> in every flophouse hotel.

Bruce always believed in our democratic system, imperfect as it is, and he always worked to make electoral politics and voting as accessible as possible. So often I've heard politicians and pundits admonish people for not voting. Usually just before or after an election. The funny thing is, I've learned that working for social justice isn't really about voting at all. Voting is an outcome of people believing they can change things. When people are turned off, beat up, or disenfranchised, or worse, suppressed from voting, we can't blame them for not voting or moralize on low voter turnout. We can only examine our own failure and responsibility to educate, empower, and mentor people around us so they can use their own voice. You can't begin at the end; you can only begin at the beginning and support people to get where they need to be. Leadership and confidence need to be developed at the most local level possible. It can't be done top-down. People at the top need to work at the bottom. Then they'll know what it takes to be real leaders.

I've spent a lifetime exploring the relationship between electoral and social movement politics, and what it is that brings transformative change. It comes down to something quite simple, but as is so often the case, difficult to attain. I had to learn that it is as much about how you work with people and build relationships as it is about the outcome you desire. It wasn't an easy lesson— and certainly not something I understood in the early days in the Downtown Eastside. Change can take place in many ways, sometimes rapidly, sometimes painfully and slowly over a lifetime, but the relationship and trust you have with your allies and even your adversaries is always at the core of that change.

When I decided to leave politics in 2015, I was ready to leave behind the parliamentary life after thirty-one years of elected office at the civic and national level. Politics and big-picture change remains a huge part of my life. I want to see transformative change take place in the political arena. I want to see people as fired up as they were for Bernie Sanders, but here in Canada. I want to be part of something that I know is possible and realistic. And I want to defeat the hatred, misogyny, racism, and xenophobia that kills people and shatters lives and communities.

I've been an activist for forty-plus years; I have no degrees and no formal training. I've been called radical left, crazy, powerful, visionary, grassroots, kind, wilful, cherubic, passionate, strong, and more. At the end of the day, like many of you, love, work, and wanting a better world is what I strive for. Sometimes the path is wide and open and full of sunshine; at other times it is so narrow and steep that I fear I will fall off the precipice. Transformative change is not an abstract theory. It is an attainable and decent way of working together that infuses hope for the future. When we work together, we have the power to change everything and anything.

Epilogue

Official Report (*Hansard*)
Tuesday, June 2, 2015; *Speaker:* The Honourable Andrew Scheer

Mr. Speaker, this is an excerpt from *Being True to Ourselves*, by poet Sandy Cameron:

"The map we inherited
isn't any good.
The old roads mislead
and the landscape keeps changing.
People are confused
and drift from place to place,
clothes scorched by fire
eyes red with smoke.

The old map tells us
to look for gold
in the city,

so we go to the city
and find the garbage dump.
We need a new map
with new roads
and a new destination.

Some people fear a new map, and
they cling to the old one
like flies to fly paper....

I don't have a new map,
so I write stories.
The stories draw lines
dig holes
and above all, remember....

'And in this harsh world draw your breath in pain
to tell my story,'
Hamlet said to Horatio.

'I seem not to speak
the official language,' the poet
Adrienne Rich said, so
she created an unofficial language,
the language of the heart..."

Mr. Speaker, it has been an honour to serve the people of
Vancouver East and the NDP for the past 18 years. Thank you.

Acknowledgements

I always had this book in my head, but the writing of it took some time with the encouragement of many people and friends along the way. Many thanks to Am Johal, Cynthia Flood, Duncan Cameron, and Matthew Adams, who gave me early support and encouragement, and to Barbara Pulling, editor, who looked over the very first draft and set me on the right course, encouraging me to write more personally. Mandy Len Catron's memoir writing course at UBC opened up new ideas and techniques that resulted in a wonderful ongoing group of us, who have met regularly to encourage each other in our writing—it's been a delightful source of support and camaraderie. Thank you, Pauline Buck, for your technical help in rearranging material for the book, and Luiza Shamkulova, Alexandra Wilson, Margaret Stott, John Perkins Jr, and John Perkins Sr, whose gentle and kind soul left us too early. To Michael MacDonald, senior archivist, Library and Archives Canada, for inviting me and encouraging me to organize decades of material for storage and use at the national archives in Ottawa and providing generous assistance at short notice. To Joe Comartin, Bill Siksay, Chris Charlton, Jean Crowder, and Rob Sutherland, thank you for collectively getting together to recall important details of events on Parliament Hill and our experiences as part of the NDP caucus. I am indebted to the loyal and utterly competent staff who worked with me on Parliament Hill and in Vancouver—your support and care made all the difference: Glen Sanford, Catherine Prince, Chris Dendys, Melissa Hunter, Karen Philp, Adele Tate, Rob Sutherland, Christian Brideau, Andrew McNeill, Della Kirkham, Emily Watkins, Leanne Holt, Sara Bergman, Andrew Cuddy, Karyne Vienneau, Adam Moore, Janet Woo, Phyllis Loke, Megan McKinney, Theresa Ho, Remick Lo, Anne Vavrik, Sam Monckton, Carli Staub, and Julius Fisher. A special thank you to the good people of east Vancouver who gave me the privilege of representing our community in Ottawa for eighteen years, and who inspired me to keep going no matter what.

Most of all to Kim Elliott, my dear partner: I am so grateful for your constant and never failing love and help. Your support kept me going when the going was tough. You have been so generous of your time and spirit, and your expert help with edits, assembling photographs, and providing a solid critique kept me moving forward. Thank you, Kim, for your enduring patience, good humour, and putting up with those moments of doubt where I felt overwhelmed.

To all the good folks at Between the Lines, notably Managing Editor Amanda Crocker, thank you for helping a novice with many questions, and especially Julie Devaney who provided guidance and suggestions for improvements. Thank you, Tilman Lewis, for your precise and wonderfully skillful editing, creating a much better book to be read.

This book is in memory of Bruce Eriksen—I feel in my heart he lives on in the community of the Downtown Eastside, where he changed the course of history and showed me the richness of his love. Our son, Lief Eriksen, displays the strength and care of his father in all ways.

Photo Credits

* Material republished with the express
permission of: *Vancouver Sun*, a division of
Postmedia Network Inc.

Index

Photographs are denoted by *italicized* page numbers.

Connolly, Michael, 153
Conservative Party of Canada: government of, 161–168, 174–175, 212, 218–219; policies of, 151–152, 182–183, 188–189, 201–202, 204–205, 227–230, 250. *See also* individual MPs
constituent mailings, 164
Controlled Drugs and Substances Act, 182
Coombes, Peter, 105–106
Co-operative Commonwealth Federation (CCF), 256
COPE, *see* Committee of Progressive Electors (COPE)
Corbyn, Jeremy, 219
Costello, Sharon, 77, 126
Council of Canadians, 105
Courage, 263–264
Criminal Code, 131–132
Crowder, Jean, 189, 238, 256
Crowder, Rachel, 130
Crowe, Cathy, *101*
Crowe, Earl, *229*
Cuba, 58–59
Cullen, Nathan, 217
Cyprus, 26–28

Davies, Helen, 32, *37*
Davies, Jane, *37*
Davies, Libby, about: with Bruce and Lief, 10, *45*, 60–62, 76–77; Cyprus, 26–29; early childhood, siblings, parents, *28*, 32–40, *35*, *37*; early employment, 66, 70; education, 31–32, 40–42; Germany, 29–30; Malaysia, 30–31; in Ottawa, 88–90, 107–108, 236; relationship with Kim, 122–127, 236, 237–238; shooting in Centre Block, 236–237; in Vancouver, 10, 16, 39, 82. *See also* Davies, Libby, politics, publications; individual family members
Davies, Libby, politics: budget deal with Conservatives, 154–157, 162–163; Citizens Weapons Inspection Team, 105–106, 147–148; city councillor and bid for mayor, 44, 63–65, *65*, 69; on community lobbying, 247–249; as critic for NDP, 114,

122, 238; on drug reform policies, 90–92, 181–182, 242–243, 250–251; on economic policies, 175–176; federal elections, 109–111, 149–151, 160, 208, *209*, *210*, 212–213, 241–242; as House leader, 142–146, 151, 179; and Jack Layton, 138–139, 195, *214*; Joel Harden campaign, *265*; Kennedy Stewart campaign, *267*; leadership, list of qualities, 120–121; on the Leap Manifesto, 259–264; on the media, 252–253; on Middle East issues, 190–206, *203*, 235, 251; as MP, 73–83, 84–86, 86–88, *145*, 240; on politics and political life, 178–181, 244–247, 254, 265, 268–269; on safe-injection sites, 93–100, 111–114, 227–231, *228*, *229*; on sex-worker rights, 53–56, 130–131, 132–133, 166–167, 221–227; on social housing, 47, *56*, 74–75, 100–104, 115–116, 187; on thalidomide survivors, 238–240; Travelling Community Offices, 169–172. *See also* Committee of Progressive Electors; Davies, Libby, about, publications; Downtown Eastside; drugs; Middle East issues; NDP; peace activism; sexism; sex workers; individual MPs
Davies, Libby, publications: *Downtown East*, 7, 13, 16; "Homelessness: An Unnatural Disaster," 101–102; "Ode to East Van," 210–211; *Peacemaking in the 1990s* (Perry), 197. *See also* Davies, Libby, about, politics
Davies, Margaret, 26, 32, 34–35, *35*, 40, 48, 209
Davies, Peter, 26, *28*, 32–34, 197–198
Davis, Angela, 59
day care facility, 63
Department of Foreign Affairs and International Trade (DFAIT), 202
DERA (Downtown Eastside Residents Association), 7–8, 11–17, 20, 24, 45–46, 62–63, 266–267. *See also Downtown East*
development interests, 20, 24, 48, 56–57, 64–65
Dewar, Paul, 194, 217
Diewert, Dave, 233

Toms, Marcy, *9*
Topp, Brian, 215, 217
Toronto Disaster Relief Committee, 101, 103
Torsney, Paddy, 113, 257
Townsend, Mark, 84, 97, 111
Tremblay, Suzanne, 143
Trudeau, Justin, 242. *See also* Liberal Party of Canada
Turmel, Nycole, 216

Unemployed Citizens Welfare Improvement Council (UCWIC), 40
"Unfair" Elections Act, 218
Union of BC Municipalities, 60
unions, 12, 21, 57, 70, 119, 248. *See also* Stanford, Jim; individual unions
United Church of Canada, 205
UNAIDS, 233–234
United Nations Decade for Women, 59
United Nations Declaration on the Rights of Indigenous Peoples, 165
United Nations Relief and Works Agency for Palestine Refugees in the Near East (UNRWA), 200–202
Urban Native Youth Alliance (UNYA), 136
USS *Independence*, 51–52

Valentine's Day Women's Memorial March, 54, *186*
Valeri, Tony, 154–156
Vancouver Aquarium, 47
Vancouver Area Network of Drug Users (VANDU), 94–97, 111, 114, 132, 181–182
Vancouver Art Gallery, *135*
Vancouver East, 75–76. *See also* Davies, Libby, politics
Vancouver Police Department, 112–113, 128–129
Vancouver Sun, 65, 91, 92, 125–126
Vancouver Winter Olympics (2010), 185–187
Vander Zalm, Bill, 23, 61–62
VANDU, *see* Vancouver Area Network of Drug Users
VanDusen Botanical Garden, 47

Veterans against Nuclear Arms, 105
Victoria Daily Times, 23
Vision Vancouver, 68–69. *See also* Committee of Progressive Electors
Volrich, Jack, 46

Walker, Amy, 186
Walk for Peace, 1982, *49*
War Measures Act, 243
Washington Hotel, 97, 134
Wasylycia-Leis, Judy, *107*, 256
Watkins, Mel, 147
Watson, Rodney, 170
weapons of mass destruction, 105–106, 147
Webster, Jack, 15
West Bank, *see* Middle East issues
What Can You Do: Stories (Flood), 68
White, Randy, 113
Williams, Blake, 72
Wilson, Dean, 228
Wilson, Fred, 77
Wilson, Patricia, 47, 51, 64
women's conference, 119
Women's International Democratic Federation, 59
Women's Memorial March, Valentine's Day, 54, *186*
Woo, Janet, 169, 209
Woodward's Department Store, Vancouver, 5, 62–63
World AIDS Conference, 234–235
World Health Organization (WHO), 233–234
World Trade Center, 115
World Trade Organization (WTO), 106–107
Wright, Ann, 178–179
Wrzesnewskyj, Borys, 201
Wyder, Fred, 18

Xtra West, 126–127

Yaffe, Barbara, 91–92
Yamashiro, Takeo, 79
Yee, Bill, 49
Yes/Oui coalition rally, *177*
Yorke, Bruce, 48, *50*, 51, 53, 57, 64